RENEWALS 458-4574
DATE DUE

WITHDRAWN
UTSA LIBRARIES

Liberals, Marxists, and Nationalists

LIBERALS, MARXISTS, AND NATIONALISTS

Competing Interpretations of South African History

MERLE LIPTON

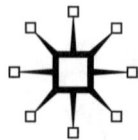

LIBERALS, MARXISTS, AND NATIONALISTS
Copyright © Merle Lipton, 2007.
All rights reserved. No part of this book may be used or reproduced in any manner whatsoever without written permission except in the case of brief quotations embodied in critical articles or reviews.
First published in 2007 by
PALGRAVE MACMILLAN™
175 Fifth Avenue, New York, N.Y. 10010 and
Houndmills, Basingstoke, Hampshire, England RG21 6XS.
Companies and representatives throughout the world.

PALGRAVE MACMILLAN is the global academic imprint of the Palgrave Macmillan division of St. Martin's Press, LLC and of Palgrave Macmillan Ltd.
Macmillan® is a registered trademark in the United States, United Kingdom and other countries. Palgrave is a registered trademark in the European Union and other countries.

ISBN-13: 978-0-230-60059-1
ISBN-10: 0-230-60059-X

Library of Congress Cataloging-in-Publication Data
Lipton, Merle.
  Liberals, Marxists, and nationalists : competing interpretations of South African history / by Merle Lipton.
      p. cm.
  Includes bibliographical references and index.
  ISBN 0-230-60059-X
  1. Apartheid—South Africa—History. 2. Apartheid—South Africa—Historiography. 3. South Africa—History. 4. South Africa—Historiography. I. Title.

DT1757.L57 2007
968.05072—dc22   2007009937

A catalogue record of the book is available from the British Library.

Design by Scribe Inc.

First edition: September 2007

10 9 8 7 6 5 4 3 2 1

Printed in the United States of America.

Contents

List of Abbreviations		vi
Acknowledgments		vii
Chapter 1	Is Historical Truth Possible—And Does History Matter?	1
Chapter 2	The Debate about South Africa I: Selected Issues before 1910	7
Chapter 3	The Debate about South Africa II: Selected Issues, 1910–90	33
Chapter 4	The Debate about South Africa III: Other Factors Eroding Apartheid	81
Chapter 5	Theory, Politics, and Psychology of the Debate	107
Chapter 6	How Historians Shape the Future	137
Appendices to Chapter 3		175
Notes		191
Reference List		203
Index		219

List of Abbreviations

ANC	African National Congress
AHI	Afrikaanse Handelsinstituut (business organization)
Assocom	The Associated Chambers of Commerce
BEE	Black Economic Empowerment
Cosatu	Congress of South African Trade Unions
CP	Conservative Party
DA	Democratic Alliance
FCI	Federated Chamber of Industries
HNP	Herstigte (purified) National Party
NP	(Afrikaner) National Party
PAC	Pan Africanist Congress
SACP	South African Communist Party
Seifsa	Steel & Engineering Industries Federation of South Africa
TRC	Truth & Reconciliation Commission
UDF	United Democratic Front
UP	United Party

Acknowledgments

I am indebted to Kenneth Hughes, Michael Lipton, and Jack Spence for their helpful comments on the manuscript and for their moral support and encouragement. The UK's Economic and Social Research Council (ESRC) funded my Senior Research Fellowship at Sussex University, Brighton for the first phase of work on this book. An Associate Fellowship at Chatham House (the Royal Institute of International Affairs) in London provided a useful base for work on the international issues.

CHAPTER 1

IS HISTORICAL TRUTH POSSIBLE— AND DOES HISTORY MATTER?

This study examines conflicting historical accounts of the origins, evolution and, especially, the undermining of apartheid. The process culminated in South Africa's relatively peaceful transition, during 1990–94, to a nonracial democracy and to much continuity with its political, economic and administrative institutions, shorn of their racist features. South Africa still has deep socioeconomic inequality, closely correlated with race, but the legally enforced racism that led the international community to stigmatize apartheid as uniquely offensive was ended by this negotiated settlement.

This relatively peaceful transition astonished not only the general public, but also most scholars working on South Africa. They had anticipated that apartheid could only be ended by a violent revolution, or at least an East European-style velvet revolution, with the ruling Afrikaner National Party (NP) collapsing in the face of mass demonstrations. Instead, apartheid was ended by negotiations initiated by President de Klerk when he released Nelson Mandela from prison and unbanned the African National Congress (ANC) and other proscribed organizations in February 1990.

At almost the same time as these dramatic events in South Africa, scholars and public opinion were surprised by another unanticipated, relatively nonviolent handover of power by a seemingly well-entrenched ruling elite: the leaders of the Communist

Party of the Soviet Union, whose action was followed by the collapse of the USSR and the transition from communism in Russia and other eastern European and central Asian states. What was the reaction to these unanticipated events of the scholars whose professional role is to provide their peers and the public with understanding of the dynamics of these societies? Within a few years, some plainspoken Sovietologists challenged their reluctant colleagues to stop ignoring this embarrassing issue and confront the painful question, "How could we have been so wrong?" Michael Cox (1998) dismissed as self-serving the excuse that historians are not concerned with prediction, arguing that to be so completely taken by surprise suggested a failure to understand the underlying dynamics of Soviet society. He, and the contributors to his book, warned that the intellectual shortcomings accounting for this failure were leading to a swing in the opposite direction, evident in euphoria about the Gorbachev and Yeltsin reforms, based on a continuing failure to grasp the significant trends in Russian society.

But almost two decades later, South African scholars show little sign of a similar serious retrospection to confront and learn from their past mistakes. This is particularly striking as the South African "miracle"—unlike the events in the USSR—did not come out of the blue. From the mid-1960s, a minority of South African scholars argued that economic growth was placing increasing pressure on apartheid and they predicted that continued growth would undermine it. Moreover, their argument received support from the reforms gradually introduced by the NP after the 1970 election. The cumulative effect of these reforms was such that, by the time de Klerk freed Mandela in 1990, few of the pillars of apartheid remained in place (this process is documented in Chapter 3).

Prima facie, the outcome in South Africa should not have occasioned such astonishment. Part of the reason why it did was because the significant reformist trends were obscured by the opposing, more widely accepted argument that these reforms—which included abolition of job color bars, social segregation, and restrictions on black trade unions and property rights—were cosmetic changes or adaptations that were "restructuring," and thereby even strengthening, apartheid.

These conflicting interpretations of socioeconomic trends in South Africa, and of the related economic interests and political pressures of its major classes and ethnic/racial groups, were at the center of an intense, bitter debate that reveals much about the nature of historical and social research and raises basic questions about the methodology and professional conduct of historians (and other social scientists).

Scholars who argued that significant reformist trends were emerging in South Africa were accused of being apologists for the apartheid regime and, particularly, for business. This accusation was most forcefully expressed by a group identifying itself as "neo-Marxist revisionists." From the early 1970s, the revisionists became influential in scholarly and public debates and acquired dominant positions in leading universities in the United Kingdom, South Africa, and elsewhere—positions many of them still retain.

The revisionists rejected what they termed "the conventional liberal version" of South African history. They argued that this portrayed South African society as shaped by the "irrational racism" of the Boers/Afrikaners, while obscuring the material, class interests of capitalists and British imperialists, whose interests were the real driving force behind segregation, and its later version, apartheid. The revisionists argued that South Africa's institutionalized racism had been "tailored" to suit the interests of capital; that English-speaking liberals had played a leading role in evolving the policy of segregation; and that all this had been obscured by (past and contemporary) English liberal historians who served as apologists for capital and for British imperialism.[1] The revisionists also maintained that their reinterpretation was creating a new paradigm that was transforming and revolutionizing the study of South African history. As shown later, this claim was and remains widely accepted by many scholars outside their ranks.

Thus, this debate is not only about the substantive historical issues: the origins, evolution, and demise of apartheid and the respective roles in this process of Blacks and Whites, Capital and Labor, Afrikaans and English-speaking South Africans, locals and foreigners. The debate is also about the historiography: the role of historians in shaping perceptions about South Africa's past.

* * *

How do students of history—which aspires, at least in part, to be a science—construct their analyses and form their views and verdicts? Science involves not only establishing "facts," but also explaining them by formulating and testing hypotheses. That the accounts of historians differ more radically than those of scientists is partly due to the nature of the discipline: the past cannot be tested in the laboratory. This contributes to the tendency of many historians to ignore or dismiss evidence that does not support, or even contradicts, their hypotheses. This study explores the extent to which, in the South African case, this widespread tendency was due to the historian's commitment to theory (models of how society evolves and functions), to ideology (justificatory beliefs about how society should function), to political agendas (commitments to particular political organizations), and/or to the historian's professional and personal interests and ties.

History matters because it forms an important part of our consciousness, contributing to our beliefs about who we are, who our friends and enemies are, and how our societies might and should evolve. The past is continually cited in relation to claims and entitlements, to grievances and responsibilities. The fact that history is invoked in this way shows that it is widely perceived as relevant and that it has significant psychological, moral, and political effects, influencing our values, social relations, and policies. And this is certainly evident in post-apartheid South Africa.

But even if history matters, is historical truth possible? Are there criteria for determining that A's account is closer to the truth than B's, or is there no answer to the claim of extreme relativists (now termed postmodernists) that historical truth is impossible, and that, to take a famous case, the version of "holocaust deniers" is of equal value to analyses based on detailed documentation of the extermination camps of the German Reich?

Richard Evans (1997), among others, convincingly rebuts extreme relativism, showing that it is often feasible to establish significant degrees of historical truth. This argument receives support from the tendency (though not inevitability) of the truth to exact recognition—even when opposed by strong convictions and powerful vested interests. This tendency is gradually emerging in the bitter, polarized South African debate. The neo-Marxists (who now refer to themselves as progressives or radicals) remain silent about their past record. They now mostly prefer to engage in "reconceptualizing modernity," rediscovering "culture," and exploring new areas such as gender and the environment. But when they venture into what has become the sensitive terrain of race, class and the struggle for power, there are signs of a significant—though unacknowledged—shift in their interpretation toward the "conventional liberal version," particularly of twentieth-century South Africa, and even toward the adoption of liberal values and policies, such as market mechanisms and "bourgeois" political institutions.

But although the weight of evidence is forcing the neo-Marxists/progressives to make this shift, it has not, paradoxically, ended their hostile rhetoric toward those they identify as "liberals." Nor has it ended their claims of transforming South African history, or the credence accorded to these claims by others. Even after the peaceful inauguration of post-apartheid South Africa in 1994, the neo-Marxist interpretation continued to be reflected in academic and public discourse, for example, in the Report of South Africa's (in many ways exemplary) 1997–98 Truth and Reconciliation Commission, particularly in the sections on the conduct of business and the English media under apartheid.

This paradox of continuing acrimony despite narrowing differences stimulated this book. Its aim is not only to review the contending historical analyses of how economic and other pressures—whether from business, armed struggle, mass action, or international sanctions—shaped South African development, especially the unexpected ending of apartheid. The aim is also to address *the paradox of the continuing acrimony among historians, despite the narrowing differences* among them over "the facts," the interpretation of these facts, and in many of their underlying values and policies.

Chapter 2 examines conflicting interpretations of selected themes from South Africa's colonial history before the formation of the Union of South Africa in 1910. It is argued that neo-Marxist claims of transforming the history of this period are largely based on misrepresentation, and/or misunderstanding, of the work of liberal and nationalist historians.

Chapter 3 addresses the central issue in the liberal–neo-Marxist debate: the evolution of apartheid during the twentieth century, especially the relationship between capitalism and apartheid. It focuses on conflicting historical analyses of three crucial periods: the 1922 rebellion over the job color bar on the gold mines, the abortive reforms of the 1940s, and the reforms that gradually began after the 1970 election. The liberal argument that the costs of apartheid were rising, and business pressures against it growing, is contrasted with the revisionist argument that capital had been, and remained, the main pressure for apartheid, and that capitalism and apartheid were inextricably linked, comprising a combination that rendered South Africa unreformable, so that the system could only be ended by revolution. This chapter also discusses contending interpretations of the roles of white labor, the bureaucracy, and Afrikaner nationalism in the evolution of apartheid.

Chapter 4 examines contending interpretations of the role played in apartheid's demise by other factors, particularly, international sanctions, armed struggle, black trade unions, and mass actions.* Chapters 2 through 4 also discuss alternative (African and Afrikaner) nationalist interpretations of the rise and decline of apartheid, highlighting their greater emphasis on the salience of racial/ethnic, as distinct from class, factors in shaping South African development. The neo-Marxists' damaging allegations against the professional and political conduct of liberal historians and social scientists are examined in the Appendix.

Chapter 5 discusses the underlying assumptions and values shaping these conflicting interpretations. The influence of theory, ideology, and political commitment on the work of historians is well recognized. However, in the South African case, the influence of theory and ideology seem less important than the heated, inflated rhetoric suggests. What seems more relevant are underlying, though largely implicit, differences in assumptions about individual and social behavior, such as the role of self-interest and the nature of social change. Insufficient attention has been paid to the influence on historians of their professional and personal ties and animosities, evident in rivalries for jobs, status, and power. These factors were magnified by the neo-Marxists' self-identification as a distinctive school; their effective group mobilization; and their insistent, often arbitrary, political categorization of all historians.

Chapter 6 examines the influence of historical misunderstandings, grievances and fears on social and political relations in post-apartheid South Africa and the role of intellectuals, especially the growing group of black historians and social scientists, in shaping perceptions about the past and expectations about the future. The influential social role of historians confronts them with the challenge of reconciling their professional duty to uncover and disclose the truth with their ideological commitments and their professional and personal ties, especially in situations where they feel the need to be politically *engagé*, and/or become polarized into rival coteries or "schools."

Chapter 2

The Debate about South Africa I: Selected Issues before 1910

Great is the power of steady misrepresentation
—Charles Darwin

The claim of the neo-Marxist revisionists that they transformed South African history by exposing the inadequacies and fallacies of "the conventional liberal version" rests on their contention that earlier and contemporary liberal historians:

1. ignored the role of economic and class interests in explaining racism, attributing this instead to "irrational" ideological and psychological factors;
2. portrayed the eighteenth-century Boers/Afrikaners as the originators of racism, thereby obscuring the origins of racism in twentieth-century industrialization;
3. obscured the fact that English-speaking liberals were among the originators and promoters of segregation;
4. acted as apologists for British imperialism.

As these claims indicate, this debate is not only about the substantive historical issues, particularly the origins and evolution of segregation/apartheid. The debate is also about the historiography: how historians portrayed the past. This is underlined by the further accusation that contemporary liberal historians, without acknowledging the neo-Marxist research, have "quietly shifted" toward recognizing that there was a major economic dimension to apartheid, and that capitalists, the British government, and English-speaking whites have a more malign record than in the liberal portrayal of them as "friends of the natives." This bald summary brushes over recent minor qualifications of these claims by some revisionists. But, as will be shown later, the main thrust of their claims continues to be reiterated by analysts both within and outside their ranks.[1]

THE ECONOMIC DIMENSIONS OF RACISM

The claim that liberal—and all other—historians ignored the material and economic dimensions of racism is a foundation stone of the neo-Marxist critique, and the basis of their claim of transforming South African history. In her widely quoted surveys of South African historiography, Shula Marks (1981, 1986) wrote that the revisionists "questioned many of the basic assumptions of earlier writing on South Africa. . . . [formulating] an alternative conception. . . . that transformed South African historiography. . . . and challenged the stranglehold of ruling class orthodoxies and mythologies. . . . breaking with the notion that racism was simply an atavistic carryover from the eighteenth century. . . . The revisionists exploded these comfortable myths . . . broke the hold of dominant, pluralist models of race relations in South Africa . . . with their demand for . . . a materialist analysis of race and class."

Other revisionists constantly reiterate this claim. For example, Nigel Worden (1994, 2) writes, "Our understanding of the South African past has been transformed by . . . the 'historiographical revolution' of . . . historians who were influenced by a neoMarxist or revisionist paradigm, which explained apartheid not by the irrational racism of a preindustrial colonial frontier, but as the direct product of industrialisation. . . . Apartheid resulted from class domination by capitalists, rather than from broad race domination by whites." And, three decades after the first neo-Marxist claims, Paul Maylam (2001, 216) wrote, "Both Afrikaner nationalist and liberal writers operated within the paradigm of racial pluralism, assuming race groups to be real categories and discrete entities. . . . while generally neglecting economic interests."

This claim has also been widely accepted outside neo-Marxist ranks. The influential historiographical survey by Christopher Saunders (1988, 168, 179) attributed to "the new revisionist perspective. . . . a challenge to liberal historians who, by concerning themselves exclusively with 'race,' obscured or ignored the fundamental transformation that flowed from the spread of capitalist social relations. . . . Whereas for liberal historians, irrational race prejudice, explained in mere psychological terms, was often cited as the reason for segregation and apartheid, for the revisionists, racism itself had to be explained." John Lonsdale (1983, 67), though less dismissive of the liberals, agreed that, following the neo-Marxist transformation, "among liberals there [is now] . . . increasing awareness of the need to study the material necessities of production and its contradictory social relations."

It is surprising that such credence has been given to claims that conflict with evidence readily available from the publications of many (liberal and other) historians, such as MacMillan, de Kiewiet, Frankel, Hutt, Neumark, Robertson, van der Horst, Salomon, Horwitz, van der Merve, and Wilson. Even a cursory examination of their work shows that, in analyzing race relations, they accorded a central role to economic interests, both in their competitive and cooperative aspects.

Emphasis on the economic interests underlying racism is evident in the work of the nineteenth-century liberal intellectual and missionary, John Philip, who highlighted the desire of white colonists for black labor and land and rejected the white settler version of benign whites bringing order to aggressive, savage blacks. The colonists were angered by Philip's references to "forced labour" and by his argument that differences between whites and blacks were due to educational and environmental factors, not to "race." Philip (1828) advocated social, legal, and economic reforms that would integrate blacks into a common society as producers ("with the power to bring their labour to a fair market"), consumers, and citizens. Philip's twin themes of the economic as well as moral dimensions to racist policies established the framework for the liberal analysis of South Africa.[2]

Philip's papers were used by W. M. MacMillan (1927, 1929), the founder of liberal South African history, who took up Philip's twin themes of the common humanity and shared material interests underlying race relations. MacMillan, like Philip, highlighted the poverty of blacks and explained differences between blacks and whites in material, not racial, terms. MacMillan's argument that it would be both morally right and economically efficient to move towards a common society was not based on naïve ignorance of the material interests underlying racist policies. He noted that whites employed "distinctions of race and colour as devices for social and economic discrimination." His approach was structural, that is, he explained historical evolution primarily in terms of sociological and economic, rather than racial or ideological, factors.

MacMillan considered that "the South African colour question is only one phase of the World Problem which arises from the economic competition of peoples . . . complicated by racial misunderstandings, and distorted by fear." He paid close attention to agrarian poverty, initially of poor whites (mostly Afrikaners), but increasingly of blacks. A major MacMillan theme was the loss of land by blacks: "European land-hunger has forced [blacks] into a position of economic dependence and impotence." Consequently, blacks were transformed into poor peasants and farm laborers and forced to migrate to the cities, where they came into competition with poor rural whites. MacMillan's writing on twentieth-century South Africa highlighted the socioeconomic transformation effected by the mineral discoveries, the creation of new markets and new forms of competition, and the acute social problems wrought by industrialization and urbanization.

MacMillan influenced the work of de Kiewiet, Frankel, Neumark, Robertson, van der Horst, and others. De Kiewiet's concise *History of South Africa* (1941) focuses on the three-way struggle among the Dutch (and later British) authorities, white settlers, and blacks over land, water, cattle, and labor, as well as on physical and ecological conditions: the climate, tsetse fly and phylloxera, and the malnutrition that affected both poor whites and poor blacks. De Kiewiet argued, "White dependence on black labour was the most significant social and economic fact of eighteenth- and nineteenth-century South Africa. . . . [White society] set out deliberately to create a black proletariat. Its legislation sought to restrict and bind, not to relieve or liberate. . . . The leading theme of South African history is the growth of a new society in which white and black are bound together in the closest dependence."

Robertson (1934) stressed that white pressures for restrictions on black landholding were driven by the twin desires to acquire black land and increase the supply of black labor.[3] Hutt's *The Economics of the Colour Bar* (1964) was subtitled "A study of the economic origins and consequences of racial segregation." Hutt (27) attributed these origins primarily to "the determination [of whites] to defend their economic privilege" against competition from blacks and, secondly, to white fears of black political domination. Far from giving weight to "colour prejudice," Hutt argued that "in a free market system, the rising economic standards of non-Whites would have led to a gradual dissolution of prejudice."

S. H. Frankel (1930) regarded "the premier issue" in South Africa as neither social nor political but economic, arguing that white policy was shaped by "a calculating desire" for black land and labor, combined with "an instinctive military attitude" that feared and did not understand blacks. White policy, he wrote, was focused on "only one problem—the supply of cheap, unskilled docile labour . . . [leading to] the diseconomy and appalling wastes involved in unduly low wages and the exploitation of large masses of wage earners. . . . [White policy] fears the development of natives as [farmers] . . . taking no account of the possible beneficial reactions of such a development on the general economic condition. [Pass laws] waste the time and effort [of blacks]. . . . The cheap Native labour policy [amounts to] slave labour" and leads to low productivity and inefficiency for the whole society.

A final example: in the preface to her pioneering *Native Labour in South Africa* (1942, 133–34, 137, 147f.), Sheila van der Horst wrote that the desire of whites for black labor was "foremost among the forces" shaping South African history. Her documentation and analysis of measures, such as the 1856 Masters and Servants Laws, the 1913 Land Act, and the job color bar, showed keen awareness of the economic interests served by these measures. She documented, *inter alia*, the role of the Chamber of Mines in drafting the 1895 pass laws in the Transvaal (then the South African Republic) and the monopsonistic deal among mineowners to reduce black wages below market rates.

In support of the claim that liberals ignored economic issues, Marks (1986) and many others cite Wilson and Thompson's 1971 *Oxford History of South Africa*, which they describe as the culmination or "apogee" of the liberal tradition. This is misleading. The 1948 victory of the NP shifted the attention of many scholars—liberal, Marxist, and nationalist—to the NP's political onslaught with its intensified race policies and associated historical myths, particularly the claim that, when whites arrived in South Africa in 1652, much of the land was empty. These political preoccupations were reflected in the *Oxford History*, in which there was less of the distinctive liberal focus on socioeconomic issues (except for pioneering chapters on white farming by Francis Wilson and on urbanization by David Welsh). The major contribution of the *Oxford History* was in countering the NP's political myths and insisting on the central role of Africans in South Africa's common society. It was for this, that J. M. Coetzee (2002, 342) described it as "the first . . . new revisionist history of colonial South Africa."[4]

The *Oxford History* thus reflected the concerns of its time. However, liberals such as van der Horst, Doxey, Salomon, Neumark, and Horwitz continued to focus on economic issues and, in this, they were soon followed by the next generation of scholars. This refocusing, too, reflected the preoccupations of the time, including the influence of modernization theory and development studies.

There were, and still are, liberals who focused primarily on political, military, and ideological issues, such as Leonard Thompson, Rodney Davenport, Dunbar Moodie, and Peter Walshe. But their existence does not negate the fact that the "structuralist" liberals pioneered socioeconomic analysis in South Africa. Subsequent historians are right to challenge the inevitable shortcomings in their work, but there can be little question about their pioneering role. The neo-Marxists diverged from these "structuralists" in rejecting their arguments that 1) apartheid delivered not only gains to whites, but also imposed costs, directly on some employers and indirectly on the whole society; and 2) as the South African economy modernized, becoming more skill intensive and in need of a larger domestic market, these costs would rise, forcing the ruling whites to choose between continued economic growth and apartheid. This is what de Kiewiet meant when he wrote (1957, 65): "Apartheid is at variance with many of the essential requirements of a growing modern industrial society. . . . It inhibits the full development of the productive powers. . . . the more effective utilization of the native labour force. That the laws of economics and requirements of industrial efficiency are at war with the laws of Parliament is a notable cause for hope."

It could be argued that liberals were mistaken in believing that racist policies were inefficient, and/or that they failed to recognize that repression was essential to raise the surplus for investment (an argument used to justify labor-repressive policies in both socialist and capitalist societies). But this was not the neo-Marxist argument, which was that all historians of South Africa, particularly liberals, ignored the economic dimensions of racist policies. Among the reasons for the revisionists' misrepresentation of liberals is that they lump liberals together with conservatives, few of whom share their structuralist approach and none of whom share their values. This misleading categorization obscures the distinctive role of liberals in pioneering socioeconomic analysis and in challenging the real "conventional white version," produced by conservative (English and Afrikaans) historians, such as Theal, Cory, Muller, van Jaarsveld, and Preller. These historians, with their emphasis on the security problems, and the racial superiority, of whites, dominated official discourse and school and college textbooks.[5] The revisionists ignore this major liberal challenge to the conservatives. Instead, they bracket liberals together with conservatives as architects of the conventional version, while claiming the role of challengers for themselves.[6]

This misrepresentation of liberal historians was attacked by a few critics, such as Harrison Wright (1977) and Lipton (1977, 1979). The revisionists dismissed these criticisms as "character assassination," but thereafter recategorized a couple of liberals, as "radicals."[7] However, what is required are not grudging, patronizing concessions about the modest contribution of a couple of liberals coopted as radicals, but a reassessment of the sweeping neo-Marxist claims about South African historiography. This need is reinforced by their other widely accepted and equally dubious claims.

LIBERAL HISTORIANS AND THE BOERS/AFRIKANERS

Martin Legassick's article, "The Frontier Tradition in South African Historiography" (1980) was hailed as "standing most of the liberal findings on their head [and marking].... the rout of the conventional liberal wisdom [by refuting] the Anglophone liberal" argument that racist policies were a victory for the attitudes of Afrikaner frontiersmen, and showing, instead, that racism was forged by the British.[8]

Maylam (2001, 218) wrote that neo-Marxists "rejected the liberal notion that the racial order evolved over a long period of time. . . . [Instead, they revealed racism] as an essentially modern phenomenon, integrally bound up with the development of industrial capitalism." Marks (1981, 299f.) wrote that Legassick contradicted the liberal view that "the origins of racism [should be] sought . . . in the formative influence of the 'frontier' . . . [thus] averting attention from the way in which forms of racism developed within the capitalist economy. . . . [Liberals] persist in attributing the present situation in South Africa to the peculiar vices of the Afrikaner. . . . and ignore the role of imperialism in the creation of contemporary South Africa."

In his suggestive, stimulating article, Legassick (60f.) argued that: 1) The origins of racism did not lie on the Cape frontier, which was a more "fluid zone of social relations," including cooperation with blacks, than the longer settled Western Cape; instead, the origins of racism lay in twentieth-century industrialization. 2) Frontier conflicts were due to class, not race. Indeed, Legassick denied the frontier-fostered racism: "The last thing that can be said about the eighteenth- and early nineteenth-century frontier was that it fostered 'group consciousness.'"

Critical scholarly work on the frontier preceded the neo-Marxists and was produced not only by liberals such as MacMillan, Marais, Reyburn, and Neumark, but also by 'conservatives' such as P. J. van der Merwe and van der Walt, who wrote pioneering studies based on archival material that challenged the 'white settler' versions of Theal, Cory, and Walker, who depicted the frontier primarily as a zone of conflict between hostile 'races' with white pioneers defending themselves against savage, thieving blacks.

MacMillan (1927, 12) wrote, "The frontier wars are properly to be understood as the struggle for . . . valuable land." Neumark (1957) argued, "Whatever role noneconomic factors are supposed to have played [in frontier relations], the predominance of economic motivation can hardly be in doubt." Neumark was so focused on the economic determinants of frontier expansion that he paid little attention to differences between Boers and Brits, blacks and whites. It was relations between pastoralists and traders that interested him. His emphasis on economic and ecological conditions was shared by van der Merwe (1938), notable for his analysis of the emerging class of Afrikaner *bywoners* (landless white squatters).[9] Instead of viewing the frontier primarily as a clash between white and black, Christian and heathen, these historians viewed it as a site of both competition and cooperation among traders and pastoralists over land, cattle, and water and as an area of growing economic integration.

The difference between Legassick and these historians does not lie in their failure to recognize the fluid, complex situation on the frontier or the role of material factors in shaping social relations—although Legassick contributed to work on these aspects. The difference lies in Legassick's insistence that the origins of racism did not lie in seventeenth- and eighteenth-century South Africa, but in the twentieth-century mining and industrial economy, and his contention that the frontier did not intensify group consciousness. Liberal, conservative and (African and Afrikaner) nationalist historians, believed racism had deeper roots and that the racist assumptions and behavior of preindustrial South Africa carried over into the twentieth century. De Kiewiet argued that the frontier intensified white group consciousness and that "in the face of the native population, their sense of race and fellowship was exceedingly keen." He did not see this as contradicted by the existence of trade and cooperation, nor by the fact that, in the absence of effective administration, social relations were often more fluid.

An exception to the liberal emphasis on economic factors was I. D. MacCrone, a psychologist who worked on the ideological and psychological roots of racism. MacCrone (1937) did not dismiss the importance of the struggle for resources, but his interest was in ideas and feelings. He located the roots of racism in the early history of the Cape Colony, particularly the influence of seventeenth-century Calvinism and of almost two hundred years of slavery, and he argued that these racist views were "stiffened" and group consciousness "intensified" by the frontier situation. MacCrone was ridiculed by the revisionists as an "idealist," but he helped steer South African psychological research away from the allegedly physical basis of racial differences (size of the cranium, etc.) toward the sociological and cultural roots of group conflicts.

The influence of preindustrial South Africa, including the frontier, on shaping racism remains a subject of scholarly debate. Since 1970, much new research has been quietly produced by Peires, Ross, Guelke, Shell, Frederickson, and others. Surveying this work, Elphick and Giliomee (1988, 522f.) argue that "the racial order was largely in place by the end of the eighteenth century" (that is, before the British takeover), and that there was by then a close correlation between race and class that "reinforced each other and. . . . had overlapped for so long. . . . [that they were regarded as] natural or God-given," even though these divisions were neither total, nor as formally institutionalized, as they became during the twentieth century. Elphick and Giliomee give weight to the influence of slavery as well as to the feeling among frontier people of "alienness" from the indigenous blacks and to white fears of "gelykstelling," that is, of becoming like blacks and "reverting to barbarism," despite (or perhaps because of) their similar lifestyles.

The view that racist attitudes were deeply established among the frontier Boers by the end of the eighteenth century receives support from the Boers' own statements and actions. These include their resistance to measures of the new British regime, such as Ordinance 50 of 1828, which increased mobility, for and ended indenture of, the Khoi; the abolition of slavery in 1834; and sporadic attempts by the British administration to constrain settler expansion beyond the colonial frontiers. The declaration of the Voortrekkers in 1836 (and of leaders of earlier rebellions in frontier districts such as Graaff Reinet) set out their objections to measures that resulted in people of color "being placed on an equal footing with Christians, contrary to the law of God and the natural distinction of race and religion. . . . Therefore we withdraw [on the Great Trek] to preserve our doctrines in purity."[10] All this happened before the mining and industrial era.

It would indeed be striking if it were shown that the two and a half centuries following the arrival of white settlers, marked by the conquest of black and brown indigenes and discriminatory policies against them, did not leave a legacy of racism. It would be surprising if the competition for land, water, cattle, and labor between often warring groups, differing in language, customs, and physical appearance, was not marked by group stereotyping and hostility. These hostilities existed on both sides, evident in the desperate action of the Xhosa in 1856–57 of destroying their own cattle and crops in the messianic belief that their elders would arise from the dead and drive whites into the sea.[11] These hostile aspects of frontier relations seemed to have deep roots in mutual feelings of fear, territoriality/acquisitiveness, and aggression, features of human nature lacking from neo-Marxist analyses, which assume that, in the absence of capitalist relations of production, all human relations would be peaceful and benign (these behavioral assumptions are discussed in Chapter 5).

The industrialization that began in the late nineteenth century added to these racist attitudes its own distinctive forms of conflict and discrimination—as well as new forms of contact and cooperation. Liberal (and other) economists and historians did not fail to notice that competition for jobs and other urban resources both integrated people more closely into the economy and fuelled group conflicts. In their view, racism became more institutionalized precisely because attitudes and social relations that had been "treated as normal and taken for granted" were undermined by industrialization and urbanization. These threats to the racial hierarchy led to increasing resort to legal measures to shore them up.

MacMillan, van der Horst *et al.* recognized that modernization can exacerbate inequality; far from having a "rosy Whig view" of industrialization, they documented its harsh effects and were not so obtuse and insensitive as to be unaware of, and unconcerned about, these. Racism in South Africa was overdetermined, with material, security, ideological, and status concerns reinforcing each other. It would indeed transform our understanding of the evolution of race/class relations in South Africa if the neo-Marxists showed that the extreme (though not total) racism of colonial South Africa did not carry over into the twentieth century, where it was in some respects strengthened and in others, challenged. But they have not shown this.

THE MISTREATMENT OF AFRIKANERS BY LIBERAL HISTORIANS

The belief that English liberals were biased against Afrikaners is summed up in the accusation by Dan O'Meara (1983, 2; 1996, 13) that liberals portrayed Afrikaners as "virulent racists. . . . The peculiar vices of Afrikaners . . . are held responsible [for apartheid]. . . . On Afrikaners alone lies the onus." O'Meara maintains that apartheid was universally portrayed as "the simple product of Afrikaner racist paranoia" until neo-Marxists revealed that "the racial order was not an outgrowth of Afrikaner ethnicity, but a product of material forces. . . . the necessary historical condition for the development of capitalism in South Africa."

Among English historians, there were both critics and defenders of Afrikaners. The defenders included conservatives, such as Theal, as well as liberals such as MacMillan, de Kiewiet, Thompson, and Davenport, all of whom recorded and criticized the injustices done to Afrikaners by British administrations. De Kiewiet (1941, 129) described the machinations of Cecil Rhodes and Joseph Chamberlain before the Anglo-Boer War as "a sinister alliance between the British Government and capitalistic finance to destroy the independence of a proud people [and as] placing a stigma upon Imperial statesmanship" from which it never recovered.

Some conservative English historians, such as Walker and Cory, were more hostile to Afrikaners than these liberals, despite sharing the racist views of many (though by no means all) Afrikaners. The fact that Afrikaners were both victims and perpetrators resulted in many liberals—as well as Marxists and African nationalists—becoming almost schizophrenic about them. There were thus complex relations between Afrikaners and English and a confusing mixture of views among the historians writing about them.

Liberal historians did not exonerate English whites from their share of blame for racist policies. MacMillan (1927, 24) noted that "colour prejudice is very far from being a monopoly of the Dutch population" and that many Afrikaners supported the Cape's nonracial franchise.[12] David Welsh (1971b) documented the racism of English settlers in Natal and the role of the British Commissioner Shepstone in evolving segregationist policies there. Welsh commented, "It is a myth that apartheid is the exclusive product of Afrikaner nationalism. . . . A long line of segregationist writers and politicians from Natal did much to [promote] . . . segregation." Thompson (1971, ch. 7) documented the racist policies of the (English) Natal delegation at the negotiations for South Africa's 1910 Constitution. Van der Horst (1942, 133–34, 137, 147f.), Horwitz (1967, 80f.), and Francis Wilson (1971, 1972) were among those exposing the support of English mineowners for measures such as the Land Acts and pass laws that forced rural blacks onto the labor market and depressed their wages. Meanwhile (as discussed in Chapter 3) many Afrikaner intellectuals were anti-British, with a particular hatred of the English liberals who denounced racist policies.

The picture is therefore mixed, with anti-Boers and anti-Brits in all camps. Singling out liberals as anti-Afrikaans ignores the role of some liberals in defending Afrikaners and gives a distorted, partisan picture of a complex web of relations involving resentments and hostilities on all sides. Even more questionable is the revisionist claim that liberals were responsible for the ideology and policy of segregation.

LIBERALS AND SEGREGATION

Legassick (1973, 1976) charged that not only capitalists, but also liberals "served to reproduce racially differentiated structures" and "racial categories." This charge was elaborated by Saul Dubow (1995, 4), who maintained that liberals not only "placed the sole responsibility for segregation onto Afrikaner nationalism. . . . They [also] sought to avert the largely justified accusation that [some English liberals] . . . played an instrumental role in the formulation of segregationist ideas."

In support, Dubow (1989) cites the activities of the 1903–05 South African Native Affairs Commission (SANAC), which drafted the framework for much segregationist legislation. Dubow maintains that in the early 1900s, the basic segregationist ideas were propounded by a group he terms "liberal segregationists." This group included Howard Pim, Maurice Evans, C. T. Loram, and Edgar Brookes. However, writes Dubow, "by the 1930s, some of these liberal segregationists were changing their tune and going against segregation because they saw it was not practicable." Marks and Trapido (1987, 6f.) Worden (1994, 72), and Maylam (2001, 172) are among numerous revisionists who reiterated this accusation that segregation was expounded by "liberal segregationists . . . [who only] moved away from segregation because they saw economic and social integration becoming a reality."[13]

Maylam (2001, 167, 216f.) also maintains that liberals "operated within the paradigm of racial pluralism, assuming race groups to be real categories and discrete entities. . . . while generally neglecting economic interests. . . . [The neo-Marxist] challenge was a forthright rejection of these pluralist and idealist assumptions. . . . which rested on the false presupposition that the racial order was essentially a political and ideological phenomenon." O'Meara (1979) adds that liberals disseminated the very ideology they professed to condemn by their use of racial categories, which buttressed the racial system, and that their analysis "places [them] squarely on the side of those who . . . defend this brutal society."

The earliest records of the Cape Colony refer to "swart volkje [black people]. . . . kaffirs, Mulattoes, Mesticos" (Giliomee, 2003:17). Subsequently, racial categories were used by everyone, including the African National Congress (ANC) which organized its Congress Alliance into African, Indian, Coloured, and White branches. In 1930, the South African Communist Party advocated the establishment of a Black Republic, rejected at the time by breakaway dissident members who wanted a workers' republic irrespective of color.[14] Despite this use of racial categories across the whole political spectrum, including Marxists, O'Meara's nailing of this on liberals is reiterated by others.[15] Thus are myths established and "reproduced."

The revisionist claim—that liberals advocated segregation, only "changing their tune when they saw it was not practicable"—seriously misrepresents their record as advocates of a common society. Even Saunders, usually the revisionists' chief praise-singer, rejects this, pointing out (1988, 70) that it distorts the "defensive segregation measures" advocated by John Philip and Alfred Hoernlé.

During the nineteenth-century frontier wars, Philip advocated drawing a line to protect black land from further encroachment by whites. Philip, who promoted the spread of education and Christianity, could be accused of eurocentrism and meritocracy, but he was neither a racist nor segregationist. Instead, he argued consistently for a common society in which individuals would be judged on merit.

During the 1930s, against the background of intensifying racism not only in South Africa but also in Europe, Alfred Hoernlé agonized over the prospects for liberalism in multiracial societies. In his 1939 Phelps-Stokes lectures, Hoernle argued that in view of "the determination of the white minority to remain dominant," the only moral options were *either* total assimilation *or* total separation because "half-way measures [would perpetuate] the present system of domination-cum-trusteeship." As noted by Mark Sanders (2002, 64f.), "For Hoernle, the goal of any scheme of racial separatism was the ending of white domination; a policy that failed to achieve this goal had no justification." Hoernle also addressed the question whether, in a common society, there could be parallel "group rights." Hoernle's conclusions were pessimistic: he could not envisage how these problems could be resolved in a morally defensible way in South Africa.

But while Hoernle despaired of a liberal solution to South Africa's problems, his ideas attracted the attention of Afrikaner nationalists such as the poet N. P. van Wyk Louw (who urged Afrikaners to find "survival in justice") and F. R. Tomlinson, chairman of the NP's 1956 commission proposing enlargement of the African reserves as a first step towards separation. Their interest led some to associate Hoernle with the NP's "grand apartheid" schemes, an association Mark Sanders describes as "a travesty" that twists Hoernle's views to justify racist policies (on Hoernle, see also Charles Simkins 1986). Whatever one's view of "defensive segregation," it is very different from the discriminatory segregation designed to favor whites, which was justified by conservative historians such as Theal, Preller, and Muller. The SANAC Report was the work of paternalist conservatives such as Nicholls, Loram, Evans and, in their early years, Pim and Brookes. They urged preservation of the "native reserves" (in opposition to white farmers who wanted to appropriate this land) under a separate system of "native administration" based on the chiefs, whom they viewed as a bulwark against proletarianization and radicalization. The fact that—unlike Philip and Hoernle—they combined this policy with support for discriminatory measures such as pass laws, job bars and continued white political control, contradicted their claim that segregation was designed "to protect the interests of the natives."

Nevertheless, Maylam (2001, 173) justifies classifying these paternalist segregationists as liberals for the following reason: "They have been labelled 'liberal' because their ideas were tinged with benevolent paternalism [and] they themselves saw their policies as moderate." But, as Rich noted (1993, 16), these self-styled moderates themselves described their policy as a middle way between the "repressionists" (who wanted to appropriate the African reserves) and the "assimilationists or equalists," whose model was the Cape non-racial franchise—that is, the liberals! Thus, while the segregationists would not reduce and might even expand the African reserves, they wanted *more separation* between the "races," not the common society advocated by liberals, including Philip and Hoernle.

"Defensive segregation" does not fit well with liberal principles, based on individual rather than group rights, and most liberals, including MacMillan and de Kiewiet, opposed Hoernle's approach, fearing it obscured the need to recognize the growing integration of blacks and whites in a common society. The rejection of segregation by liberal politicians such as Sauer and Merriman was set out in their testimony to SANAC, in their speeches to the Cape parliament, and at the negotiations for the new Union Constitution. Their arguments for a non-racial franchise in a common society for all South

Africans and their opposition to pass laws, job color bars, and restrictions on African land ownership and business activities is documented by Thompson (1960, 117f., 145f.), McCracken (1967, ch. 7), Lewsen (1972; 1982, 271f.) and many others.

Later, two of the SANAC segregationists, Brookes (in 1927) and Pim (in 1929), reversed their positions stating they had come to realize that SANAC segregation was not protective, but exploitative. It was *at this stage* that they became liberals, with Pim abandoning his former opposition to black political rights, and Brookes later joining the Liberal Party.[16] It is misleading to cite the early, and subsequently rescinded, views of Pim and Brookes as examples of liberal thinking.

Policy towards the African "reserves" or "homelands" remained a thorny issue, particularly the problem of how to respond to the periodic, modest proposals to enlarge them, because the NP (under Hertzog in the 1930s and Verwoerd in the 1960s) used such enlargements to justify the exclusion of Africans from political rights in "white" South Africa. Saunders (1988, 183, 217) aptly terms this dilemma the "ethnic trap." The intensity of this dilemma is illustrated by the fact that John Dube, first President of the ANC, initially said he did not object in principle to separation of the races "as far as it can be fairly and practically carried out." Dube later rescinded this view when it was contested by many within the ANC (Gumede 2005, 6; Walshe 1970, ch. 2 and ch. 3). However, this dilemma was not due to liberals, but to the NP's policy of denying Africans land and citizenship while continuing to want their labor.

The issue of using ethnically based policies for defensive reasons remains contentious, as can be seen from the ANC's "affirmative action" or Black Economic Empowerment (BEE) policy. The circumstances and rationale for this policy are very different, but the policy illustrates the complexity and ambiguity that often surrounds this issue—for liberals as for everyone else. Segregation/apartheid, as envisaged by ideologists such as Shepstone, SANAC, and later Verwoerd, was more complex than straightforward white *baaskap* (domination). But whatever the intentions of these ideologists— rendered suspect by their support for blatantly discriminatory policies—segregation and apartheid came to signify discriminatory, racist policies. Nailing segregation on liberals by "labelling as liberal those who termed themselves moderates" misrepresents the record of liberals as advocates of a common society.

Assessing Cape Liberalism

The approach and values of liberals also need to be assessed in the context of their stance on a range of other issues, including their pressures for the abolition of slavery, support for Ordinance 50, and advocacy of a non-racial franchise for the Cape Colony's 1853 Constitution establishing representative government. Other measures that liberals campaigned for were equality before the law, open courts, and freedom of the press.

Revisionists dismissed these measures as limited and marginal. Stanley Trapido (1980) accuses liberal historians of accepting nineteenth-century Cape liberalism at face value and of failing to recognize the self-interest involved in their advocacy of a stable, free African peasantry, able to participate in the market and qualify for the nonracial franchise. Trapido argues that, as the interests of liberals changed, they diluted or dumped these measures. His dismissive assessment is widely accepted. Maylam (2001, 235) maintains the abolition of slavery "only brought to an end an extreme form of labour oppression. . . . The Cape non-racial franchise did not prevent white domination of the political system [which] firmly belies any idea of British imperialism as a liberalising force." Similar assessments are made by nonrevisionists who question whether Cape liberalism was "really humanistic" and describe it as "shallow and idiosyncratic."[17]

Trapido makes some valid points about the limitations of nineteenth-century Cape liberalism. However, these limitations were recognized—and deplored—by many later liberals.[18] And, far from concealing the enlightened self-interest underlying these nonracial policies, John Philip was the first in a long line of analysts who stressed the benefits for all of a common society with equality before the law. Trapido lumps together liberals and conservatives, failing to recognize that the later attacks on the Cape franchise, and pressures against a free African peasantry, did not come from liberals, but from conservatives, including Afrikaners and English settlers in the eastern Cape—although the attack on the Cape franchise was closely linked with the growth of Afrikaner nationalism.

This conservative attack on the franchise was resisted by liberals such as Solomon, supported by growing mercantile interests in the Cape Colony. This resistance puzzles Trapido, who writes (1980, 247, 253f., 269) of their battle against dilution of the Cape franchise—and subsequent struggle for a nonracial franchise in the 1910

Union Constitution—as follows: "It is difficult to account for the heightened support the franchise was given. . . . [Was this because liberals] reconciled themselves to a free peasantry . . . who might be their allies against white labour in the Transvaal [anticipating that]. . . . only propertied and skilled blacks would be included in the franchise?" Trapido speculates that liberals were probably envisaging only political and legal, not social, equality and assuming that blacks would confine themselves to "a passive and deferential role."

What Trapido does not envisage is that liberals might have believed in the principle of nonracism—even if they often fell short of this ideal in practice. Nevertheless, his puzzled comments on their determined struggle confirms that this belief had a powerful hold on them. To Trapido's credit, while he misunderstands and denigrates liberals, he does not ignore evidence that conflicts with his view—hence his bafflement at what he regards as their contradictory behavior.

The neo-Marxists also present liberal attitudes out of their historical context. During the nineteenth and early twentieth century, the qualified franchise was the general rule in the world's few democracies. In South Africa, whites only got universal suffrage in 1931. Initially, the ANC itself advocated a qualified franchise, with universal franchise only becoming part of its demands in 1943. That most Cape liberals were men of their time is evident from the exclusion of women from the vote, as well as from W. P. Schreiner's statement that "We [whites] shall, if we deserve it, remain dominant. But it must be a dominance in a free country where career is open to talent and to civilised men with no discrimination or distinction upon such grounds as colour or race" (McCracken 1967, 102). This attitude is arrogant, meritocratic and sexist, but it is not racist. More plausible than the revisionists' ahistorical view is the assessment of Giliomee (2003, xiv) that the measures introduced into the Cape Colony by the British, in response to liberal pressures, amounted to "a near social revolution"—an assessment congruent with the objections of the voortrekkers to legal measures that placed people of color "upon an equal footing" with whites.

Judgements as to whether liberals overvalued the Cape's nonracial franchise and legal equality depend upon beliefs about the desirability, and difficulty, of establishing these institutions. In South Africa, these did not spring up unaided, but only after intense struggles. These struggles preceded the British takeover of the Cape, though the few rights conceded by the Dutch were restricted to whites. The rights extracted from the British were limited and imperfect, but they established liberal principles and institutions that persisted despite their attenuation under attacks from conservative (English and Afrikaans) whites, especially during the upheavals from the late nineteenth century as the colonies, republics, and African kingdoms underwent wars, industrialization and, in 1910, consolidation into the Union of South Africa.

Thereafter, blacks and their white supporters fought a long rearguard action to preserve, and build on, the remnants of this fragile inheritance. The failure to extend nonracial institutions to the rest of the Union in 1910 was not the fault of liberals, who barely succeeded in retaining these for the Cape. The revisionists habitually exaggerate the power of the liberals. But they were seldom able to get their way, and their few successes usually depended on external intervention. The practice of appealing for outside support was initiated by Philip, and by African leaders such as the Basotho King Moshesh, and further developed by the ANC after its establishment in 1912. The hope of those who mounted these pressures was that, over time, the influence of antiracist ideas would grow, supported by principled arguments and reinforced by evidence of the socioeconomic benefits of a common society.

The view that this approach was based on naïve, wishful thinking was understandably reinforced during the twentieth century, as South African governments responded to pressures for more racist policies from white voters, particularly the increasingly mobilized Afrikaner nationalists, supported on race policies by the conservative English. However, even in these unfavorable circumstances, liberal ideas and institutions lingered on and (as argued later) contributed to South Africa's remarkable transition to democracy. J. S. Mill was the first in a long line of theorists who believed that "free institutions are next to impossible in a country made up of different nationalities" (Lewsen 1972, 79). Their partial establishment in the nineteenth-century Cape Colony, and remnants in South Africa's 1910 Constitution, were unusual achievements for the time.

The Cape principles of equality before the law and the nonracial franchise, and the rejection of these by the trekboers whose republics embodied the explicitly racist principle of "no equality in church or state," came to symbolize the options open to South Africa, referred to rather simplistically as the Cape and the 'frontier' traditions. The main thrust of liberal analysis and policy prescriptions was the belief that "South Africa could not survive half slave, half free," but would have to extend legal and political rights to all citizens, and that this would bring economic and social benefits to the whole society.

This was the view not only of historians, but also of other liberal social scientists. Adam Kuper (2003, 164) wrote, "Mainstream social anthropologists at English universities in South Africa were committed to the study of South Africa as a single social system, a perspective developed most powerfully by the historian W. M. MacMillan and endorsed by Radcliffe Brown at UCT . . . and Winifred Hoernle at Witwatersrand. . . . The common society was conflict-ridden and divided, but it was riven by conflicts precisely as a consequence of the very nature of the overarching social structure itself, not because of any primordial and intractable 'cultural' differences." Leo Kuper (1974, 263) identified the core of South African liberalism as "the fostering of racial contact and [their recognition] that the origins of racially structured societies [lay] in conquest and exploitation and [rest] on the structures of power."

It is a travesty of the truth to depict liberals as proponents of segregation rather than as supporters of a common society, which accorded with their basic principle of individual, as distinct from group, rights. Their despair at the evolution of South African policy was expressed by de Kiewiet's dismay at "the great inequities in social and racial policy . . . the danger and folly of white policy. . . . of which much of South African life is an indictment" (Smith 1988, 116).

LIBERALS AND BRITISH IMPERIALISM

Timothy Keegan (1996, 4, 6) maintains that "the British imperial factor was overwhelmingly portrayed by liberal scholars as on the side of the good. . . . that the 'advance of civilisation' entailed conquest, coercion and cultural suppression was never recognised by liberals." Shula Marks (1981, 300f.) states that "liberals took the ideology of imperial humanitarianism at face value," portraying the British as humanitarian and negrophilist. Atmore and Westlake (1972, 2) maintain that "liberal ideology in South Africa presents modern capitalism as resulting in. . . . the peaceful interaction of, mutual cooperation between, and equivalent benefit to all participants."

But it was not liberals who praised the British government as "humanitarian and negrophilist." It was (Afrikaans and English) conservatives who *accused* it of this in response to the abolition of slavery and establishment of equality before the law. These policies—Giliomee's "social revolution at the Cape"—were lobbied for by liberals such as Philip and then defended against attack by champions of white interests such as George McCall Theal and William Boyce. The Atmore/Westlake claim that liberals viewed capitalism and imperialism as having "wholly benign effects" is nonsense. From MacMillan onwards, they showed a keen awareness of its negative features. Indeed, Adam Smith, founder of neoclassical economics, was a leading critic of imperialism, arguing that it led to "dreadful misfortunes [due to] . . . the superiority of force of the Europeans . . . enabled to commit with impunity every sort of injustice in those remote countries [which will only end] when those countries grow stronger [and there is] equality and . . . respect for the rights of one another."[19]

Far from being uncritical apologists for imperial rule, liberal historians attacked many imperial policies toward both blacks and Afrikaners. So too did liberal Cape politicians such as Solomon, Rose Innes, and Sauer, as recorded by, *inter alia*, Trapido (1980, 253, 247, 269). MacMillan (1929, 73) denounced "the blundering" management of frontier conflicts by the British. De Kiewiet (1929, 7) judged "the shortcomings of British policy . . . many and grievous," deplored the British government's "very hesitant and timid humanitarianism," and regretted that it was "at no time after 1854 prepared to sacrifice men or money in pursuit of purely native interests. In consequence a large proportion of South Africa's native population was subjected to the 'colonist' point of view . . . that the native held too much land, and that the white man was a superior being."

Leonard Thompson (1971, 321, 265, 313f.; 1960, 16f.) criticized Britain's "Machiavellian behaviour" toward the Zulu King Cetshwayo, attacked the conduct of Chamberlain and Rhodes in the events leading to the Anglo-Boer War, and accused the High Commissioner Alfred Milner of "the chauvinistic assumption that the 'British race' had . . . a moral right to rule other peoples [and of having] wrought harm in South Africa . . . [making it] more difficult to establish a stable and humane society."

The role of Chamberlain and Rhodes in precipitating the Anglo-Boer War was exposed and denounced by liberals. De Kiewiet (1941, 129f.) condemned "the greed of the financial interests that confronted [Kruger's] inexperienced government," maintaining that this conduct "placed a stigma upon Imperial statesmanship from which it never recovered." This conduct also led to sympathy for the Boers in both South Africa and in Britain, where opposition to the war contributed to Chamberlain's 1906 defeat by Campbell-Bannerman's Liberal Party. This sympathy complicated the task of countering the racist elements in the Union Constitution demanded by the Afrikaner republics, supported by Natal conservatives. Thompson concluded (1971, 364) that in attempting to reconcile the Afrikaners, Britain withdrew from South Africa, leaving behind "a caste-like society, dominated by its white minority. The price of [white] unity and conciliation [of Afrikaners] was the institutionalisation of [racism]." Thus, both contemporary and later liberals recognized and condemned the imperial government's failure to oppose the entrenchment of a racist order in South Africa.

Atmore and Marks—in an article described by Bozzoli (1990) as "a seminal re-evaluation of the imperial factor"—argued that whites were weak and evenly matched by the independent black kingdoms until British intervention tilted the balance in their favor. Atmore and Marks suggested (1974, 110) that without British intervention, the Afrikaners "left to themselves" were likely to have merged with the indigenous blacks, "as did the Portuguese *prazeros* in the Zambezi valley," and that this was likely to have resulted in a less racist society.

Counterfactuals can provide a sense of perspective and of alternatives in reflecting on the historical paths that evolved. Colonization has been a ubiquitous feature of human history, occurring into and out of all major regions and continents. A feature of many of these expansions and migrations—by the Persians, Romans, Mongols, Mughals, Incas, Han Chinese, Muslims, and Europeans—is how relatively small numbers of settlers and troops, based in distant metropoles, often conquered and ruled over large, sometimes well-populated regions.

In the seventeenth century, when white colonists numbered less than four thousand, the Dutch Governor Simon van der Stel complained that if the Boers were not constrained from trekking, "all of Africa would not be enough to suit and satisfy [them]" (Giliomee 2003, 21). The restless, energetic Boers/Afrikaners defied the efforts of both Dutch and British governments to rein them in. On occasions, the Afrikaners defeated African and British armies and (in what they termed Africa's first war of independence) Afrikaners held at bay a huge British force from 1899–1902. When effectively mobilized, the Afrikaners often demonstrated a capacity to cause more trouble than, not only the small group of white liberals, but also than the far more numerous Africans, despite the formidable military capacity of some African kingdoms. This was partly because intra-African divisions meant the Boers were seldom on their own against a united Africa. Many Boer conquests were aided by their manipulation of divisions among Africans—for example, their alliance with Maroka's Baralong against Mzilikazi's Matabele, with Prince Mpande against King Dingane and, on occasion, with Griquas against Xhosa. Conflicts within southern Africa were seldom simply along black and white lines: many of the fiercest were intrawhite and intrablack, with the Anglo-Boer War probably the most destructive.

Atmore and Marks do not consider whether, without British financial and administrative muscle, a united South Africa, with a well-developed infrastructure and economy, would have emerged. Along with the upheaval and suffering European settlement inflicted on the indigenous societies in what became South Africa, the country experienced a relatively broad development and escaped becoming a narrow enclave economy, as happened in the colonies of, especially, Portugal and Belgium.

Boer resistance to the British "social revolution in the Cape" suggests it is by no means certain that, under Afrikaner aegis, a less racist society would have evolved, a la Mozambique or Brazil (whose nonracism some regard as bogus). It also seems unlikely that institutions of representative government would have taken root to the extent that they did. Attenuated though these became under NP rule, they provided what Daryl Glaser (2001, 88) describes as "experience in operating democracy. . . . a cultural transmission system for British parliamentary and civic norms, such as the rule of law and press freedom." The difficulty of establishing these institutions elsewhere suggests these benefits should not be taken for granted. It is by no means certain that the "'Afrikaner mestizo" model of the Atmore/Marks counterfactual would have evolved, nor that the institutions introduced into Africa and Latin America by the Iberian monarchies, which later evolved into fascist dictatorships, would have provided a better inheritance than those of Victorian Britain—flawed though these undoubtedly were.

African historians have varied and often nuanced views of South Africa's colonial inheritance. According to Lodge (1991b, 127), popular oral traditions include heroic versions of precolonial history, although these idealized versions are less evident in the written literature. From the late nineteenth century, writers such as Sol Plaatje and Modiri Molema combine regret for lost communitarian features of African social life with an eager embrace of much Western technology and culture—though not of the accompanying racist policies, such as the Land Acts to which Plaatje, among others, recorded a shocked, angry reaction. Their work also reveals a close personal rapport with many individual whites.[20]

These nuanced attitudes are reflected in Albert Luthuli's view that "two cultures met . . . and both profited" alongside his fierce attacks on white racism (Lodge 1991b, 128). The ANC leader and scholar, Z. K Matthews, noted benefits as well as costs and misdeeds, commenting that many Africans "willingly and even eagerly accepted the white man's world of literature and science [but it was quite another matter] to accept his account of how we all came to occupy the places in life now assigned to us" (Magubane 2002, 268). Njabula Ndebele, author and vice chancellor of Cape Town University (*Mail & Guardian*, April 30, 2004), referred to "the abusiveness of colonialism which, in the total scheme of things, could be seen as ultimately progressive [because] at the time the European colonial powers had travelled the road of technical development much further than their colonial subjects." (Ndebele added that this gave them an authority to lead that the United States currently lacks.)

These mixed, qualified assessments are challenged by others. Bernard Magubane (1979, ch. 2 and ch. 3) denounces colonization for its destruction of "traditional African social structures [leading to] atomisation, rootlessness . . . cultural pauperisation, alienation . . . and the disorientation and psychological enslavement of Africans." Magubane attributes a major role in this process to missionaries (and also presumably to both liberals and Marxists?), who "undermined African societies from within, while military force overwhelmed them from without." He argues that mission schools alienated their pupils from their own traditions and society, converted their values into Western values, and created in them a desire for Western goods: "The missionary's desire to abolish slavery was only matched by his concern to advance British commerce" by exhorting his converts to acquire books, tools, and clothes. Magubane considers the difference between the Boers and British to be that: "the Boers stood for outdated slavery on a petty scale . . . [the British for] largescale capitalist exploitation . . . and bourgeois-democratic liberalism" (43).

Magubane's own counterfactual is of a South Africa united under Zulu aegis, which, he argues, was emerging in the late eighteenth century (1979, 25). That this was unlikely to be welcomed by all Africans is evident from Sifiso Ndlovu's recent analysis (2006)—in a paper "challenging the dominant Eurocentric orthodoxy"—of the conflicting interpretations that revisionist African historians are now producing of the Zulu Kings Shaka and Dingane, whom some depict as liberation heroes and others as tyrants.

Colonization was a brutal process. The "international community"—an entity that only began to emerge in the mid-twentieth century—is struggling to bring such processes to a close (as well as debating how to deal with the current "counter-colonizations" of Western countries from Africa and Latin America). But South Africa's nineteenth- and twentieth-century liberals were not shallow optimists who viewed colonialism through "rosy-tinted glasses." Despite their undoubted shortcomings, they were ahead of their time in recognizing and trying to constrain some of colonialism's brutal effects. The tragic liberal view was expressed by de Kiewiet as "a certain inevitability of conflict and misunderstanding . . . so that no single man, nor party, idea, nor set of principles was solely responsible either for effecting any solution, nor for producing any tangle." De Kiewiet also believed that along with the appalling injustices perpetrated (which he recorded) there were achievements to build on.[21]

The neo-Marxist partisanship towards Afrikaners is presumably due to Afrikaner opposition to British (though not to their own) colonialism and to the fact that, during the early twentieth century, Afrikaners comprised the most militant, well-organized section of unionized labor in South Africa. This stance won plaudits for the neo-Marxists from some Afrikaner historians. F. A. van Jaarsveld declares that he prefers Marxists to liberals because Marxists blame the British and capitalists for South Africa's problems (Smith 1988, 94).

But not all Afrikaners connive at this attempt to shift the blame for racism not only to the British, but also to English liberals. Hermann Giliomee and Andre du Toit follow P. J. van der Merve and

J. S. Marais in demythologizing Afrikaner history and warning that the close identification of Afrikaner rule with segregation/apartheid holds grave dangers for their future, committed as they are to South Africa. They recognize that, while not all Afrikaners were racists, racist policies were the hallmark of the Afrikaner republics and of post-Union governments dominated by Afrikaner nationalists.[22] B. J. Liebenberg wishes it were true that Afrikaners were not responsible for apartheid, but unfortunately, "the Afrikaner is the principal inventor and maintainer of apartheid, and all the attempts of O'Meara and his kindred spirits to place the guilt on the English and Jewish (sic) capitalists are doomed to failure" (Smith 1988, 94, 101, ft52, 211). In the light of the support of the conservative English for racist legislation, including the Union Constitution, this assessment lets them off too lightly. But it is a measure of the integrity of many Afrikaner intellectuals (whose contribution to ending apartheid is discussed later) that they confront the past honestly and do not resort to creating historical myths that will serve as future sources of resentment and acrimony.

To conclude: the neo-Marxist revisionists misrepresent the position of earlier and contemporary liberals and understate their scholarly contribution. Liberals did not ignore the material interests underlying racist policies; they were among the first to highlight their salience. Far from being uncritical apologists for imperialism, liberals were among those exposing many of the misdemeanors of the imperial government against both blacks and Afrikaners. The claim that liberals were originators and promoters of segregation distorts their beliefs and seriously misrepresents their role as advocates of a common society.

The revisionists reacted to challenges to their sweeping claims by arbitrarily recategorizing a couple of liberals as "radicals" and by quietly dropping a few specific allegations. But they have ignored most challenges and have neither modified their claims of "transforming" South African history, nor their damaging misrepresentation of other historians. Consequently, these claims remain part of what the admiring Saunders (1988, 195) proclaims as "the new orthodoxy in South African history." A similar situation prevails in relation to the history of twentieth-century South Africa, discussed in Chapter 3.

Chapter 3

The Debate about South Africa II: Selected Issues, 1910–90

The election in 1948 of the Afrikaner National Party (NP) focused scholarly and public debate on whether the NP's determination to reinforce apartheid would hinder economic growth. Hendrik Verwoerd (Minister of Native Affairs, then prime minister until 1966) insisted his reformulation of apartheid—his "separate development" policy—would make apartheid compatible both with continued growth and with the increasingly antiracist norms of the international community.

Separate development would achieve this in the economic sphere by decentralizing labor-intensive industries to the African reserves or "homelands." This would simultaneously reduce African numbers in "white" areas and provide Africans with economic opportunities in their "own" areas. Politically, separate development would provide Africans with their own representative institutions in what would become independent homelands (nicknamed Bantustans). Coloureds and Indians, too, would have their own separate political institutions. These measures would justify exclusive white control of South Africa's central political institutions, thus ensuring the survival of white, particularly Afrikaner, identity.

The NP's critics rejected this new version of apartheid as racist and fraudulent. But the critics disagreed about whether the policy could work. Some liberal analysts and businessmen argued that if economic growth continued, it would undermine the hierarchical racial system. In his seminal 1964 paper, Michael O'Dowd, an economist and director of Anglo-American Corporation, argued that the interests of the (white and black) industrial and middle classes generated by economic growth would increasingly conflict with apartheid, and that pressures from these classes would "usher in a new period of progress and reform, initially highly equivocal but gradually gathering momentum until the mutual antagonism between rulers and ruled . . . diminishes . . . [and they] find it preferable to compromise. . . . Constitutional reform in a democratic direction will begin. . . . [out of] bitterness and struggle . . . [and] will emerge some form of welfare state." Clearly, O'Dowd did not view South Africa as a uniquely evil society dominated by irrational Afrikaner racists. He viewed it as "a particularly fierce class system [in which] discrimination is more blatant and statutory than . . . in most other countries." Reviewing his predictions a decade later, in 1974, O'Dowd maintained that the erosion of apartheid was under way.

O'Dowd's analysis was challenged, not only by the NP, but also by liberals like Herbert Blumer (1965), who feared Verwoerd's malign strategy might work. Blumer agreed that continuing capitalist growth would generate pressures against South Africa's hierarchical racial system, but he argued that, faced with a determined, ruthless government, capitalists would adapt to and operate within the apartheid structures: the NP might thus succeed in reconciling apartheid and economic growth.

The opposing hypotheses of O'Dowd and Blumer set the parameters for the debates of the 1970s and '80s, to which liberal, Marxist, and (African and Afrikaner) nationalist scholars contributed, as did many people in the churches, business, trade unions, and media. This was never a debate confined to the academy.

In 1966, Verwoerd was assassinated and succeeded as prime minister by the thuggish, but pragmatic, John Vorster. To the surprise of many, Vorster slowly and cautiously began to make concessions on some apartheid policies. These provoked a breakaway from the NP by the ultraconservative Herstigte (purified) Nasionale Party (HNP), which Vorster defeated in the 1970 election. Thereafter, Vorster stepped up his concessions. These precipitated political turmoil, including a growing struggle within the NP, between the *verligtes* (enlightened) and *verkramptes* (ultraconservatives). Vorster's measures also stimulated debate outside the NP, particularly between those liberals who viewed these measures as reforms initiating the retreat from apartheid, predicted by O'Dowd, and the neo-Marxist revisionists who, building on Blumer's thesis, argued that Vorster's changes were cosmetic adaptations that would merely "restructure," and thereby even strengthen, apartheid.

Once again, this debate was not only about the substantive issues but also about the role of historians and social scientists. The neo-Marxists accused liberals of whitewashing the interests not only of business, but also of the South African government, arguing that O'Dowd's analysis "conceals or obscures the fundamental relations of capitalist exploitation . . . [and places liberals] squarely on the side of those who . . . defend this brutal society."[1] They also accused liberal academics of making covert, unacknowledged use of the revisionist research that, they claimed, was "transforming" the understanding of modern South Africa—as it had of colonial South Africa. In his influential historiographical survey, Chris Saunders wrote that the revisionists "won all the arguments [which liberals] did not even challenge"; instead they "quietly shifted to adopting neo-Marxist positions" while "striving to avoid" any reference to their work.[2] As will be shown later, these claims are a caricature of the truth.

The conflicting revisionist and liberal analyses were developed not only in their interpretations of Vorster's post-1970 policy changes, but also of earlier twentieth-century history. This chapter examines their contending interpretations of:

1. the struggle over the job color bar on the gold mines in 1922–24;
2. the abortive pressures for reform during the Second World War;
3. the changes to apartheid from 1970 to 1990;
4. the role of racism/ethnicity, particularly Afrikaner nationalism.

Conflicting Interpretations of the Struggle over the Job Color Bar

The establishment of the job color bar, and other racist measures, on the diamond and gold mines was among the foundation stones of apartheid. And, as Neville Alexander (2002, 34) noted, the conflict over the job bar posed "the single most difficult sociological and political problem" for Marxists. This is because capital and labor seemed to be on the wrong sides in this conflict, with capital urging relaxation of the job bar (which reserved skilled jobs for whites), while white trade unions mounted the barricades to defend the job bar in 1907, 1913 and in the 1922 Rand Rebellion.

The resulting conflicts between white and black workers challenged Marxist beliefs in the shared interests of labor against capital, and their explanation of social conflicts in class, not racial, terms. Moreover, as the outcome of this conflict was the maintenance of the job bar, against the wishes of mineowners, this outcome challenged Marxist beliefs in the state as the committee of "hegemonic capital," which in South Africa at that time was mining capital.

Neo-Marxists claimed they resolved these dilemmas and transformed the understanding of these events. Marks wrote (1981, 303f.; 1986, 167f.):

> It is in the interpretation of the . . . [mining and industrial revolution] that the revisionist interpretation differs most dramatically from the liberals. [Revisionists showed that] it was in deep-level gold mining . . . with its huge demand for labour and vast sums of international investment. . . . and in the policies of the Chamber of Mines, with its drive to cut costs, that the origins of many of the critical constituents of contemporary apartheid were found: the migrant labour system . . . pass laws and compounds; the policy of setting aside reserves. . . . to reduce the welfare costs borne by the mines; the division of the working class into skilled, highly paid white labour and unskilled, superexploited black labour.

This "paradigm shift" revolutionized conventional versions of the roles of capital, labor and the state by revealing "the instrumental quality of both racist and liberal ideology" and of measures such as the job bar, for the functioning of the mines.[3] Worden (1994, 39f.) is among the many who reiterate that it was the early revisionist historians who revealed that the unusual cost structure of the gold mines led to its distinctive labor policies, such as the job bar, compound migrant labor and ultraexploitable unskilled wages.

These claims are surprising. It was widely agreed—indeed the conventional wisdom—that the exceptional depth, thin spread, and low grade of the Rand gold deposits accounted for the huge amounts of both capital and labor required to mine them. The subsequent link between the mines' technical and economic requirements and their labor policies was recognized by, inter alia, S. H.

Frankel (1938, 80f.), de Kiewiet (1941, ch. 5 and ch. 7), van der Horst (1942, 125ff.), Doxey (1961, ch. 3), Horwitz (1967, 26, 80, 167ff.) and Francis Wilson (1972, chs. 2 and 8). This included recognition of the fact that the initial scarcity and high cost of skilled (white) labor and, later, the fixed price of gold led to intense downward pressure on the wages of unskilled (black) workers and to other labor-repressive policies. It was not the case, as revisionists also claim, that liberals focused narrowly on the job bar and ignored other relevant aspects of apartheid, such as the restrictions on African land ownership and mobility aimed at increasing the supply of unskilled labor. On all these issues, there was a well-established scholarship to which post-1970 liberal, Marxist, and other scholars added.

The distinctive neo-Marxist contribution, and basis for their claims of transforming the subject, must rest on their undoubtedly novel arguments that:

1. mineowners really wanted to retain the job bar, despite their attacks on it;
2. the claim that white labor gained from the job color bar was a "myth";
3. the division between black and white workers was based on class, not race;
4. the South African state, despite its eventual support for the demand of white unions that the job bar be maintained, was really acting in the strategic, long-term interests of capital;
5. the African reserves were retained to subsidize the costs of black labor for mineowners.

The neo-Marxists resolved the seeming contradictions over the positions of mining capital, white labor, and the state by the following "reconceptualizations." Davies (1979, 32, 100, 308, 337, 362) and others redefined white workers as a "petty bourgeoisie" and then reinterpreted the divisions between white and black workers as class rather than race conflicts—"not as a struggle of white against black, but of capital against two different groups of workers." They argued that this class division was deliberately created by capital and that, after the upheavals of 1922–24, there evolved a tacit "alliance between mining capital and white labor" against black labor, which included acceptance of the job color bar (Johnstone 1976; Greenberg 1980).[4]

The neo-Marxists argued further that liberals misrepresented the position of mineowners, who did not want to abolish the job bar but merely shift it upwards, so as to substitute (cheaper) black for white workers. Davies, Kaplan, Morris and O'Meara (1976) rejected the "myth" that white labor gained from the job bar on the grounds that, after its re-entrenchment in 1926, the ratio of white to African miners "only increased" from one white to nine African miners to one white to eight African miners.

Davies et al. also argued (1976, 11) that the differences between mineowners and the state were marginal: "minor points of method and the incidence of the costs burden." Using the new "sophisticated, nuanced and theoretically conscious" frameworks of Althusser and Poulantzas, they argued that, even when the state appeared to be acting against the wishes of capital, it was really taking a more strategic, long-term view of capital's interests. In support, they cited the adaptation of capital to the state's insistence on maintaining the job bar and their shared interest in keeping the mines operating. Saunders (1988, 180) is among the many applauding this revisionist transformation of our understanding of the mining industry.

The Liberal Analysis

The recurring struggles over the job bar were a major pillar of the liberal argument that there were significant conflicts of interest within the white oligarchy over apartheid. Liberals pointed to the implications of the job bar for a range of other policies, such as access to education and training and to family housing (skilled workers require training and low job turnover, hence employers want them settled in family housing rather than in migrant compounds). Thus, seemingly marginal differences over the job bar had dynamic implications for other apartheid policies.[5]

This was among the reasons why relaxation of the job bar was resisted by white workers who feared this would be the first step toward replacing them with cheaper, often abler blacks. In this stance, white labor was consistently supported by Afrikaner nationalist governments, particularly the 1924–33 Nationalist-Labour-Pact and the post-1948 NP, which rejected renewed pressures from mineowners in the 1950s and '60s for relaxation of the job bar and of restrictions on black access to training and to family housing.

The surprising claim that white labor did not gain from re-entrenchment of the job bar—on the grounds that this "only increased" the ratio of white to African miners from one to nine, to one to eight—ignores what would have happened if the bar had not been shored up. An indication of this is that, during the brief victory of the Chamber of Mines in 1922, the ratio rose to eleven Africans to one white miner (i.e., the employment of more Africans and less whites). After the Labor-Pact victory in 1924, the ratio was pushed down again to eight Africans to one white. This higher ratio of white to African miners was not only maintained, but rose further, reaching a low point of six to one in 1953.

This trend occurred *despite* the widening wage gap, as the wages of white miners rose faster than those of Africans, with the wage ratio reaching a peak of twenty-one to one in 1969 (Wilson 1972). The widening wage ratio obviously increased the incentive to replace white with black miners. It is unlikely this high level of white employment—in the face of their large wage increases—could have been sustained without shoring up the job bar. The Chamber of Mines frequently stated "there was not the slightest doubt" that it would prefer to employ "a materially smaller number" of whites and larger number of Africans, who could then receive higher rates of pay. The effect of the job bar on this acutely cost-conscious industry was significant. S. H. Frankel (1938, 94ff.) calculated that it contributed to "significant disinvestment" in South African mines after 1924 and to investment abroad by South African mining companies.

The mines were the main generators of wealth in South Africa, and it was not only the state and mineowners who had an interest in their operation, but also mineworkers and employers and workers in the numerous industries servicing the mines. But this did not rule out disagreements about how the mines should be operated and their profits distributed. The shared interest in keeping the mines operating imposed constraints on the room for maneuver of all parties, with each having to settle for less than they wanted, unless they were prepared to precipitate major upheavals. The point is, what did they want?

The differences between white labor and mining capital were sufficiently large to precipitate recurrent conflicts, and it is a static analysis that depicts as "merely marginal" differences that were perceived by both parties as having dynamic long-term implications likely to undermine the position of white workers, not only in relation to the job bar, but also their privileged access to education, training, housing, and other amenities. Without political protection, white workers would be undercut by cheaper blacks—unless they were willing to unite with them against capital. This was an option white labor rejected for reasons that are difficult to interpret as other than racist.

This racism was testified to by trade unionists, such as Solly Sachs (1957), who attempted to set up nonracial trade unions but, even in the few cases where progress was made (notably with women in the garment industry), found himself forced to organize these unions into racially segregated branches. The recent study by Jeremy Krikler (2005, ch. 5) of the 1922 Rand Rebellion casts doubt on the claim that the racism of white workers was stirred up by capital. Krikler documents how mine managers, supported by the police, attempted to restrain attacks and lynchings by white miners on African workers, during which scores of Africans were killed. The appeals from some trade union leaders to their members to cease these murderous assaults confirm their occurrence. Both government and mineowners feared this descent into vigilantism and anarchy.

It does *not* follow that white workers were "irrational" racists and mineowners principled antiracists. Both workers and mineowners revealed a reprehensible readiness to resort to racist measures when it suited their interests. Thus, mineowners supported major aspects of apartheid, such as the Land Acts and pass laws (discussed later). But in relation to skilled work, the interests of mineowners clashed with the job bar. But white workers benefited from the job bar: thus their interests and prejudices coincided. Some (liberal and Marxist) analysts described their behavior as "irrational" because of their support for racist policies that divided workers; but their stance was driven by "rational," material self-interest.

The deal over the job bar was neither easily arrived at, nor readily acquiesced in by capital, which returned again to this issue in the 1950s, '60s, and, finally and successfully, in the '70s. The claim by Davies et al. (1984, 11) that, after 1922, there was "an alliance between mining capital and white labor" is a misleading depiction of the tense relationship between mining capital and white unions.

Reams of neo-Marxist theses, and sophisticated theoretical reconceptualizations, have not resolved the conundrum of why capital kept returning to this explosive issue; why white labor resisted so tenaciously; and why the state invariably backed white labor. Despite the concern of South African governments of all political persuasions to keep the mines operating, they did not give mineowners their way on this, but imposed on them policies designed to take account of the interests of the white electorate, of which white labor was a major component. This suggests that the neo-Marxist model of the state as capital's agent is a misleading guide to the balance of political power within South Africa's distinctive system of democracy for whites.

This argument is strengthened by *a range of other policies* that imposed heavy costs on the mines, such as the ambitious plans of South African governments for an infrastructure that went well beyond the needs of the mines, but was financed by their taxes. Despite protests from mineowners, South African governments also set up parastatals, such as the Iron & Steel Corporation (Iscor), and imposed protectionist duties to nurture domestic industries, all of which raised the input costs of the mines. These policies were nationalist rather than racial, and many local whites (including some liberals) supported them on the grounds that they would produce more broadly based economic development.

Later, as mining capital became indigenized and began to invest in these sectors, their opposition to policies that nurtured the non-mining economy declined. But at the time, mineowners opposed these measures, and their imposition was further confirmation that, in South Africa's whites-only democracy, mineowners had less power and the white electorate more power than assumed in neo-Marxist models of the state as "fundamentally and in the final analysis serving the interests of international monopoly capital."

The revisionist depiction of white workers as passive and manipulated, rather than active agents fighting for their interests, is challenged by the success of the well-mobilized white unions in maintaining the job bar against recurrent attempts by capital to erode it over the next half century. The fact that white workers were politically quiescent after 1924 is not, as Johnstone, Davies, and O'Meara argue, because these "subordinate and supportive" classes were politically castrated, but because they had got what they wanted. The revisionist reconceptualization of white labor as a petit bourgeoisie is *ex post facto* reasoning: membership of the petit bourgeoisie was what white labor was fighting for and what apartheid delivered to them.[6]

From 1924, there was a cessation of the often violent labor disputes that wracked the gold mines because, as Horwitz noted (1967, 217), the Chamber of Mines recognized that the job bar was "not an agenda item". The white unions remained strong enough to head off recurrent attempts to undermine the job bar until 1983 when, some years after its formal abolition in all other sectors, this first, most strongly entrenched bar was the last to go—an indication of the continuing veto power of the white unions.

The neo-Marxist analysis also understated the growing influence of Afrikaner nationalism in mobilizing support for racist, as well as protectionist, economic policies. The governments that promoted these protectionist policies—and shored up the mining job bar and extended it to the expanding state, parastatal, and private sectors—were the Afrikaner Nationalist-Labour Pact government that replaced Jan Smuts in 1924 (after the 1922 rebellion) and the Afrikaner NP that came to power in 1948 (replacing Smuts's United Party). Their policies were not totally different from those of the Smuts governments they ousted: the policies of successor governments seldom are. But in relation to the job bar, the allegedly marginal differences between them pointed in different directions, deriving from the conflicting demands of capital for erosion of the job bar and from white labor not only for its maintenance, but also for its extension to other sectors—a choice that had implications for other apartheid policies, particularly those affecting African education, housing, and mobility.

The Competition for Cheap Unskilled Labor

The claim by Marks, and others, that liberals failed to recognize the link between the Land Acts and the demand for cheap black labor is contradicted by the record. Sheila van der Horst headlined her discussion of the Land Acts, "Official attempts to increase the supply of native labour" (1942, 291). Monica Wilson wrote, "The argument that land should be limited so that African men might not 'live in idleness' but go out to work for Europeans has been repeated again and again. . . . Peasant production was 'idleness' to the white man in need of labour" (1971, 65). Horwitz wrote, "Prohibiting the sale of land to Africans was . . . aimed at restricting land utilisation by Africans so as to increase labour utilisation of Africans" (1967, 47, 80f.). Francis Wilson noted that the Land Acts were "far more concerned with the problem of labour supply than anything else" (1971a, 127f.)

What *was* a neo-Marxist innovation was the argument by Harold Wolpe (1972) that the African reserves were retained in order to subsidize the labor costs of the mines. Wolpe's article—described by Beinart and Dubow (1995, 8) as "central" to the revisionist analysis—argued that "the mines favoured the retention and expansion of the reserves as they reduced welfare costs, relieving them of the need to provide social security. . . . This was much cheaper than allowing African families to settle around Johannesburg, where the employers would have been responsible for supporting the families."

Far from ignoring Wolpe's provocative analysis (as Saunders alleged), liberals responded to it directly, raising the following challenges:[7]

1. That retention of the reserves was largely due to *political factors*, including African agency in the form of resistance to giving up further land and white fears of being "swamped" by greater African urbanization
2. That retention of the reserves, far from enabling the mines to pay lower wages, *increased the opportunity cost of Africans* by providing them with alternatives to minework. This, and the fact that white farmers had priority in access to black workers, led to the growing reliance of the mines on foreign migrants. Hence, although mineowners supported the 1913 Land Act and pass laws, white farmers were their main beneficiaries.[8]

Neither Wolpe, nor other neo-Marxists, responded to these challenges to an argument central to their analysis and widely cited by them. Wolpe never addressed the crucial issue of opportunity cost that undermined his thesis.[9] (Nor, it might be added, did he explain what model of late nineteenth-century capitalism he had in mind that would have required acceptance of responsibility for the welfare function he assumed mineowners would undertake had the reserves not been retained.)

But there has been a significant shift from Wolpe's analysis in relation to African agency. Marks and Rathbone (1982, Introduction) later wrote, "The evolution of the compounded migrant system [was not simply due to mineowners but was] . . . as much a response to the resistance of African social formations to full proletarianisation [i.e., their desire to retain land in the reserves] as any thought-through scheme by mine magnates to cheapen costs. . . . The origins of migrant labour . . . did not necessarily . . . accord quite so neatly with the needs of capital. . . . [Nor was] racism simply the invention of capitalists."

Maylam described this significant shift by the neo-Marxists as the outcome of their "critically re-evaluating some of [their] earlier revisionist assumptions" (2001, 222). However, it could also be said—pace Saunders—that this, and their subsequent shifts towards giving weight to political and even cultural factors, were made "quietly" and without reference to the liberals, conservatives, and nationalists who had long made these points. Instead, the neo-Marxists treated their reevaluations as yet further "breakthroughs and paradigm shifts," resulting from entirely intrarevisionist debates to which outsiders made no contribution.[10] And this set the pattern for their treatment of their challengers in the debate on post-1910 South Africa. They seldom attacked them directly, as they had the earlier liberals. They usually airbrushed them out of existence, seldom referring to their work in print, though denouncing it in the seminar room (discussed in the Appendix).

CONFLICTING INTERPRETATIONS OF PRESSURES FOR REFORM BEFORE 1970

After the Rand Rebellion and the victory of the Nationalist-Labour Pact in the 1924 election, the trend toward racist policies intensified. This trend reflected pressures from various white interests, including the conservative English, but most forcefully and consistently from the NP, mobilizing Afrikaners in support of its dual policies of anti-imperialism (against the British) and apartheid (against blacks, including Afrikaans-speaking coloureds). However, this racist trend was briefly and partially interrupted during the Second World War, when the Smuts-Hofmeyr government introduced reforms, including relaxation of job bars and "pass laws"[11]; the inclusion of blacks in expanded welfare and education programs; and an abortive bill to extend trade union rights to Africans. During this period, real black wages rose, linked to rapid economic growth and the relaxation of job bars and "pass laws."[12]

These reforms were the result of pressures from employers in South Africa's growing manufacturing and commercial/services sectors, and from the growing black urban workforce, as well as the influence of the welfarist and antiracist norms of the war years. These norms were reflected in numerous official reports, such as those by the van Eck, Smit, Gluckman, and Fagan Commissions, whose analyses deepened the empirical and analytical basis for understanding the social impact of industrialization and urbanization and the adverse effects of racist policies. They highlighted the poverty of blacks and urged increased education, health, housing, and job opportunities, as well as a shift away from migrant labor towards acceptance of the permanence of urban Africans.

These arguments echoed the traditional liberal case for a common society for reasons of both morality and economic efficiency. Prime Minister Smuts was not a liberal, but he allowed his liberal deputy, Jan Hofmeyr, to introduce reforms that, though modest, pointed in a different direction from the racist trend of post-Union policies. In parliament, Hofmeyr denounced the "herrenvolk mentality" of many whites, stating, "I take my stand for the ultimate removal of the colour bar from our constitution." Hofmeyr shifted the financing of African education to the general revenue account—a measure reversed by the successor NP government, which limited expenditure to the revenue raised from African taxes. Hofmeyr also laid the basis for a social welfare system that included Africans and which the NP eroded but did not abolish (Lipton 1985, 21, 267, 274–48; Paton 1971, chs 11–13).

Hofmeyr's reforms were disliked by conservatives within the United Party (UP), notably its rural Afrikaans supporters, the Natal English and, on black trade unions, the mineowners, who brutally suppressed a strike by African miners in 1946.[13] Thus, there is no guarantee that, if reelected in 1948, the UP would have persevered with Hofmeyr's reforms. But, whatever the UP might have done, there is no doubt about the rejection of this tentative new policy direction by the NP, which strengthened and extended job bars, pass laws, and segregation in housing, education, and social life. The NP also froze the value of welfare payments to blacks, while increasing those of whites, and excluded blacks from new measures such as school feeding, thus increasing the gap in state expenditure on blacks and whites.

The NP's racist policies aroused intense opposition, to which it reacted with harsh repression against the black and nonracial opposition, as well as electoral gerrymandering and (un)constitutional amendments to the legislature and judiciary to preempt challenges from within the white oligarchy. These measures smashed all effective opposition and created an atmosphere of fear and crisis that consolidated the NP's support and led to a rightward shift in white politics, including within the opposition UP.

But even during the most repressive period of NP rule, there were continuing pressures for a different policy direction not only from blacks, but also from within the oligarchy, from liberals and, on some issues, from business. In 1952, Harry Oppenheimer, heir to the Anglo American and De Beers companies, pressed for relaxation of the job bar and for family housing, instead of compounds, for skilled black miners on the new Orange Free State gold mines. In 1951, when the NP reexamined the question of African unions, the Federated Chamber of Industries (FCI) and Associated Chambers of Commerce (Assocom) pressed for their recognition and opposed the 1957 amendment to the Industrial Conciliation Act, which closed the door to this. In arguing for recognition, they referred to the contribution of unions to more orderly industrial relations and to the need to improve African wages and productivity. Businessmen set up the Association for the Improvement of Wages and Productivity to encourage better training and higher wages for black workers, and FCI and Assocom opposed the restrictions on black business demanded by the Afrikaanse Handelsinstituut (AHI). Assocom's criticisms led to Verwoerd's refusal to receive its representatives and to the NP's threat that if they continue "to go against the stream of an overwhelming White Volkswil.... the Volkswil must be called in against them."[14]

In March 1960, police shot unarmed demonstrators against the pass laws at Sharpeville. This provoked widespread demonstrations and strikes by blacks, the flight of domestic and foreign capital from South Africa, and representations for reform by Assocom and FCI—on this occasion, joined by the more conservative Chamber of Mines, Steel and Engineering Industries Federation and, for the first time, by the AHI.[15] Sharpeville was followed by public criticism of NP policy by prominent Afrikaner nationalists, such as Anton Rupert of Rembrandt, and intellectuals and clergymen like Beyers Naude, Jan Sadie, Nick Olivier, and Jappie Basson, some of who left the NP. During the temporary incapacity of Verwoerd (due to an assassination attempt by a white liberal), the acting prime minister, Paul Sauer, conceded that blacks had serious grievances that should be addressed. But when Verwoerd recovered, he rejected any suggestion of reform. Instead, the ANC and PAC were banned; the security forces strengthened; and in response to his critics, Verwoerd launched his separate development policy (see p. 33).

The NP also took drastic measures to deal with the economic crisis, introducing exchange controls to stem the flight of capital; increased protection for local industries; and policies to stimulate growth, including the establishment of heavy industries such as fuel and armaments, in the state sector. The aim of these measures was to increase South Africa's self-sufficiency so that it could resist the growing attacks on apartheid, both from within and outside South Africa. The NP's success in restoring political stability and economic growth led Verwoerd to claim that his separate development policy was working.

The liberal and neo-Marxist interpretations of the wartime reforms, and of the renewed pressures for reform after Sharpeville, reflect their contending models of the interests and power balance shaping policy. Liberals viewed these events as indicative of significant divisions of interest among whites that held the potential for a different policy direction: "an opportunity . . . [for] laying new foundations on which might be built a better society" (Ballinger 1969, ch. 9). Neo-Marxists stressed the shared policies of the UP and NP. Thus, O'Meara, in comparing the UP's Fagan Report (which urged relaxation of pass laws and more family housing for urban Africans) with the NP's Sauer Report (which urged tighter influx control and migrancy), stressed their "common ground. . . . The major difference lay in policy towards the site and size of the reserve army of labour [and] . . . forms of labour control . . . of which capital was to be the major beneficiary" (1983, 235f.). In his study of this period, Davies does not even refer to reforms, maintaining that "industrial capital's position on the . . . [racial structure] . . . remained fundamentally the same" (1979, 288f., 308).[16] These conflicting interpretations were more fully developed in response to the unexpected changes introduced by Verwoerd's successor, Vorster.

Conflicting Interpretations of the Post-1970 Reforms

The modest concessions in sport and social policy introduced by Vorster, and his connivance at renewed attempts to relax the job color bar, precipitated the 1969 breakaway of the ultraconservative HNP from the NP.[17] In the 1970 election, Vorster defeated the HNP and gradually introduced further changes. To assess their significance—whether they were (as liberals argued) reforms that began to erode apartheid, or (as revisionists argued) cosmetic changes that merely adapted and "restructured" apartheid—we need, briefly, to recall the key apartheid measures introduced or extended by the NP after 1948. By 1970, these measures encompassed:[18]

Social apartheid: In 1949–50, the NP tightened prohibitions against interracial sex and marriage. The 1950 Population Registration Act classified the whole population by race. The NP also extended or introduced restrictions on interracial sport, restaurants, beaches, etc.

Economic apartheid: The NP extended the job color bar and restrictions on black apprenticeship, training, and education. This contributed to the widening differential between white and African wages which, by 1970, reached six to one in manufacturing and twenty to one in gold mining. The differential in state spending on white and African education widened to sixteen to one.

Influx controls over Africans were tightened: in 1970, pass law prosecutions reached an annual peak of almost 0.7 million. The 1967 Physical Planning Act introduced controls over capital in an attempt to force business to decentralize labor-intensive production to the Bantustans.

Restrictions on African property and business rights in "white" areas were tightened, and "surplus" blacks (the families) repatriated to the Bantustans.

Political apartheid: The NP removed the remnants of black political representation in South Africa's Parliament and Cape Provincial Council as a prelude to establishing independent "homelands" for Africans and separate representative councils for Coloureds and Indians. The NP rejected recognition of African trade unions and banned the South African Communist Party in 1950 and the ANC and PAC in 1960. The 1968 Improper Political Interference Act made nonracial political parties illegal, leading to the voluntary dissolution of the Liberal Party. Police acted harshly against black and nonracial NGOs.

The following changes indicate the turnaround in NP policy from 1970:

Social apartheid: Restrictions on interracial sport, social mixing, and sharing of public amenities (transport, restaurants, beaches) were first eased, then abolished, culminating in the 1985 removal of the laws prohibiting interracial sex and marriage.

Economic apartheid: The job color bar and restrictions on black training and apprenticeship were first eased, then repealed by the 1979 amendment to the Industrial Conciliation Act. In 1972, Verwoerd's cap on expenditure on African education was removed. Thereafter, the differential in state spending on white and African education halved from sixteen to one in 1970 to seven to one in 1983. The number of Africans in secondary education rose from 122,489 in 1970 to one million in 1984 and, at universities, from under two thousand to almost fifty thousand. The 1983 de Lange Commission recommended gradual equalization of expenditure on education and establishment of a single, national education department. White/African wage differentials narrowed: on the goldmines from twenty to one in 1970 to five and a half to one in 1982, and in manufacturing from six to one to 4.4. to one. The white share of total personal income declined from 72 percent in 1970 to 54 percent in 1990. Racial differentials in state spending on health, pensions, and welfare also narrowed although, in all these cases, the absolute gap remained wide.

The pass laws were eased: prosecutions declined from 0.7 million in 1970 to 0.2 million in 1982. But for much of this period, the NP attempted to enforce the Physical Planning Act and to remove "surplus" Africans from "white" areas. This policy ended in 1985, when the President's Council recommended abolition of the hated "pass laws" and an end to forced removals. By then, an estimated two to three million people had been so removed.

From 1975, restrictions on African ownership of property and business were eased, and construction of African family housing in "white" areas recommended, hence signaling acceptance of the permanence of urban Africans.

Political apartheid: Repression of black and nonracial political activity was sporadically eased, facilitating the growth of trade unions, independent media and NGOs. In 1977, the Wiehahn Commission was appointed to consider recognition of African trade unions, which were legalized in 1979. In 1985, the Prohibition of Political Interference Act was repealed, legalizing the formation of nonracial organizations. However, the media, unions and opposition NGOs remained subject to periodic, often vicious, crackdowns. Vorster persisted with Verwoerd's plan to establish "independent" homelands for Africans and separate councils for Indians and Coloureds. Vorster's successor, P. W. Botha, began to shift from these Verwoerdian principles by moving towards "power-sharing." The 1983 Tricameral Constitution replaced South Africa's all-white parliament with three separate, but linked, chambers for whites, coloureds, and Indians, although on terms designed to secure continued domination by the white parliament and still excluding Africans. In January 1985, Botha stated that Africans would be included in these constitutional arrangements, which would lead toward "a united South Africa, with one citizenship and universal suffrage." Botha also announced the establishment of a National Statutory Council to negotiate new political arrangements and offered to release Mandela and other political prisoners on condition they eschewed violence—an offer they declined. In February 1990, Botha's successor, F. W. de Klerk, unconditionally unbanned the ANC and other organizations; abolished the remaining apartheid laws; and initiated negotiations for a new constitution.

Thus, by 1985—before the mid-1980s uprisings and imposition of limited economic sanctions by South Africa's major trading partners—practically all *socioeconomic* aspects of apartheid had been relaxed or abolished. But *political* change was still limited and ambiguous. Until 1985, despite some concessions (recognizing trade unions, expanding space for NGOs), the NP attempted to salvage the geographical and demographic basis of "separate development" (to reduce African numbers in 'white' areas) and, until the accession of de Klerk, insisted on separate, though increasingly linked, political institutions for the different 'races.'

These tumultuous, confusing changes occurred against a background of growing unrest, both within South Africa as the lid was lifted, and in the Southern African region, as independence was achieved by Mozambique and Angola in 1975 and Zimbabwe in 1980. The South African liberation movements began to use neighboring countries as bases for the armed struggle, and the NP reacted with harsh economic and military countermeasures—its "destabilization" strategy. Thus, while the NP was introducing major socioeconomic reforms, it was also often cracking down on opposition and hitting out at neighboring states. It is hardly surprising that analysts produced such conflicting interpretations of these developments.

In comparing the revisionist and liberal interpretations of this period, the focus will be on their differences over substantive historical issues, particularly the roles of capital, labor—and the state, and the relative importance of economic interests, ideology, and race/nationalism in shaping policy. Historiographical issues—revisionist claims of transforming the subject, and their allegations against liberal and other historians—are discussed in the Appendix.

THE NEO-MARXIST REVISIONIST INTERPRETATION

The neo-Marxist interpretation of the post-1970 period underwent a series of major shifts. Initially, Legassick (1973), Wolpe (1970), and others argued that—far from being in conflict with economic growth—*apartheid was "tailored to the needs of capital,"* and that Vorster's changes were not eroding, but intensifying apartheid.[19] Rejecting O'Dowd's argument that economic growth was now producing material gains for urban blacks, the revisionists maintained that trends in South Africa were, instead, confirming Gundar Frank's model of "underdevelopment" and "immiserisation of the masses." In support, they claimed that, while South Africa had achieved exceptional growth and profit rates since the Second World War, real black wages had declined.

This analysis was challenged by Bromberger (1972), Bell (Bromberger and Bell 1974), Lipton (1974a, 1974b, 1976) and others.[20] They showed that, since 1960, real wages of many blacks had risen, not fallen, and that significant shifts were occurring in the occupational structure, with blacks advancing into more skilled jobs and eroding the hierarchical racial structure.[21] They also pointed to Vorster's policy shifts (relaxation of the job bar and social apartheid and removal of Verwoerd's expenditure cap on African education) as the first signs of the shift away from apartheid, and an indication of the growing influence of *verligtes* within the NP.

Following these challenges, the neo-Marxists abandoned their immiserization hypothesis tacitly accepting that many blacks were making economic gains. They also tacitly recognized that Verwoedian apartheid imposed some costs on urban business and that some unexpected policy changes were underway. Immiserization theory was replaced by an elaboration of Blumer's *accommodation thesis*, which held that, despite some inconveniences, business could and would adapt to apartheid, and that the NP's concessions on the job bar, black education, and wages would facilitate this. Indeed, these "marginal and cosmetic" adaptations would make apartheid more flexible, thereby strengthening it—as well as hoodwinking the NP's critics. The accommodation thesis was cogently set out by Greenberg (1980, 189, 194, 207, 385), who depicted it as "an easy accommodation" by urban capital not only to the racial order, but also to "the full complement of labour-repressive policies [thus confirming]. . . . that the historic process of . . . capitalist development . . . carries forward and elaborates racial distinctions." In this, and their subsequent shifts, the revisionists—with the partial exception of Legassick (and later Posel)—did not refer to the research findings and direct challenges of their critics.[22]

Nevertheless, continued challenges from these critics led to the revisionists' third shift, to their *theory of the restructuring of apartheid*. Davies, O'Meara and Dlamini wrote, "Monopoly capital [wanted] increased repression with some attempt to restructure, or in their terms 'reform,' some of the institutions of apartheid" (1984, 37). Greenberg explained that the aim was "to rationalise, centralise and obscure the [labour] control machinery. . . . from a rudimentary bureaucracy concerned with expelling redundant labour to a sophisticated regulative and allocative apparatus" (1987b, 107). Thus, what was happening was not merely cosmetic, but nor was it reform. The NP's concessions were interpreted as further evidence of apartheid's functionality for capital and confirmation of the revisionist thesis that capitalism and apartheid were inextricably linked.

The final revisionist shift, to their "*theory of the security state*," tacitly recognized the growing conflicts over economic policy between capital and the state. Their argument now shifted to capital's support for apartheid for *political* (rather than economic) reasons. Davies, O'Meara and Dlamini argued (1984, 38) that Botha's succession "marked the consolidation of a new political alliance of monopoly capital and the military," which instituted so-called "reform" as part of Botha's counterrevolutionary Total Strategy, which aimed at preserving the apartheid regime. Davies et al. (69) singled out the policy of the Anglo-American corporation, headed by Harry Oppenheimer, as "not differ[ing] markedly from the strategic thinking underlying Total Strategy. O'Meara (1983, 253) noted some business pressures for "reform" but depicted these as emerging very late, only after 1979, and as sinister in intent: "An effective political alliance between the military and the most powerful sections of the capitalist class began to take place. . . . [At] precisely this stage of direct military intervention in the political struggle, leading businessmen became directly and stridently involved in a vigorous campaign for 'reform' [sic]." This late dating of the emergence of business pressures, and emphasis on their political rather than economic motives, was subsequently adopted by all revisionists.[23]

Following the huge support from business for de Klerk's release of Mandela in 1990, and for negotiations for a new constitution, *the revisionist paradigm gradually disintegrated.* The most widely cited revisionist on the post-1948 period is O'Meara, and his 1996 book, *Forty Lost Years*, reveals a major shift toward the liberal argument that there were growing business pressures for reform *from the 1940s*, as well as increasing and fundamental conflicts over apartheid between business and the NP.

This willingness of some revisionists to shift their views is commendable. But the fudged way in which they did this—without reference to and, instead, continued denigration of the liberals whose analysis they came to share—led to confusion about what their view now was of the relationship between capitalism and apartheid. Hence, it is hardly surprising that O'Meara's clear, early portrayal of the active role of business in supporting apartheid to the bitter end remains widely cited, both in the academic literature and in public discourse, despite his own break from this view.

An example is the testimony presented to the Truth and Reconciliation Commission (TRC) by, S. J. Terreblanche and by the trade union confederation, Cosatu. In a paper reflecting O'Meara's early analysis (although citing his later 1996 book!), Terreblanche argued that business: "enthusiastically supported . . . the relentless attempts to make a success of Verwoerdian separate development. . . . The Total Strategy project and the neo-apartheid strategy, launched on the request of the business community, were definitely not anti-apartheid [but intended to] *perpetuate the life of the Botha government and with it, also apartheid*" (Terreblanche's emphasis).[24] This argument was reflected in the TRC's findings and is still widely cited, even though it has been largely (though "quietly") abandoned by O'Meara and some other revisionists. This major shift in O'Meara's analysis, and the seeming unawareness of it by those citing him, is discussed in the Appendix.

The Liberal Interpretation

The neo-Marxists—scrambling to keep up with the new research findings and the course of events—insisted that no one could have envisaged South Africa's evolutionary outcome. However, this possibility was envisaged by some: it occurred close to the date predicted in O'Dowd's 1964 paper (see p. 34) and via a negotiating process similar to that sketched out by David Welsh and Frederik van Zyl Slabbert, who became leader of the Progressive Party in 1979.

The liberal argument was *not* that capitalists led a long, heroic struggle to end apartheid. Nor did liberals argue that apartheid had always obstructed economic growth. Their argument was that apartheid always had costs as well as benefits for capital, and that the rapid growth and diversification of the South African economy raised the costs, especially for employers in manufacturing and services. Since the election of the NP in 1948, economic growth had both strengthened the apartheid state and intensified the costs of policies that restricted the employment of blacks in more skilled jobs. The poverty of the black majority limited the domestic market, as well as the size of production runs in South African manufacturing. As manufacturing and services overtook the primary sectors in their contribution to GDP, these costs rose.[25]

The limited domestic market was less problematic for employers in agriculture and mining, who were more export oriented and more dependent on the cheap, unskilled labor apartheid provided. Nevertheless, the costs of excluding blacks from skilled work had already led mineowners to challenge the job bar early in the century—with results that deterred them from mounting another frontal attack on the bar for the next half century. But by the 1960s, both mining and agriculture were mechanizing, thus increasing the need for skilled workers. Hence the limitation of skills to the shrinking pool of whites was becoming more costly for them too. By the mid-1960s, the economic costs of apartheid were rising for all employers and for producers who needed a domestic market.

The O'Dowd liberals argued that these problems could not be solved by Verwoerd's separate development policy which, far from being "tailored" to the needs of business, was acting as a straitjacket and worsening South Africa's skill shortages and high cost structure. Most employers resisted the NP's attempt to force them to decentralize labor-intensive production to the Bantustans. They also complained that the counterpart of decentralization—tightening influx control and migrantizing urban Africans—hindered production in the industrial centers. (The neo-Marxist claim that employers merely wanted the adjustment and streamlining, not abolition, of influx control and decentralization, is discussed in the Appendix.)

Liberals also argued that the hothouse growth nurtured behind the NP's protectionist barriers was worsening South Africa's high cost structure and its balance of payments. They maintained that Blumer (see p. 34), and his liberal and neo-Marxist followers, had posed the wrong question: the issue was not just growth, but *what kind of growth*. If this required large numbers of unskilled workers and was export oriented (as in mining and agriculture), then it could coexist with, and even benefit from, apartheid. But growth that required skills and a wider domestic market was inhibited by apartheid. Ironically, the NP's encouragement of mechanization, to reduce dependence on Africans in "white" areas, increased the demand for skills.

The O'Dowd liberals concluded that apartheid and its separate development version were unworkable and that, unless the NP chose to sacrifice economic growth, it would be forced to acquiesce in apartheid's erosion. Some of us (Lipton 1985; Lundahl 1992) analyzed the choice facing whites in terms of a Becker-type trade-off between economic interests and racial preferences (Becker 1957). The economic interests of employers, and of professionals with scarce skills, conflicted with racist policies, while the interests of less skilled, less affluent whites were served by racism. Hence, as on the goldmines in 1922, the material interests of white workers reinforced their racist tendencies, while the interests of employers and professionals conflicted with racism. For both capital and white labor, there was thus a correlation between economic interests and attitudes to apartheid, although this correlation was the opposite to that posited by the neo-Marxists.

Another issue stressed by liberals—and even more by Afrikaner *verligtes*—was the changing population balance. Two key trends were involved: First, the declining white share of the population. At Union, whites constituted 20 percent of the total. This began to decline from about 1960, reaching 16 percent in 1980 and a projected 11 percent by 2000. The ruling Afrikaners constituted about 63 percent of whites, so their share of the total population declined from 12 percent at the time of their 1948 election victory to a projected 6 percent in 2000. By then, the African share of the population was projected to rise to 80 percent (coloureds and Asians accounted for the remaining 9 percent). The second major demographic trend was that, from around 1960, South Africa's perennial shortage of unskilled labor turned into a surplus, resulting in rising unemployment among the unskilled, alongside the growing skill shortage. Afrikaner demographers and sociologists like Jan Sadie (1971) and S. P. Celliers (1972), who were taken more seriously by the NP than their English counterparts, drew attention to the declining white share of the population and to its implications, viz that the acute skill shortage, and new problem of unemployment among the unskilled, would worsen if the exclusion of blacks from skilled work continued.

These demographic and economic trends raised stark questions about the security of a privileged white minority amidst an impoverished black majority, and prompted doubts, including in military circles, about whether a policy so economically costly and lacking in political legitimacy was functional, let alone essential, for Afrikaner survival. NP generals began to warn that "the struggle for Afrikaner survival" would be 80 percent political and only 20 percent military.

The liberals linked their analysis of economic and demographic trends closely to political developments, including the growing pressures for reform from business. Assocom and FCI began to receive more support from the hitherto conservative Chamber of Mines, Steel & Engineering Industries Federation (Seifsa) and the politically crucial AHI, as well as from managers in the state sector and parastatals, such as South African Railways, Eskom (electricity), and Sasol (oil). Employers also began to emphasize the need for wider socioeconomic reforms as awareness grew of the links between skill shortages, low productivity, and South Africa's limited domestic market and the poverty, lack of education, housing, and health services for most workers.

But business remained cautious and divided over black political rights. Among the few businessmen who addressed this issue publicly was Harry Oppenheimer, who supported Helen Suzman's Progressive Party (established in 1959), which advocated a nonracial franchise, abolition of color bars and pass laws, and recognition of African trade unions. From the late 1960s, Afrikaner businessmen, such as Jan Marais of Trust Bank, began to speak out publicly about the long-term political problems raised by apartheid.

Business organizations are set up to lobby on issues directly related to their members', which operations, usually tried to avoid sensitive political issues. But the logic of the reforms and sporadic black unrest—at Sharpeville, the 1976 Soweto riots, and during the mid-1980s—pushed business into confronting political issues. In 1981, Jan Steyn, director of the Urban Foundation (established jointly by English and Afrikaans business in 1976) urged removal from the statute book of all institutionalized discrimination. In 1983, Assocom called for "a common citizenship" for all in an undivided South Africa, while the FCI's Business Charter called for legal equality and universal suffrage.[26]

However, even liberal business remained nervous and suspicious of South Africa's premier liberation movement, the ANC, until the mid-1980s. This was partly because of the ANC's close alliance with the South African Communist Party (SACP), evident in the latter's large representation on the ANC's National Executive Committee, the ANC's commitment to "nationalisation of the mines, banks and monopoly industries" and the involvement of senior SACP/ANC members in implementing socialist policies in Mozambique after its independence in 1975.

However, the ANC/SACP alliance, in turn, was largely due to the reluctance of Western countries to provide tangible support for the ANC's struggle against the apartheid regime. This began to change after the accession of President Gorbachev in 1985 and the collapse of communism in Eastern Europe and in Mozambique and elsewhere in Africa. These events contributed to shifts in ANC policy, evident in its 1988 Constitutional Guidelines, and in its increasing reliance on support from Western rather than Soviet sources. These international developments (discussed in Chapter 4) reduced the apprehensions of business about the consequences of black majority rule.

CHALLENGES TO THE LIBERAL ANALYSIS

While revisionists such as O'Meara have now (as documented in the Appendix) adopted large swathes of the liberal analysis, others continue to maintain that, until 1990, business continued to support at least two major aspects of apartheid. First, it is argued that business opposed recognition of black trade unions, only accepting this when "forced to by union militancy." Second, it is argued that there was a last-ditch "political alliance between capital and the military" as part of a counterrevolutionary strategy to preserve the Botha regime.

The claim that business *only recognized African trade unions* because they were forced to by union militancy is *ex post facto* reasoning, based on the later strength of the unions. During the 1970s, African unions—decimated by the NP's bannings and intimidation—were too weak to force recognition. The 1973–74 Durban strikes, which placed the issue of union recognition back on the agenda, were spontaneous wildcat strikes: membership of African unions at that stage was only about twenty thousand. The NP would not have appointed the 1977 Wiehahn Commission without pressures from liberal (South African and foreign) business. The appointment of Wiehahn signaled that union recognition was likely and stimulated their growth. Yet, by 1979, when the Industrial Conciliation Act was amended to legalize unions, the leading black trade union federation, Fosatu (which later became Cosatu), had only forty-five thousand members. After 1979, black unions grew rapidly: by 1984, Fosatu/Cosatu had four hundred thousand members (10 percent of the formal African workforce) and by 1989, almost one million.

By the mid-1980s, the unions were a significant factor on the industrial and political scene. But this was not the case during the 1970s, when their weakness and vulnerability was recognized by leading trade unionists and sympathetic observers. Leading Cosatu official, Alex Erwin, said that during this period, the unions avoided "dangerous activities which would divert resources and provoke state action against our embryonic movement." Jay Naidoo described the unions' "initial . . . position as essentially 'anti-political'" because of their continuing weakness and vulnerability (Marx 1992, 196). Steven Friedman noted that the unions remained aloof from overtly political actions because "they knew it would be tactical suicide" to challenge the state on political rights when they were not yet strong enough to win rights in the workplace (1987, 430).[27]

Some employers, especially farmers and some mineowners (the Chamber of Mines was divided over the issue), remained opposed to unionization, and many employers continued to have conflictual relations with them. But the revisionist insistence that all capitalists must be opposed to trade unions was contradicted by the record in South Africa and elsewhere. Employers in South Africa's garment industry had been dealing with African unions since the 1940s, when Assocom and FCI supported the abortive legislation to recognize them. As noted previously (p. 46), Assocom and FCI opposed the NP's 1957 amendment to the Industrial Conciliation (IC) Act, which removed the issue of African unionization from the political agenda.

After the 1973-74 Durban strikes, Oppenheimer called for a commission of enquiry into African unionization and set out the classic reasons why progressive employers favor institutionalized means for negotiating wages and settling grievances and conflicts.[28] South African employers had the added incentive of acquiring an ally in their struggle against the job and apprenticeship color bars and in securing acceptance of the permanence of the urban African industrial and middle classes.

Assocom, FCI, and some leading South African and foreign companies supported Oppenheimer's call for union recognition. But this was opposed by the South African Agricultural Union, Afrikaanse Handelsinstituut (AHI), SEIFSA, and by some members of the Chamber of Mines—who were either opposed to worker organization or preferred the NP's alternative of a separate committee system for Africans. Some employers began to experiment with the committees, and this experience did not deter many of them from later agreeing to the full trade union rights demanded by African workers once the issue was on the agenda again. Indeed, some employers began to deal with the emerging unions ahead of the 1979 legislation. The ensuing relationship proved both difficult and constructive, providing, *inter alia*, experience in interracial bargaining and negotiating that later facilitated the process of negotiating South Africa's new constitution (discussed in Chapter 4).

Recognition of African unions was opposed by the white unions linked to the Afrikaans labor confederation, SACOL, which later said it had been misled by the NP. The white unions' shock at official recognition of African unions led many of them to switch their support from the NP to Andries Treurnicht's Conservative Party, when he led the second *verkrampte* breakaway from the NP in 1982. Thus, recognition of African unions was a momentous step for all parties: the NP, employers, and black and white workers. Support from liberal capital and opposition from white labor were significant features of this process.[29]

The second challenge to the liberal analysis is the claim of "a *political alliance between business and the military*" in defense of apartheid—a claim made by Davies, Kadar Asmal, et al., the early O'Meara, and many others. The evidence produced in support of this is that: during the 1980s, "business supported NP crackdowns" against anti-apartheid activists and protestors; business was involved in South Africa's defense industries; some businesspeople sat on committees of the National Security Management System, which was attempting to deliver more efficient services to the black townships; and that business only began to support "so-called reform" from 1979 as part of Botha's counter-revolutionary strategy to prop up apartheid against the Total Onslaught.

These claims are discussed in detail in the Appendix (which also discusses more fully the position of business on freedom of movement and political rights). Here it should be briefly noted that, against a background of growing internal unrest and external pressures, Botha attempted to win support from English whites, particularly business, courting them during the early years of his presidency and taking the unprecedented step (for an NP leader) of addressing two business conferences. Botha also introduced some of the reforms that business and others were pressing for, such as abolition of job bars, extension of property rights, abolition of the sex and marriage acts, and recognition of black unions.

But the fact that business welcomed these measures, and also wanted the maintenance of law and order during the mid-1980s uprisings, does not mean they supported all other aspects of Botha's policy, including his Total Strategy, which involved intensified domestic repression and a confrontationist foreign policy toward neighboring countries. On the contrary, from 1983, these aspects of NP policy led to a sharp deterioration in Botha's relations with business.

In November 1984, Assocom and FCI condemned the NP's harsh reaction to demonstrations and stayaways, protesting against "the sweeping . . . and arbitrary" powers for ministers and the detention of trade unionists and restrictions on the right of appeal to the courts (Lipton 1985, 180). Afrikaans business was more reluctant to criticize the NP on political issues but, in June 1986, some joined other business organizations—including the National African Federated Chambers of Commerce (Nafcoc), now emerging as an active public voice—in condemning the State of Emergency and calling for the release of Nelson Mandela and negotiations with the ANC. Thus, most businessmen did not support, but protested against, Botha's "crackdowns." South African capital, unlike German capital under the Nazis, did not, on the whole, support fascist policies, but spoke out in support of the rule of law.

The claim by Davies et al. (1984, 65f., 108f.), Asmal et al. (1997, 69, 120) and others that business supported Botha's *kragdadige* (ironfisted) reactions against neighboring African states conflicts with the evidence.[30] During this time of growing internal unrest and external pressure, Afrikaans business muted its public criticisms and rallied around the NP. But English businessmen stepped up their attacks, reacting angrily to Botha's 1985 Rubicon Speech, billed as launching the next round of reforms, but dominated by the image of South Africa's president wagging his finger at the international community and warning, "Don't push me too far." Business was appalled by, and denounced, Botha's 1986 military strikes against Harare, Lusaka, and Gaberone, which scuttled the visit to South Africa of the Commonwealth's Eminent Persons Group. As their relations with Botha deteriorated, some businessmen established open links with the ANC, publicly meeting exiled leaders such as Oliver Tambo and Thabo Mbeki, in Lusaka in September 1985.

These developments strained business relations with a powerful, ruthless government. Botha denounced his business critics as unpatriotic, and his aggressive attacks led to the departure from South Africa of critics such as Gordon Waddell of JCI, Tony Bloom of Premier Milling, and Chris Ball of Barclays Bank. Yet, despite the continual, bitter clashes between government and business, the revisionists insisted on bracketing them together and did not distinguish between what was wanted by business and by the NP because of their *a priori* assumption that the state would not act against the interests of capital.

However, business and the NP had *different agendas* that overlapped in some respects, but not in others. It is misleading to claim that because business welcomed some measures, such as the abolition of job bars and pass laws—reforms the ANC itself called for—they must have supported all other NP actions, including Botha's Total Strategy. These differences were recognized and encouraged by some within the ANC. By 1986, as Gumede records (2005, 39, 69), both Mbeki in exile and Mandela on Robben Island were arguing against their own hardliners for contacts with business, and with verligte Afrikaners, to explore the possibility of a negotiated settlement.[31]

The mobilization of business against apartheid was a difficult, lengthy process. Most businessmen were as feckless and disinclined to long-term thinking as other people. But there were in South Africa some businessmen who were farsighted and strategic in their thinking, as well as liberal in their convictions. Harry Oppenheimer's wide-ranging interests in both mining and manufacturing meant his commercial interests were not without their contradictions until the 1973 rise in the gold price that, together with relaxation of the job bar, reduced the cost constraints on gold mining. Thereafter, Oppenheimer pursued more boldly his long-stated opposition to apartheid, and his liberal aims were actively promoted, on and off the factory floor, by his senior executives, such as Dennis Etheredge, Nicky Oppenheimer, Bobby Godsell, Clem Sunter and Michael Spicer.

The FCI and Assocom hammered out unusually well-developed policies not only on economic, but also on social and, later, political issues, and pressed persistently for these over some decades. During the 1970s, they were joined by Afrikaners such as Andries Wassenaar of Sanlam, Wim de Villiers of General Mining, Albert Wessels of Toyota, and, later, the designers of the Nedbank scenarios (which sketched out alternative options for South Africa), who had better access to the NP and more success in shifting its policies. There was increasing business support for the Progressive Party, strengthened by the influx into parliament of senior executives, such as Zach de Beer, Alex Boraine and Gordon Waddell in the 1974 and 1977 elections, when the Progressives, committed to a nonracial franchise in a common society, replaced the disintegrating UP as the official opposition.

Foreign observers commented on the extent to which South African business was to the left of government and on the bitter clashes between them. The neo-Marxist revisionists never considered why business devoted time and money to lobbying for reform and set up well-resourced organizations, such as the Urban Foundation and Consultative Business Movement, to research and lobby not only on labor and social policies but also, increasingly, on the political alternatives to apartheid. When it became impossible to ignore these increasingly vocal business pressures, the revisionists dismissed them on the grounds that they were motivated by self-interest and aimed at adapting, rather than ending, apartheid. This reasoning raises questions about the revisionists' behavioral assumptions: how they assess intentions and whether they reject the notion that self-interest plays a major part in shaping all human behavior and does not necessarily preclude having moral and social concerns as well (discussed in Chapter 5).

Regarding the role of white labor: after the NP's 1948 victory, the neo-Marxists could no longer deny their patent support for apartheid. However, they continued to depict the white unions as quiescent and manipulated. This does not fit with research findings showing that white labor was strengthened both economically, by the growing skill shortage, and politically, by the NP's support for the white unions on the statutory Industrial, Apprenticeship and Wage Councils that policed the job, training, and wage bars. White workers were also represented on local and provincial councils and in parliament, and their political representatives, unions, and churches engaged actively in the debates about apartheid measures that provided whites with privileged access to segregated housing, education, and other facilities, which white workers were less able to secure for themselves than richer whites.

However, this research also showed that rising educational standards and prosperity were changing the interests, and reducing the opposition to black job advance, of many whites, particularly white collar workers. This process was facilitated by wage hikes and promotion for cooperative white workers. Thus, far from being dragooned by capital into supporting apartheid, white labor's opposition to the erosion of the apprenticeship and job bars was bought off by employers in both the private and state sectors. The concessions wrung from the white unions were not primarily in response to the arguments of private employers, whom the unions did not trust, but to the NP, whose assurances elicited from white workers the response, "We agree to this [black job advance] because the government says its OK."[32] However, some unions, such as Mynwerkers and Yster en Staal, continued to oppose this process and switched their political support to the *verkramptes* who broke away from the NP in 1969 (the HNP) and in 1982 (the Conservative Party).

The acquiescence of many white workers to erosion of the job bar, and other apartheid policies, was bought at a high price, evident in rising white wages and a growing white-black wage gap. It was also evident in the rising cost structure and declining competitiveness of South African manufacturing. By 1970, these costs were causing anxiety in official circles, reflected in the report of the 1972 Reynders Commission. Managers in the state sector and parastatals began to echo the complaints of private capital about the rising costs of buying off the opposition of white workers to black advance.

However, once the acquiescence of white workers was secured, and the NP had seen off the threat from the HNP, the bargaining power of white labor declined. From the mid-1970s, their wage increases slowed and the black-white wage gap narrowed. Thus, the concession by white labor on the occupational structure, access to training and unionization was—as the HNP predicted—the thin edge of the wedge in undermining their protected, privileged status.

White labor's vested interest in apartheid remained greater than that of capital. Heavily concentrated in the state sector, and owing many jobs in the private sector to political regulation, white workers remained dependent on the NP to shield them from black competition. The continued fear of a backlash from white labor secured some protection for them at the constitutional negotiations, such as the "sunset clauses" guaranteeing their jobs and pensions—a further indication of their continuing leverage until the end of white rule.

The political influence of white workers and bureaucrats cannot be assessed in isolation, but needs to be viewed in the context of their membership of the Afrikaner nationalist coalition, cemented together by the largesse that all partners shared via their control of the state. Viewed in this context, white workers—by 1970, largely transformed into a bureaucracy in the state and private sectors—had greater political influence than accorded to them in the revisionist model.

Contending Interpretations of Afrikaner Nationalism

The final neo-Marxist claim to be examined relates to their interpretation of Afrikaner nationalism. O'Meara (1983, 6f., 40; 1996, 10) insists that his analysis departs from that of both Afrikaner and liberal historians, who portray Afrikaners as "motivated purely by ideological concerns . . . [thus reducing the] disparate, differentiated and fractious Afrikaners to a static and monolithic ethnic group. . . . [This approach prevails]. . . . without exception in the existing literature." Marks, Saunders, and Smith are among the many endorsing this claim: "For the revisionists, class analysis offered an exciting new tool. . . . Afrikaner nationalism was no longer understood as a movement of ethnic mobilization, but as a class-based phenomenon" and "a unique attempt to identify the constituent material elements of Afrikanerdom . . . correcting the fallacy that Afrikaner nationalism was monolithic and static."[33]

This is a surprising claim. The importance of economic factors, and of class differences among Afrikaners and between Afrikaans and English whites, were recognized by many early and contemporary analysts. As noted in Chapter 2, MacMillan, van der Merve, and Grosskopf documented the situation of poor Afrikaners, including *bywoners* on the farms and the unemployed and disoriented in the cities. Afrikaans society was hardly treated as "monolithic and static" by Afrikaner nationalists such as Diederichs, Pauw, and du Plessis, who wrote proudly about their emerging professionals and entrepreneurs. The role of the Afrikaner Economic Movement in redressing the significant class inequalities between English and Afrikaans whites was the central theme of Laurence Salomon's 1964 essay, "The Economic Background to Afrikaner Nationalism." Critics of the NP, such as Horwitz (1967), acknowledged its "brilliant success in building an Afrikaner bourgeoisie and professional middle class" and nurturing companies such as Sanlam, Volkskas, and General Mining. The significance of non-ideological factors and intensity of intra-Afrikaans conflicts were analyzed by, among others, Welsh (1969, 1974), Bunting (1964), Nolutshungu (1971, 1972), Adam and Giliomee (1979), Slabbert (1975), Magubane (1979), Hepple (1967), and Stadler (1969).

While Roberts and Trollip (1947) focused on the political aspects of Afrikanerdom, they depicted it as "faction ridden . . . and deeply split . . . by bitter rivalries." Likewise, while Andre du Toit (1975) and Kurt Danziger (1971) focused on ideology, they portrayed Afrikaner nationalism as a modern urban, not archaic rural movement, highly flexible and owing its success more to organization than ideology. The growing conflicts within the NP from the mid-1960s were closely monitored by journalists such as Hennie Serfontein, whose 1970 book, *Die Verkrampte Aanslag*, was a significant contribution to the debate, and Wimpie de Klerk, who coined the terms *verlig* and *verkramp*.

A survey of this work reveals wide agreement about basic trends: viz, that rapid economic growth from the 1930s eliminated South Africa's poor white problem; that this was accompanied by resurgent Afrikaner nationalism; and that the NP's 1948 victory stimulated the growth of Afrikaner entrepreneurs, managers, and professionals who benefited from the NP's "Afrikaners First" policy. Afrikaners soon monopolized senior- and middle-level jobs in the expanding state sector and parastatals, and they were favored in subcontracting to the private sector. The growth of an Afrikaner business class was encouraged by Oppenheimer, who facilitated their takeover of General Mining, anticipating that this would, in the long-term, transform them into allies in the struggle to reverse apartheid. The *verkrampte/verligte* dispute that emerged in the mid-1960s was quickly linked by analysts to the changing socioeconomic structure of Afrikaans society.

O'Meara and other revisionists contributed to this body of (earlier and contemporary) work. But what was "unique" about their interpretation was, as they said, their explanation of Afrikaner nationalism "not as a movement of ethnic mobilization but as a class-based phenomenon," dismissing the importance of the racial/ethnic dimension, which other analysts believed not only held together this differentiated intraclass alliance, but also explained how it emerged in the first place.

By 1970, the NP's constituency comprised the following main elements:[34]

White farmers: despite their declining contribution to GDP, the NP, after its 1948 victory, raised the maize price, increased agricultural subsidies and protection, and tightened controls over farm workers.
White labor: the NP extended the job and apprenticeship color bars and accorded preferential access to jobs in the expanding bureaucracy and parastatals to white Afrikaners. There was discrimination against both coloured Afrikaners and against English whites, elbowed out of state-sector jobs.
Afrikaner entrepreneurs: were accorded preference in state contracts and grants, and increased protection against black and particularly Asian entrepreneurs (a policy urged by the AHI and opposed by Assocom).
Afrikaans cultural establishment: was rewarded with compulsory mother tongue education in schools (to prevent Afrikaans children attending English schools); promotion of Afrikaans as an official language; tightening of laws against interracial social mixing and sex; and establishment of a republic outside the Commonwealth.

Support for the view that power lay with this multiclass, ethnic alliance, rather than with hegemonic capital, was provided both by the NP's policies and by their outcome, viz, the disproportionate gains made by Afrikaners, whose income gap with the English *narrowed*, while their income gap with blacks *widened*. From 1939 to 1974, the proportion of Afrikaners in agricultural and blue-collar occupations halved from 73 to 35 percent. Afrikaans ownership of assets listed on the stock exchange increased from 1 to 30 percent in mining, from 5 to 21 percent in finance, and 3 to 15 percent in manufacturing and construction. The ratio of Afrikaner to English per capita incomes narrowed from 100 to 211, to 100 to 141 (larger Afrikaans families contributed to the continuing differential).[35]

Thus, all sections of the Afrikaner alliance benefited, and their interests prevailed not only in relation to blacks, but also in relation to non-Afrikaans whites. State action was required for delivery of these benefits, which could not have been secured by market forces alone. The glue that held the NP coalition together was, surely, racism/nationalism. The revisionists provided no alternative explanation for the basis of this diverse class alliance if it was not racism (against blacks, including Afrikaans-speaking coloureds) and nationalism (against English whites).

CHANGING WHITE ATTITUDES AND VALUES

> *There are two great causes for wonder: the starry skies above and the moral law within us.*
>
> —Immanuel Kant

Arguments about the rising economic costs of apartheid, and the implications of demographic trends, were widely debated in the media, including the new verligte newspapers, *Rapport* and *Beeld*. However, the arguments driving this debate were not only instrumental. The moral issues raised by apartheid were intensely discussed in intellectual and church circles, challenging traditional beliefs about the legitimacy of apartheid. A signal of *changing attitudes and values* was the 1974 speech by Ambassador (later Foreign Minister) Pik Botha to the UN, acknowledging that there was racial discrimination in South Africa, that this was unjust, and that it should be removed. Following the 1974 Durban strikes, Vorster urged his followers to recognize that blacks are "human beings with souls." When urging reconsideration of the Mixed Marriages and

Immorality Acts, Botha said that people of different races "could really love each other."[36]

Afrikaans writers such as Andre Brink, Elsa Joubert, and Breyten Breytenbach produced Afrikaans equivalents of Paton's *Cry the Beloved Country*, Huddleston's *Naught for Your Comfort*, and Gordimer's novels, which had educated and humanized an earlier generation of English South Africans. Fieldwork and public opinion surveys by Laurence Schlemmer and others confirmed the gradual shift toward more verligte views. The proportion of Afrikaners accepting blacks in the same jobs as whites rose from 38 percent in 1970 to 62 percent in 1978, while those accepting interracial sport rose from 4 to 76 percent.

These surveys also showed a strong correlation between political views and class. Verligtes were generally more educated and wealthier; verkramptes drew their support from less affluent, less educated whites and from rural areas—a finding confirmed by the verkramptes' electoral base in rural areas and in suburbs dominated by white workers and bureaucrats. Afrikaner economic advance, encouraged by the NP's 'Afrikaners First' policy, was thus accompanied by a decline in racist views and by growing acceptance of the verligte argument that apartheid was both unworkable and wrong.

These changing views were reflected in the policies of educational, cultural, and sports organizations, including the elite, secretive Afrikaner Broederbond, which had been active in drafting apartheid policies. A landmark was the Broederbond's 1985 de Lange Report, "The Basic Constitutional Values for the Survival of Afrikaners," which argued that blacks had to be incorporated in decision making at the highest political level and that South Africa's head of state might, in the future, be black.[37]

The verkramptes had their own cultural base in the media, universities and churches, which had opposed the introduction of television, fearing this would spread, corrupting foreign views. Verkramptes predicted the NP would lose control of a process that would not be limited to socioeconomic reforms and separate political institutions, but would end in black majority rule. They warned this would spell the end not merely of white supremacy, but also of Afrikaner identity and security. They urged adherence to the policies of Verwoerd (or even the straightforward 'baaskap' of Malan and Strijdom), accompanied, if necessary, by a more autarkic economic strategy.

Many observers predicted that—if forced to choose—the NP would choose the autarkic *verkrampte* route. Such a choice would not have been unique. A similar path was taken by Rhodesia under Ian Smith and by authoritarian regimes in Burma, North Korea, Iraq and, later, Zimbabwe—none of which matched South Africa's combination of economic and military capability, including nuclear weapons. An Afrikaner-led laager might have held out for many years and, even if this ended in a worse eventual outcome for them, societies frequently make self-destructive choices. History records at least as many examples of failed, as of successful, states.

A precondition for this autarkic choice was a united Afrikanerdom (reinforced by some conservative English and coloureds). Hence the importance of the *verkrampte/verligte* dispute, which opened up the political process and, within two decades, destroyed the cohesion essential for political domination by Afrikaners, who comprised less than 7 percent of the total population (though 63 percent of the ruling whites). The conversion of a significant proportion of Afrikaners to acceptance of a common society was one condition for a negotiated settlement. The other condition was the existence of black political leaders with the willingness, capacity and legitimacy to negotiate such a settlement.

The Changing Balance of Political Power

The belief of the neo-Marxists—and the NP—in the compatibility of apartheid and capitalism led them to conclude that whites would *not* be forced to chose because they could have both. The neo-Marxist belief that, despite the apparent control of the state by Afrikaner nationalists, "in the last analysis and fundamentally," power lay with "hegemonic" (English and foreign) capital meant most of them regarded the *verkrampte/verligte* dispute as a kremlinological sideshow. It was precisely because liberals believed 'real' political power lay with the Afrikaner nationalist coalition that they attached significance to the political struggle among Afrikaners.

Liberals also stressed the importance of South Africa's large state sector, dominated by Afrikaners, which meant English capital was less "hegemonic" than appeared from data based on shares of the private sector alone. Liberals also believed that neither the white nor the black opposition would be able to dislodge the NP in the foreseeable future. Thus, a split in the Afrikaner alliance was crucial for a relatively peaceful evolution from apartheid. This did not mean the attitudes of all Afrikaners had to change, but enough to make possible a change of direction—to which others, particularly blacks, could then respond.

Verligtes and *verkramptes* represented the extreme wings of Afrikaner opinion. Most people were in between, or shifting from pragmatic to principled positions. Those committed to liberal principles, such as Andre du Toit and Johann Degenaar, were uneasy about being bracketed together with tough-minded pragmatists.[38] But whatever the calculations underlying the shift to verligte policies, their adoption was crucial for changing, and dividing, the NP and loosening its grip. However, to dismiss this shift from racist thinking as merely Machiavellian misses the significant change in attitudes and values it signaled.

The victory of the *verligtes* refuted the widespread belief that Afrikaners were so much in the grip of "irrational" racism/nationalism that they would never give up apartheid.[39] But this shift did not happen suddenly or automatically. Economically, it was aided by the planning and hard work of employers and managers in the private and state sectors, whose educational programs facilitated the gradual changes in the occupational structure. Politically, this major shift was facilitated by the wide-ranging public debate in parliament, the media, universities, boardrooms, and the homes of "ordinary" people. Visitors commented that South Africans seemed engaged in a constant seminar: it was an educational process that contributed to the changes in the attitudes and values of the ruling whites.

The transformation in white attitudes is evident from the fact that the reforms were well underway before the uprisings of September 1984 and the imposition of official economic sanctions by South Africa's major trading partners in 1985–86 (discussed later). When de Klerk succeeded Botha as president in 1989, there were few legalized apartheid measures left, apart from the Land and Franchise, Population Registration, and Group Areas Acts. Inequality and discrimination remained severe, as did political repression—but these are different issues: it is possible to have deracialization without redistribution or democratization. Many of the legalized racist measures (which distinguished apartheid from racial/class discrimination elsewhere) had been removed since 1970, when the turnaround in NP policy got under way.

The 1970 election was a turning point because defeat of the HNP opened the way for reform. The shift in white attitudes was reflected in the poor electoral showing of the HNP in elections during the 1970s. The shift in attitudes was also evident in the displacement of the disintegrating UP by the Progressive Party, which became the official opposition in 1977. This meant that, for the first time since Union, a political party calling for the abolition of apartheid and nonracial franchise was well represented in parliament. These significant developments were obscured by charges that "whites notoriously and deliberately chose the NP to govern them with ever-increasing majorities . . . until the very end of the apartheid regime" (Alexander 2002, 117). This statement obscures the fact that, from 1970, there was increasing support for liberal/*verligte* policies, evident in growing support for the Progressives, as well as the rejection by NP voters of its verkrampte breakaways.

However, from the mid-1980s, there was another significant and overlooked development: a white backlash against the background of growing internal unrest and external pressures. In the 1987 election, the Progressive Party was displaced as the official opposition by the CP which (together with the HNP) won 30 percent of the white vote and over 50 percent of the Afrikaans vote. This parallels the backlash after Sharpeville, with a swing to the NP in the 1961 and 1966 elections, and Vorster's gains in the 1977 election after the mandatory UN arms embargo. Another indication of the backlash was the abortive 1987 Labor Relations Amendment bill that threatened to roll back a decade of expanding workers rights (Adler et al. 1992). The *verkramptes* also had support within the NP parliamentary caucus and state bureaucracy, including the security and defense forces. Thus, when de Klerk succeeded Botha, the NP's political dominance was eroding. This was confirmed by the 1989 election, when the NP lost support to both the CP and the Progressives.[40] The *verligtes* feared that if they did not move quickly, the verkramptes might regain the political initiative.

Meanwhile, the extraparliamentary opposition was growing and its ties with whites strengthening. In 1986, the Progressive Party leader, van Zyl Slabbert, resigned from Parliament to devote himself to extraparliamentary activity. Business also increased its involvement with civil society organizations. These developments brought the political scene into closer alignment with the profound changes in South Africa's socioeconomic structure, including the emergence of a black middle class and well-organized trade unions, both of which were positioning themselves for further evolutionary changes, rather than, as neo-Marxists insisted, for revolution (discussed in Chapter 4).

ENGLISH-AFRIKAANS RELATIONS AND ATTITUDES

The opinion polls and surveys referred to previously also revealed significant differences in English and Afrikaans attitudes on race and towards the apartheid state. Research by Schlemmer (1980), Hanf (1981), and Gagiano (Giliomee 1992, 180) shows the English as consistently less racist than Afrikaners. Part of the reason for this difference was the correlation with class: the English were better off and more educated. As Afrikaners advanced economically, racism among them declined.

Yet even accounting for class, differences remained. In 1977, Schlemmer found that 78 percent of Afrikaners still supported "a consistent policy of apartheid," compared to 25 percent of the English. In the mid-1980s, Gagiano found that Afrikaners identified more closely with the apartheid state, including its security services, than English whites—70 percent of Afrikaners compared with 22 percent of the English. In line with their dismissal of the significance of racism/nationalism, revisionists brushed aside differences between English and Afrikaans whites—except when attributing greater patriotism to Afrikaners and greater racism to the English!

The revisionists also portray anti-Afrikaner sentiment as being mainly due to English liberals, ignoring the widespread hostility toward the ruling Afrikaners, which increased during the Second World War and, especially, after the NP's 1948 victory, when anti-Afrikaans sentiment increased among all other population groups and political organizations, including Marxists. There are no studies that go further in portraying Afrikaners as "virulent racists" than Mzimela's *Apartheid: South Africa's Nazism* and *The Rise of the South African Reich* by Brian Bunting, a leading member of the South African Communist Party. But the revisionists do not highlight these.[41] They also downplay the anti-English attitudes of many Afrikaners and their intense hatred of English liberals.

Afrikaner hostility was expressed in their exclusion of the English from the civil service and from political office and in an immigration policy aimed at restricting the growth of English numbers (Wilkins and Strydom 1978, 151f.). Verwoerd's newspaper, *Die Transvaler* stated, "We completely reject the notion that all South Africans must be thought of as one *volk*. The Afrikaners are the *volk* of South Africa and the rest, so far as they are white, are either potential Afrikaners or they are foreigners." The Broederbond plan of Afrikanerizing the English (echoing Milner's policy of Anglicizing Afrikaners after the Boer War) was only abandoned after Vorster became prime minister. However, NP politicians continued to attack "Hoggenheimer" (English-Jewish) capital, which they periodically threatened to nationalize.[42]

After Sharpeville, the NP began to feel the need for allies and appointed a couple of English to their hitherto all-Afrikaans cabinet and eased their anti-English immigration policy. But this tokenism did not end English alienation, including the alienation of conservatives who agreed with much of the NP's "native policy" but disliked its attempt to enforce use of the Afrikaans language; its undermining of the independence of the judiciary and of English universities, churches and media; and the NP's breaking of Commonwealth ties.

However, the English grudgingly acquiesced in NP rule, particularly during periods of unrest, for fear of overturning the boat in which they too were stuck. But the assumption of the NP (and the neo-Marxists) that the NP could rely on the English because they had no other options, underestimated the historical animosities between the two white groups and the preference of many English for living in a society that respected the rule of law and independence of their cultural institutions. The NP itself did not dismiss these differences: Prime Minister Malan envisaged "breaking away from all that is harmful to the *volk* in the present British liberal democracy." Leading NP politician Blackie Swart denounced "the false so-called democracy of British-Jewish imperialism and its outdated form of imaginary parliamentary government" (Nolutshungu 1972, 27).

The NP's assumption that the English would fall into line behind it at the constitutional negotiations and accept it as gatekeeper to the ANC proved unfounded. Once the English felt their interests would be no less safe under an ANC government, there was no lingering loyalty to the NP, which most of them never voted for nor identified with.

NATIONALIST CHALLENGES TO LIBERALS AND MARXISTS

The bitter liberal-Marxist argument about the economic interests of capital drove into the background that other major theme of South African history: the role of racism/ethnicity, whether black/white or English/Afrikaner. While Marxists accused liberals of being obsessed with race to the exclusion of class, African and Afrikaner nationalists accused both liberals and Marxists of ignoring race and ethnicity.

Sam Nolutshungu (1982, 62) argued that not only Marxists, but also many liberals, underestimated the extent to which "race and nationality . . . [were] more than 'mere ideology'—a cover for economic exploitation, or a false understanding of it. . . . Racial or national consciousness and political action are not situational peculiarities that universalist socialism or liberalism must in its wisdom educate and transform. They are part of the political terrain. . . . Racial confrontations are not merely ideological epiphenomena but . . . integral components of the relations of domination and exploitation at their most fundamental." Nolutshungu insisted that the crucial issue in South Africa was race, not class, and predicted that liberals and Marxists would not, "as they blithely suppose . . . be able simply to uncouple race and class" and replace them with alliances across color lines, whether with black labor or with the black middle class.

Magubane (2002, 276–77) takes a darker view of the neo-Marxist/liberal emphasis on class at the expense of race. He believes this approach "liquidates the national question. . . . is status quo theorising. . . . sanitising the fact of conquest. . . . [The struggle] was not simply for inclusion in what was called 'a plural society'; it was a struggle for power in a society made of oppressor and oppressed. . . . Neo-Marxists and liberals do not capture what it means to be a member of the 'subject race'. . . . They liquidate the national aspirations of Africans in favour of a universal proletariat led by themselves."

Afrikaner nationalists also believe that both liberals and Marxists underestimate the importance of race/nationalism. Giliomee (2000) complains of their "reluctance to accept the intractable nature of racial conflicts, the incapacity of . . . [economic interests] to dissolve racial antipathies. . . . [the fact that] culture, race and nationhood will for a long time determine both political and economic action for the great mass of the population . . . the hard reality that people see themselves not just as bearers of individual rights but also as members of a particular community. . . . and the reality of race-based mobilisation and policies of patronage." Giliomee does not ignore economic interests, but maintains that political schisms among Afrikaners were "not triggered by material conflicts waged along class lines but by symbolic issues which brought to a head intra-Afrikaans conflicts about the best way of ensuring Afrikaner survival." Giliomee does not believe apartheid was primarily a means of securing Afrikaner material advance, but was a tool for mobilizing the *volk* and countering the deep psychosocial fears of an insecure minority seeking first to acquire, and then maintain, political control.

Giliomee's *The Afrikaners* is, in part, an apologia for Afrikaner rule. Apartheid, he argues, provided the political order essential for economic development and the establishment of a new state. Similar explanations have been offered of other harsh paths to modernization (for example, in the USSR, by Carr, Hobsbawm and Huntington). Many will disagree with this argument, but they are unlikely to find grounds for accusing Giliomee of suppressing evidence about the suffering inflicted by apartheid, or of misrepresenting its critics.

However, it is unclear how Giliomee's apologia relates to his other major theme: that the *raison d'etre* for apartheid was to secure Afrikaner identity and security *despite* its economic costs. Part of the explanation probably lies in the fact that apartheid's costs were not borne by Afrikaners, most of who gained from it, until economic growth reached the point at which these costs could no longer be shifted to others. Thereafter, support for apartheid gradually declined among crucial groups of Afrikaners, although those who continued to benefit—white labor, sections of white agriculture and of the political/administrative class—continued to support it.

Nolutshungu and Giliomee highlight the inadequacy of explanations of the role of racism/nationalism in shaping South African society. There is, among Marxists as well as some liberals, almost a taboo against according importance to racism (discussed in Chapter 5). However, Nolutshungu et al. overstate the extent to which liberals dismissed the salience of racism. O'Dowd, a rigorous structuralist who treats racism as a functional surrogate for class, is an exception. Most liberals, while giving relatively more attention to class, do not dismiss racism and would probably not disagree with the following formulation of the race/class issue:

> Social and political divisions tended to take place along the lines of ethnic rather than class cleavages. . . . It proved easier to forge alliances based on ethnic ties . . . which acted as a more effective cement in binding people together. . . . But [ethnicity] did not provide an inevitable or sufficient basis for political alliances . . . and was not so "natural" and strong a tie as to prevail over all other interests. . . . The

splintering [of the Afrikaner alliance] showed that, when people were forced to choose . . . ethnicity did not invariably prevail. Class conflicts within the group were not simply over-ridden by ethnic ties. . . . Both class and ethnicity are essential for understanding political behaviour. (Lipton 1985, 373f.)[42]

The fact that racial/ethnic issues have not disappeared in post-apartheid South Africa makes it unlikely that scholars will be able to continue evading this difficult, sensitive issue and to dismiss it as "an epiphenomenon of capitalism."

A MORAL CHALLENGE

A further criticism of the liberal analysis is of its portrayal of business as "progressive." Stolten (2002) regrets that liberals end up seeming to defend wealthy, powerful mineowners, rather than identifying with poorly paid (white and black) workers struggling to secure their rights. Stolten has a point: even if we cannot comfort the afflicted, should we not (as J. K. Galbraith put it) at least "afflict the comfortable."

Similar challenges were raised by black trade unionists and businesspeople who—responding to my argument about the progressive role of business—said that, while they accepted the evidence of business pressures against many apartheid policies, they found many of the issues on which business focused, such as the Physical Planning and Apprenticeship Acts, rather technical and abstruse. Meanwhile, their personal experience in factories and offices during the 1970s and '80s was that employers were still not promoting blacks as rapidly as they merited; were reluctant to support them in confrontations with white workers and officials; were often wary of, or hostile towards, their trade unions; and seldom showed solidarity with their struggles outside the workplace. Moreover, the white businessmen (and liberals) who condemned apartheid continued to live privileged lives as "fat cats on the inside, while we were suffering outside."[44]

These criticisms raise moral and psychological issues about how people do—and should—behave in situations in which they are living comfortably while others suffer. But these important issues (discussed later in Chapter 5) do not negate the fact that the structural economic and legal issues tackled by business were essential for a nonviolent outcome in South Africa. The businessmen involved in these battles probably assumed that their role in eroding apartheid was obvious. They also assumed people realized that, even if they supported the principle of trade union recognition, their relationship with the unions remained, in many respects, adversarial. Most businessmen also failed to respond to the desire of victims of apartheid for signs of moral and psychological solidarity. All this contributed to negative perceptions of their stance, notwithstanding their growing conflicts with the NP and their "objectively progressive" role in undermining apartheid.

To conclude: liberals and neo-Marxist revisionists provided conflicting interpretations of the three periods reviewed in this chapter: the 1922 Rand Rebellion, the abortive wartime reforms, and the post-1970 reforms. Liberals perceived, in each period, the possibility of a less racist evolution for South Africa and, in each case, identified the interests of progressive capital as among the pressures for this. Revisionists identified capital as the major support for the racial order; dismissed conflicts within the white oligarchy as marginal and attempts at reform as "cosmetic restructuring;" and insisted capitalism and apartheid were "inextricably linked" and the whole system unreformable.

The recent, gradual disintegration of the revisionist paradigm has left confusion about where they now stand. Some revisionists have quietly shifted towards the liberal analysis of the post-1970 period (and, as discussed in the Appendix, in some cases of earlier periods as well). But others remain committed to the belief that apartheid was merely restructured and that there remained, to the bitter end, a "close alliance between capital and the military to defend the apartheid regime."

The argument here is not that business played a heroic role in ending apartheid—it did not. Nor is it argued that business alone was responsible for ending apartheid—it was not. The argument is that, after 1948, the costs of apartheid to capital rose sharply, exacerbated by the NP's attempt to tighten apartheid and, then, to impose its "separate development" version. This attempt led to the gradual but, eventually, effective mobilization of South Africa's differentiated and divided business community, which came to play a progressive role in halting, then rolling back, Verwoerdian apartheid. In this, they were driven by self-interest, reinforced in some cases by liberal convictions and by the desire to be part of,

Chapter 4

The Debate about South Africa III: Other Factors Eroding Apartheid

What explanation is offered by those (including, but not only, neo-Marxist revisionists) who deny that pressures from within the white oligarchy, including from business, contributed to ending apartheid? Alternative explanations include the armed struggle, mass action, and economic sanctions. This chapter briefly discusses each in turn, as well as some other possible factors.

Role of the Armed Struggle

Most commentators agree that the armed struggle was psychologically important as a symbol of resistance to apartheid: a source of hope to blacks and a warning to whites. From South Africa's 1975 intervention in Angola, the armed struggle also became a drain on South Africa's budget and manpower. However, no serious commentator claims it drove the NP to the negotiating table. Nelson Mandela said, "I never had any illusions that we could win a military victory; the purpose of Umkhonto we Sizwe [ANC's armed wing] was to focus attention on the resistance movement." A 1986 report by the ANC's Political-Military Council recognized that "despite all our efforts, we have not come anywhere near the achievement . . . of our objectives." ANC Secretary General Alfred Nzo acknowledged in 1990 that the ANC did not have the capacity "to intensify the armed struggle in any meangingful way." In 1992, Joe Slovo urged the ANC "to win at the negotiating table what we failed to win on the battlefield."[1]

Dissent about the armed struggle is along different lines. Legassick (2002) regrets that "a strategy of armed insurrection was . . . never seriously implemented." Others, such as Mckinley (1997), who urged the revolutionary overthrow of the apartheid regime argue that the ANC should have continued fighting instead of compromising when "structural conditions" were becoming ripe (an argument unaccompanied by any indication of how the huge shift in the balance of power necessary for a successful revolution might have been secured, nor of the likely impact on South Africa's economy and infrastructure, including possible partition of the country). Thus, whatever the actual impact and potential of the armed struggle, it is not perceived, either by neo-Marxists or by others, as having played a crucial role in ending apartheid.

This assessment of the limitations of the armed struggle was underlined by the outcome of its high point: the 1987 battle at Cuito Cuanavale in Angola. The setback to South African forces revealed they were becoming overstretched, especially in air power. But this setback was unexpectedly followed by a shift of the military balance against the ANC when it was deprived of its bases in Angola as part of the 1989 Namibian settlement. The loss of these bases pushed the ANC further away from South Africa than it had been a decade earlier. Ellis and Sechaba write (1992, 175), "In 1985, it was still possible to believe armed struggle . . . might achieve its goal, [but] by 1988 this was hard to believe." Instead, the ANC came under increasing pressure to abandon armed struggle and enter negotiations not only from the West, but also from the (disintegrating) USSR and from neighboring African states, reeling from the effects of South Africa's destabilization strategy against them (on the changing regional and international balance of power, see Crocker 1992).

As noted by Lodge (1991a, 190), these setbacks to the armed struggle, combined with South Africa's success in quelling domestic unrest by its 1986 state of emergency, "reduced expectations of a military victory. . . . coupled with growing pressure from the Soviet Union . . . [and increased the need] to seek a negotiated solution . . . rather than a revolutionary one."

The Impact of Mass Unrest

The uprisings of 1984–86 sent shock waves through South Africa and attracted unprecedented international attention. At the time, many agreed with O'Meara's assessment (1983, 252; 1979, 258f.) that the NP was confronted by an "organised and militant working class and mass resistance . . . taking an increasingly anti-capitalist form" and increasing the likelihood of the revolutionary overthrow of the government. But these beliefs declined from July 1986 when the NP took off the gloves, declared a harsh state of emergency, and demonstrated it could halt mass action and leave the United Democratic Front (UDF) "badly battered," as Jeremy Seekings put it (2000, 293). In retrospect, most analysts, including O'Meara (1996, 5) came to agree that mass action "proved unable to . . . pose a significant threat" and that it was "hard to say the UDF played a crucial role in pushing the state to the precipice" (Etherington 1992, 118. See also Bozzoli 1990, ch. 4).

Nevertheless, even if the NP's challengers proved unable to "push it to the precipice," did the uprisings not reveal a revolutionary potential that President de Klerk adroitly deflated by his release of Mandela in 1990? Analyses of the unrest by Seekings and others reveal a process that was complex, volatile, and difficult to interpret. It is widely agreed that, initially, the uprisings were unplanned and spontaneous, with the UDF (linked to the ANC) "taken by surprise by the mid-1980s township revolts" that they and their rivals, Azapo and National Forum, tried to channel and take the credit for. Seekings highlights the minor role played by the UDF, dominated by coloureds and Indians, in the uprisings in African townships. It is also widely agreed that the causes of unrest were often specific and local, such as the sharp increases in rent and service charges for township residents in 1984 (similar to the imposition of Afrikaans as medium of instruction before the 1976 Soweto uprising).[2]

Seekings (2000, 288f.) stresses the caution of the masses when confronted with the risks and costs of revolutionary action. Anthony Marx (1992) links what he terms "mass pragmatism" to the limited time and energy most people can devote to such activities. Craig Charney (1995) argues that on many issues, the masses, while undoubtedly opposed to apartheid, were conservative and did not necessarily share the socialist aims and confrontationist approach of political activists.

suggest that the political dynamics would have worked against the gradual, evolutionary incorporation that Botha was cautiously moving towards. This approach might have worked in the 1940s; by the 1980s, it was too late.

Whatever one's assessment of the mid-1980s unrest—and the willingness and capacity of the masses to push confrontation with the state to the point of civil war—*the unrest cannot, ex post facto, account for the reforms that began around 1970*, when the NP's capacity to maintain control was unquestioned. An indication of this is the modest size of South Africa's police and defense forces before the mid-1980s. They were smaller and included a higher proportion of blacks than is often recognized.[4] The shock of Sharpeville led to expansion of the security forces but was followed by a period of quiescence among all the government's opponents. Confronted with both the mailed fist and with carrots (rising wages for urban blacks, conciliatory gestures toward English whites), most people acquiesced and got on with their lives.

Acquiescence declined after the 1976 Soweto riots, which were followed by an increase in the number of young blacks available for political mobilization, against the background of an explosive combination of rising expectations and growing unemployment. The NP responded by expanding the security forces. The unrest from September 1984 ratcheted up internal conflict, requiring armed forces on a larger scale and more extended duty. Thereafter, all analysts agree that South Africa had a serious security problem.

However, the continuing capacity of the NP to contain the situation was confirmed by its 1986 clampdown: tens of thousands of people were detained, and there were arrests, beatings, and murderous attacks on activists by both the police and vigilantes (such as the Witdoeke and the A-team), leaving the UDF "badly battered."[5] Until de Klerk's accession, it was clear the NP's challengers would be faced, not with the velvet gloves of 1989 eastern Europe, but with the guns of Tiananmen Square—based on the capacity, calculations, and political will of the Botha regime.

Botha's tough stance rested on the NP's control of the security/defense forces, which remained intact throughout the stormy processes of reform, backlash, and, later, negotiation.[6] This included discipline among the black police and troops until 1994 when this began to weaken, as shown by the action of black police during the abortive rightwing coup in Bophuthatswana, during which they shot whites involved in the coup. The main worry during the transitional period of 1990–94 was whether there was support within the defense/security forces for the white Right. (The exposure of Operation Vula in July 1990 revealed parallel plotting by a group of SACP members within the ANC, attempting "to have a last crack at revolution," reportedly without the knowledge of Mandela and Mbeki.[7])

By 1988, Botha had restored sufficient order for local elections to take place in an orderly environment, for the UDF to consider participating, and for a turnout respectable by the standards of local government elections. However, this outcome led the NP to overestimate the support for—as distinct from acquiescence in—its policy and to overestimate the support that (together with its allies) it might receive from "moderate" Africans in electoral competition with the ANC.

The belief that the NP had the capacity to hold onto power for considerably longer was shared by the ANC, which anticipated that a long, hard struggle lay ahead. The revisionists shared this assessment—hence their astonishment at de Klerk's "leap in the dark." The retention of power by Zimbabwe's government—also faced with intense domestic and international opposition and with much less economic, administrative, and military capacity than the apartheid regime—is among many examples of the extreme difficulty of dislodging well-armed, ruthless governments.

After the release of Mandela, and the unbanning of the ANC in February 1990, mass action became a significant factor in the struggle over the nature of the transition, and terms of the settlement, pushing South Africa toward a more thoroughly nonracial and democratic outcome. But mass action cannot account for the reforms of the 1970s and early '80s, or for de Klerk's "leap in the dark" in 1990. The timing, or "periodization," is wrong.

The Role of Black Trade Unions

All analysts attach importance to the growth of black unions and to their growing industrial and political power. But similar problems apply to according them a key role in initiating and driving the reforms, particularly the weakness of the unions before their legalization in 1979 and their cautious political strategy until 1990.

As noted previously (p. 58), the 1973–74 strikes, which revived the debate about unionization, were largely spontaneous, and the black unions then small and weak, with membership of less than twenty thousand. After the legalization of trade unions in 1979, their membership grew steadily, reaching one hundred and fifty thousand in 1981 and one million in 1989. By then, the unions were a significant factor on the industrial scene, represented with government, employers, and white unions on the Industrial Councils, Apprenticeship Boards, and National Manpower Commission. Nevertheless, their continuing vulnerability to government crackdowns led them to avoid political involvement—as confirmed by senior Cosatu officials (see p. 58).

After 1979, the bargaining power of the unions increased; but they remained aware of their continuing vulnerability, not only in relation to the security police, but also economically, because of rising unemployment and the fact that many union members were unskilled and thus readily replaceable. Another indication of the weakness of the unions' domestic base was their heavy dependence on foreign funding: in 1985, three quarters of Cosatu's income of Rands 2.4m came from foreign sources (Anthony Marx 1992, 202). Hence the unions' caution in responding to calls for strike action in 1976 and during the 1984–86 unrest. The unions' continuing vulnerability in the industrial sphere was illustrated by the 1987 miners strike, which led to the loss of thousands of jobs and a sharp drop in membership of the black Mine Workers Union.

Politically, the unions adopted what Adler, Webster, and Maller (1992) termed "a strategic approach." They decided to register under the Industrial Conciliation (IC) Act, against pressures from those urging a boycott of the official system. The unions also strove to avoid confrontation and to "distinguish principles from tactics . . . and choose tactics most likely to succeed, including negotiation and compromise. . . . gradualism and flexibility . . . [not] aimed at the state's overthrow." The unions also focused on specific industrial actions, usually eschewing general strikes related to political aims (on these issues, see also Martin Plaut, 1991).

This strategic approach did not reduce the unions to a tame, acquiescent role. Their increasing, now legal, strikes contributed to the rising real wages of black workers, which continued to rise despite the slowdown in growth and growing unemployment from the mid-1970s. Wages of blacks rose much faster than those of whites, narrowing the wage ratio, and the absolute gap, between them. Politically, the unions denounced apartheid and state repression, made effective use of the media coverage accorded to their activities and statements, and set up educational and other programs to press for further reform. This strategic approach did not preclude radical demands, nor did it prevent hostile reactions from some employers and, particularly, from the security services, who on occasion reacted viciously with bannings, arrests of union activists, and the bombing of Cosatu House. But the growing activities of the unions were reformist, not revolutionary. They added to pressures for reform, but did not attempt to overthrow, the apartheid regime.

This *assertive but nonrevolutionary strategy* secured some important gains, including growing unionization of urban workers at a time when unions worldwide were shrinking. This reformist strategy also contributed to the changing climate of public opinion among both blacks and whites and widened the space for political activity, which other NGOs soon used. The unions' skilful use of the opportunities and institutions open to them helped to evolve the negotiating mechanisms and skills that later produced South Africa's post-apartheid settlement, in which experienced union leaders such as Cyril Ramaphosa played a major part.

From 1990, the rules of the political game changed. The constraints on the unions eased, and they became the most disciplined element in the mass support on which the ANC could rely. During the transition, all sides were aware of their formidable potential, and this helped to shift the balance of power toward the ANC, despite the continuing loyalty of the police and defense forces to the NP. But this increased bargaining power of the unions cannot explain what happened before 1990—let alone before the legalization of black trade unions in 1979.

Even after 1994, with the unions' close ally, the ANC, in power, there remain limits to the capacity of South Africa's popular, experienced unions to get their way. These include continuing constraints on the use of their industrial muscle to oppose policies they dislike, including the fear of destroying their members' jobs or damaging the economy on which they depend. Trade unions are generally less willing or able to act effectively against strong states and employers than is imagined by those who romanticize their revolutionary potential (discussed later in Chapter 5). This is among the reasons why many employers prefer to recognize unions and battle out

conflicts with them in institutionalized settings, despite the difficulties and tensions inherent in this process.
  This record does not fit the neo-Marxist model (as in Davies et al. 1984) of how trade unions behave. Nor does the emergence of a well-organized, disciplined trade union movement fit models of a society being immiserized rather than reformed. Even after 1979, the newly legalized unions recognized the constraints on their power, especially in the political sphere, where control of the unwieldy ship of state remained in the hands of the white oligarchy, arguing among themselves about their destination and whether, and how fast, to change course. The revisionists insisted that even the reformers among them aimed at the same destination (reconciling capitalism with apartheid) but *were forced to change course—but by what?* This is unclear, and the mystery is deepened by the fact that most revisionists no longer argue that armed struggle, mass action, or trade unions forced de Klerk to the negotiating table. Far from denying he could have held out longer, they were astonished that he did not do so.

THE ROLE OF INTERNATIONAL SANCTIONS

Those who exclude a role for business in ending apartheid, and accord only a qualified role to mass actions, are left with sanctions as the main explanation for apartheid's demise. What do analysts say about sanctions as the *explanation* for this (as distinct from supporting or opposing sanctions), and what is their model of how sanctions worked?
  Many, especially foreign, observers and scholars claim that sanctions forced de Klerk to the negotiating table. Yet there has been little research on their actual impact on South Africa. Scholarly work has focused mainly on the legal issues and mechanisms involved in adopting sanctions and on setting out the case for or against them.[8] There has been little empirically-based analysis of their effects, with the exception of the sports boycott, well documented and analyzed by, inter alia, Lapchick (1975) and Guelke (1993). But while most analysts agree that this was effective, that is, sports would not otherwise have been deracialized at this early stage of the reform process, no one suggests the sports boycott forced the NP to the negotiating table. The only candidate for this is economic sanctions.

Among reasons for the paucity of research on economic sanctions are the empirical and theoretical difficulties of assessing their effects, and the extreme politicization of the sanctions debate (discussed later, p. 165f). The sweeping claims that economic sanctions had a major impact on South Africa ignore the fact that few sanctions were imposed by South Africa's main trading partners, the European Union, the United States, and Japan.[9] Moreover, these limited sanctions were imposed for only a short time, mostly from 1985, and there was little monitoring of their implementation or their impact (the arms and oil embargoes are discussed later).

The few rigorous attempts to assess the impact of *trade sanctions* revealed that South Africa was adapting to them by sanctions-busting and by finding substitutes for its imports and alternative markets for its exports. The effectiveness of these adaptations is indicated by South Africa's success in diversifying into alternative (Asian, Middle Eastern, and east European) markets. These adaptations (combined with the 1985 devaluation of the Rand) led to an *increase in South African exports* from Rand 41billion (US$18 billion) in 1985 to Rand 59billion (US$68 billion) in 1989 (Lipton 1988, 1990). This increase in the face of sanctions was described in the (pro-sanctions) report commissioned by the Commonwealth Heads of Government as "prodigious" (Ovenden and Cole, 1989).

Sanctions were more successful in stimulating *disinvestment* from South Africa by foreign, particularly American, companies, many of which left South Africa from the mid-1980s.[10] Disinvestment was a blow to business confidence. But it did not halt, or even reduce, production and had some ambiguous effects, including the acquisition of foreign assets by South African companies at firesale prices.

Arms and oil sanctions undoubtedly imposed heavy costs on South Africa and intensified the white oligarchy's sense of isolation. But they too had complex, often unintended, consequences. The UN arms embargo (imposed on a voluntary basis in 1963; made mandatory in 1976) stimulated the expansion of South African arms production: by the mid-1980s, South Africa had reportedly become the world's tenth largest arms exporter. Likewise, the threat (and later partial implementation) of an oil embargo led South Africa to expand its oil-from-coal process, in which it became a world leader. In one of the few rigorous attempts to analyze the impact of all these economic sanctions, Becker and Pollard (1990) described South Africa's reduction of dependence on these strategic imports as "stunning" and "extraordinary"—as well as economically costly and distorting because, *inter alia*, they accentuated the trend toward capital intensity in a country with a shortage of skills and capital and a surplus of unskilled labor.

The widespread belief that *financial sanctions* were more successful in pushing South Africa toward negotiations may be true, but has not yet been established. Such an analysis would need to differentiate the effects of these sanctions from market forces, such as investors and bankers fleeing the country because of perceived political instability (as after Sharpeville, when there were no sanctions). Account will also need to be taken of the fact that these financial sanctions were imposed at a time of increasing international indebtedness for many countries (Argentina, Mexico, Australia, Zambia), and that, despite being under sanctions, South Africa coped better with its debt problems than many others, leaving the post-apartheid government with a relatively low level of international debt (Lipton 1990). This is not to dismiss the importance of financial sanctions, but to note the present shallow basis for sweeping claims about their impact.

Whatever the economic effects of sanctions, their aim was not, surely, "to bring the South African economy to its knees," but to achieve the *political* goal of ending apartheid. There has been even less research on the political effects of sanctions. The limited debate has focused on two issues: first, the extent of black support for sanctions and second, whether sanctions pushed whites towards reform. Hofmeyr, Orkin, and Schlemmer used opinion surveys, focus groups, and interviews to assess black political support for, and white reactions to, sanctions. This work provides an interesting example of scholars drawing the opposite conclusions from similar findings.

In analyzing *the attitudes of black workers*, Orkin (1986) concluded that they supported sanctions, and Schlemmer (1986) that they opposed them. Yet, the research findings of both show that 1) black workers welcomed sanctions as symbols of opposition to apartheid, but 2) their support for sanctions declined sharply when asked about their potentially adverse effects on employment. Orkin found their support for sanctions declined from 73 percent to 26 percent in the case of job losses. This finding parallels the reactions of Polish workers, with Lech Walesa, leader of the trade union Solidarity, calling for international pressure on Poland but opposing sanctions that might damage the economy. Likewise in Zimbabwe, the opposition Movement for Democratic Change calls for international pressure on Mugabe but not for sanctions that might further ravage the economy. This is relevant to the question of how black South Africans might have reacted if (as was not the case) prolonged, severe sanctions had been imposed on South Africa.

Attempts to interpret the *political effects of sanctions on whites* are bedeviled by confusion over voting trends. As noted previously (p. xxx), the claim that white South Africans voted solidly for the continuation of apartheid from 1948 to 1990 is misleading. From 1970, whites voted in increasing numbers for the Progressive Party, while NP voters rejected the *verkrampte* HNP and CP and supported the NP's reforms. But in the 1987 election, this reformist trend was reversed and the electorate swung right, leading to the replacement of the Progressives as the official opposition by the CP. Other indications of the white backlash were the abortive 1987 bill to curb trade union rights and Botha's intensified destabilization campaign against neighboring African countries. Thus, the 1985–86 sanctions, and domestic unrest, were followed by a white backlash (as happened after Sharpeville with the swing to the NP in the 1961 and 1966 elections, and in the 1977 election when, following the UN arms embargo, there was an increased vote for the NP).

At the least, voting trends and Botha's *kragdadige* (ironfisted) reactions, both domestically and regionally, challenge the argument that sanctions drove whites to the negotiating table. The political effects of sanctions seem contradictory: as the surveys of Hofmeyr (1990) showed, *verkramptes* cited sanctions as evidence that "the outside world is out to get South Africa whatever we do" (i.e, despite the reforms), while business and liberals/*verligtes* cited sanctions as an additional reason for reform. Thus, external pressures seem to have reinforced the convictions of both sides.

Could sanctions have pushed South Africa toward reform over a longer period? This assessment needs to take account not only of their contradictory and often perverse effects (increased exports, white backlash), but also of their timing. Apart from the voluntary 1963 arms embargo (made mandatory in 1976) and boycotts of oranges, wine, etc., official economic sanctions were only applied by South Africa's main trading partners from 1985 and were never made mandatory by the UN. These limited measures (see footnote 197, no. 9) seem unlikely to explain what happened in South Africa, especially before the mid-1980s.

Nevertheless, the *mere threat* of sanctions did serve to focus minds in ruling circles on growing international hostility to apartheid and they intensified the crucial domestic debate about apartheid. But the threat also had some unintended consequences: economically it was cited as justifying increased arms and oil production; politically it was cited by Verwoerd as a major reason for his separate development policy, particularly the need to establish "independent black homelands . . . in the light of the pressures being exerted on South Africa . . . [so as to] buy for the white man his freedom and right to govern himself" (Lipton 1985, 306).

To argue that sanctions played the key role in apartheid's demise is to assume that they precipitated a change of direction that would not otherwise have occurred—in other words, that trends in South Africa were not eroding apartheid and that sanctions, reinforced by mass action and armed struggle, *forced the white oligarchy to change course*. This hypothesis needs to take account of the following counterindications: 1) the wide-ranging reforms introduced before the economic sanctions of the mid-1980s; 2) the unintended effects of these (and earlier) sanctions, including the white backlashes that followed them; 3) the NP's success in halting domestic unrest and the weakening of the ANC's military position following the collapse of the USSR and 1989 Namibian settlement; and 4) the increasingly fluid international situation after 1989, in which it became uncertain whether the international community would impose further sanctions on South Africa.[11]

The difficulty of making sanctions "work" (i.e., of securing their *political* goals) is demonstrated by the cases of Rhodesia under Smith and by Iraq, Burma, and North Korea—all of which were less well-equipped than South Africa to resist sanctions, yet did so for many years. It seems inadequate to explain the watershed decision by South Africa's ruling elite in 1990 as the outcome of the limited economic sanctions imposed a few years earlier, especially when these had contradictory and, as yet, little studied effects.

There is an alternative interpretation of the role of international factors in undermining apartheid, based on giving weight to *a wider range of international influences*. These include 1) the effect on all countries, including South Africa, of the changing international *zeitgeist* and balance of power, linked to increasing global economic and cultural integration, and 2) pressures on South Africa from its "friends in the West" who opposed sanctions and isolation but (pressured by their domestic lobbies) urged South Africa to abandon apartheid and tried to secure this by "engaging constructively" with the ruling elite and, increasingly, with its challengers (Lipton 1990; Guelke 2005). This strand of international pressure on South Africa was evident from the time of MacMillan's 1960 speech to the South African parliament, urging it to heed the "winds of change" sweeping through Africa. As international revulsion against institutionalized racism grew, the NP became anxious to avoid being isolated, particularly from foreign investors. To improve South Africa's image abroad, lobbies such as the South Africa Foundation were set up. However, they themselves began to lobby the South African government for reforms that would "help our friends in the West to help us."

Constructive engagement was not limited to argument and persuasion but had concrete, material dimensions. The Sullivan and EU Codes of Conduct for foreign companies were backed up by planning and resources to promote black job advance and provide support and resources for black trade unions, the independent media, and NGOs such as the UDF. Many people worked hard not just to isolate, but to deracialize, South African sports, churches, and other institutions.

The likely influence of these wider international forces on South Africa receives support from the similar transitions from authoritarian rule that occurred elsewhere, notably in the USSR, where a strongly entrenched ruling elite also voluntarily abandoned its distinctive ideological and social system in a relatively peaceful way. Attempts to understand the role of international pressures in ending apartheid need to take more account of these complex, subtle cultural and psychological ways in which international forces were affecting societies worldwide. The question of whether these factors played a role in pushing South Africa toward reform is relevant to the application of sanctions elsewhere and to the usefulness of carrots as well as sticks, contact as well as isolation, in pushing states in breach of international norms toward reform.

Despite the paucity of evidence on the complex effects of economic sanctions, they are widely cited—especially outside South Africa—as *the* (or at least *a*) crucial factor in ending apartheid. Indeed, this has become the default position for those lacking other explanations. However, as discussed in Chapter 6, the sanctions debate has been driven by political considerations, not evidence.

Attempts at more serious analysis will need to take account of, rather than ignore, some perverse effects of sanctions and some positive effects of constructive engagement. The jury is still out on the role of sanctions in apartheid's demise.

OTHER POSSIBLE FACTORS

There are some other factors whose possible role in contributing to apartheid's relatively nonviolent demise have received little attention. These include the role of blacks functioning, or simply working, 'within the system' and, more generally, the role of institutions and human agency.

The extent to which blacks categorized as working within the system may have contributed to apartheid's demise is a taboo subject, presumably because it raises the sensitive question of complicity and/or is viewed as detracting from the contribution of activists and revolutionaries. Nevertheless, according to Central Statistical Services data, by 1989 two thirds of the 1.7 million employees in the public sector (including parastatals and Bantustans) were black. Moreover, their skill levels were rising, as were their numbers and skill levels in the private sector. By 1990, the National African Federated Chambers of Industry and Commerce (Nafcoc) and its affiliated chambers had thousands of members; black journalists and professionals also had their own organizations.

What impact did this socioeconomic advance have on South Africa's hierarchical race structure and its underlying justificatory norms? This includes the effect on NP officials, some of whom were now facilitating black advance and hoping to win over the black vanguard as allies, or at least avoid their becoming a 'fifth column.' Did not such people, as Francis Meli (1988) wrote, "by their very existence, and without doing anything except working in their professional occupations, help to shatter the racist myth of the inherent or biological inferiority of Africans?" Did they not contribute to what Kane-Berman (1990) termed South Africa's "silent revolution"? The South African transition was, in fact, noisily debated and fiercely contested, but it had this quieter, less-explored dimension.

A structuralist analysis would anticipate that the growth of these skilled industrial and middle classes would, *per se*, pose a challenge to the racial hierarchy, making it more difficult to treat blacks as serfs and inferiors. Interviews with the advancing black vanguard in both the private and state sectors, including the Bantustans, never gave the impression of pliable, willing collaborators. On the contrary, they were usually forthright in denouncing apartheid. But there has been little investigation of their role in undermining, or propping up, apartheid.[12]

Insufficient attention has been accorded to the rivals of the ANC and UDF. These include the Pan Africanist Congress (PAC), Black Consciousness Movement, Azapo, and the National Forum. Africanist organizations played a key role in sparking the Soweto riots and inspiring the post-Soweto generation and, although they performed poorly in post-apartheid elections, many of their ideas, such as their black empowerment policies, have been taken over by the ANC. Likewise, many leading activists, such as Saki Macozoma, Barney Pityana, Joel Netshitenzhe, Mojanku Gumbi and Itumeleng Mosala have been incorporated into leading positions in the post-apartheid government. The revisionists, in particular, were markedly less sympathetic towards Africanism than to Afrikaner nationalism and usually ignored or sidelined the Africanists, which gives a misleading picture of black political evolution.[13]

The question whether Bantustan institutions and leaders contributed to apartheid's erosion is understandably sensitive, as it raises the dilemma of the ethnic trap: the NP's unjustified use of the Bantustans to exclude blacks from political rights in "white" South Africa. Some Bantustan politicians attempted to subvert this aim by refusing to accept "independence" (which the NP tried to force on them) while using the Bantustans as platforms from which to attack apartheid and mobilize their followers. From 1970, speeches attacking NP policy by Gatsha Buthelezi and others received front-page coverage in the South African and international media. Such coverage of black attacks on apartheid were unprecedented in South Africa; but their effect on politicizing blacks and changing white attitudes has been little explored.

Any use of the "separate development" institutions was ruled out in principle by Steve Biko and the Black Consciousness movement. Indeed, they focused their ire on Buthelezi precisely because (as Biko said) his critical stance on apartheid and his effective mobilization of a power base aroused fears that he was giving credibility to the Bantustans. But the potential of using the unintended consequences of the Bantustans was taken seriously by Mandela on

Robben Island, and by some ANC leaders in exile, who were in contact with Buthelezi until their breach with him in 1979—though contacts continued with Bantustan leaders such as Enos Mabuza and Bantu Holomisa.[14]

The recognition of Buthelezi's usefulness was accompanied by growing fears that he might build a power base rivaling that of exiled and imprisoned leaders. This contributed to the breach with him and to his becoming the most reviled Bantustan leader. Buthelezi's angry reaction to this, and his later acceptance of covert support for Inkatha from the South African security forces, intensified the reaction against him and contributed to the spiraling violence and high death toll in KwaZulu-Natal, where Inkatha became locked in bloody conflict with the equally confrontationist ANC regional leader, Harry Gwala. After 1990, Mandela and Mbeki tried to reconcile Buthelezi, who was later included in the ANC cabinet. Mbeki's recent attendance at the funeral of Kaiser Matanzima, who, unlike Buthelezi, bowed to NP pressure to accept "independence," may signal a shift in attitude toward Bantustan politicians and lift the taboo on considering the complex role some of them played (though scholars should not await such political signals before studying these issues).

South Africa provides an interesting case-study of the relationship between political unrest and economic conditions. Yet there has been surprisingly little research on this, including by Marxists.[15] Research cannot proceed if it is deemed improper to recognize that significant numbers of blacks were gaining from improvements in their wages and occupations, and that what was happening was not immiserization, but growing class differentiation. Research unimpeded by political taboos could shed light on whether unrest followed worsening or improving conditions; whether it was due to intensifying social dissonance (advances in economic but not social and political conditions); and the extent to which the impetus came from the emerging middle, rather than the industrial, class.

The point being made here is *not* that blacks "working within the system," or simply functioning and even making gains under apartheid, played a role in eroding apartheid. The point is that the question of how they affected the process—*whether they delayed or accelerated it*—has not been addressed. Their role is often dismissed by describing them as 'coopted,' that is, as passive or active collaborators. This, in turn, raises questions about the difficult, tangled notions of cooption and complicity, and about the underlying model of how politics works (discussed in Chapters 5 and 6). Many scholars remained silent, or even participated, in the demonization of blacks categorized as 'working within the system.' Indeed, those who suggested that they might be playing a subtle, long-term role were themselves demonized.

Both Marxists and structuralist liberals give a low weighting to *institutions and agency*, although public opinion ("ordinary people") attaches importance to the role of individuals in shaping history. South Africa was relatively well endowed with institutions of representative government: an independent judiciary, media, universities, and NGOs. Most of these institutions were tarnished by racism and undermined by the NP's growing authoritarianism, but they survived and, even during the worst periods of NP rule, vigorous criticism of apartheid continued in parliament and the media. These institutions, in the form in which they continued to evolve in democratic countries, remained the model many South Africans aspired to, and built on, when constructing their post-apartheid constitution.

South Africa's relative abundance of institutions compares favorably with those in many other societies undergoing major transitions. Commenting on Gorbachev's attempt to inaugurate reform in the USSR after 1985, Eric Hobsbawm wrote, "By the 1980s . . . the Soviet economy was unreformable. If there were real chances of reforming it in the 1960s, these were sabotaged by the self-interest of a nomenklatura [party and state bureaucracy] that was firmly entrenched and uncontrollable" (1985). Hobsbawm added that "political and juridical liberalisation was the major . . . achievement of perestroika." However, recent authoritarian trends in Russia cast doubt on this too. The record in Russia, and in many Latin American and African countries, illustrates the difficulties of such transitions—and South Africa's unusual achievement.

Institutions depend on *human agency*, and South Africa has been fortunate in many of its leaders. Despite the NP's abhorrent race policy, and the increasing corruption associated with its lengthy monopoly of power, the Afrikaners did not become gangster politicians who bled the country dry, leaving the national treasury denuded and the country undeveloped. Likewise, English South Africans, in addition to enriching themselves, contributed finance and entrepreneurship toward development of the infrastructure and nurtured the skills, ideas and institutions required for a productive economy and, later, a liberal democracy.

Mercifully, the NP did not eliminate most of its opponents. Despite harsh repression, many survived in exile or prison and some had the opportunity to study and plan for the future and, from the mid-1980s, to engage in exploratory (often secret) talks with business, *verligtes*, and, later, representatives of the regime, despite the intensifying domestic and regional conflict.[16] During this process, relationships evolved that encouraged both sides to enter negotiations and avoid a destructive civil war. Personal agency facilitated the South African transition, in contrast to the hatreds and acrimonies that impeded similar processes in Northern Ireland and the Middle East.

Both de Klerk and Mandela were intelligent and humane enough to recognize and balk at the terrible costs of worsening repression and revolution. Both were capable of acting disinterestedly and taking a long-term view beyond the immediate interests of themselves and their coteries. Each had authority over a disciplined political organization and proved able to secure acceptance of a settlement involving difficult, unpopular compromises on all sides. They were also both team players rather than autocrats, which helped to nurture the depth of political leadership around them. Alongside Mandela were, *inter alia*, Mbeki, Ramaphosa, Lekota, Zuma, and Slovo. De Klerk was backed up by Coetzee, Meyer, Viljoen, and Heunis and supported by able civil servants like Simon Brand, Chris Stals, and Niels Barnard, who could be relied on to continue operating the country during and after the negotiations. Even Vorster and Botha—who had much to answer for—took the first difficult steps away from Verwoerd's *cul-de-sac*, though each in turn balked at following through the logic of a path contrary to his background and beliefs.

The NP's liberal critics also included able, dedicated people such as Suzman, Slabbert, and Eglin, while numerous members of churches, universities, trade unions and businesses devoted time and energy to the struggle to rid South Africa of apartheid without a civil war. Such diligent, intelligent citizenship is not to be taken for granted, as can be seen in the fate of countries lacking this.

There are less positive perceptions of South African politicians and activists. Heribert Adam (1971, 1993, 1997) is among those who portray the South African settlement as the outcome of two

Machiavellian elites successfully hoodwinking their followers and attempting to do likewise to each other. Adam's analysis deflates the self-righteous, moralizing rhetoric in which much South African political commentary is clothed. His analysis is also evenhanded and based on universal behavioral assumptions that apply to all parties. However, Adam surely underestimates the capacity for at least sporadic feelings of altruism and patriotism that, alongside self-interest and cynicism, motivate many people. It is difficult to understand the behavior of Mandela, de Klerk and others who struggled to achieve South Africa's settlement without giving weight to their fear of anarchy and civil war, their desire for a good future for their country, and the feeling of satisfaction that comes from avoiding disaster and achieving a constructive outcome. This is not to assume they did not take advantage of opportunities to advance the interests of themselves and their group/coterie. But faced with grave situations, some people can—at times and for a while—rise to the occasion.[17] This is what outsiders salute as South Africa's 'miracle,' for there are many countries whose leaders lack this sporadic capacity, or where the rule of law is not sufficiently entrenched to protect such leaders from being assassinated by opponents of negotiated compromise. (The 1993 assassination of ANC leader Chris Hani was among the exceptions during the South African transition.)

The major debate that began from the mid-1960s helped to shift public opinion and to create an atmosphere in which reform became not only acceptable, but expected. Fieldwork visits to South Africa were like being engaged in a constant seminar, not only in the universities and media, but also in offices, factories, farms, and the homes of 'ordinary' people. There was no such wide-ranging public debate in the Soviet Union. Gorbachev's *glasnost* emerged out of the blue a few years before the collapse of communism in 1989. This abrupt turnabout was followed by confusion, social anarchy and an abortive military coup in 1991. The fact that these issues were intensely debated in South Africa over almost three decades; that new institutions grew out of the old; and that choices were made via a political process involving a wide range of people and organizations helped to provide continuity and stability during an inherently difficult, destabilizing process.

The lessons of South Africa's transition are that shifts in public opinion take time, and that social change is cumulative and multifaceted, involving many aspects of social life, with changing economic interests an essential, but not the whole, part of the process. Thus, the initial modest changes in sport and social policy were not merely marginal and cosmetic, but indicators of significant underlying social shifts. Another lesson is the importance of institutions through which social changes can be mediated and of leaders with the intelligence, will and capacity to push through these difficult reforms. The survival of South Africa's parliamentary, judicial and other independent institutions, and the continuing aspirations to universal standards of many of its people, made it possible to build on these institutions and processes with which people were familiar. This made it easier to take advantage of the openings that emerged, gradually and erratically, from 1970, and to make the huge adaptations that followed. These imperfect institutions served as useful building blocks for post-apartheid South Africa rather than being merely eccentric nineteenth-century hangovers.

The advent of post-apartheid South Africa was a miracle in the sense that such successful transitions seldom occur, especially in multiracial societies with a history of conflict. But this achievement did not arrive out of the blue, nor did it occur automatically as a by-product of economic development with the superstructure adapting to underlying structural changes as though by osmosis. There have been many situations that seemed structurally "ripe for reform" but failed to adapt successfully, instead stagnating or regressing into anarchy and collapse—as many expected South Africa to do. It was a process spread over almost three decades that involved intense discussion and hard work by many people. The role of institutions and agency in shaping South Africa's social evolution, especially its recent transition, has been underestimated. More generally, there has been insufficient research on all the factors discussed in this chapter, particularly the complex role of mass actions in contributing to relatively peaceful, rather than revolutionary, change.

Summing Up the Debate

Apartheid was not ended by a war of liberation, although armed struggle challenged and alarmed the oligarchy. Nor was apartheid ended by an east European-style velvet revolution with the government collapsing before mass unrest. South Africa had a different transition. By 1990, most major apartheid laws had been abolished, except for the Population Registration, Group Areas, and Land Acts. After 1990, these remaining measures were removed by the NP, which also initiated negotiations for a new constitution. The negotiations, which began formally and publicly in 1992, involved an unusually wide range of agents: not only political organizations, but also people from business, trade unions, and NGOs. Their influence was reflected in South Africa's liberal democratic constitution and choice of a market economy with social democratic features, including retention of a strong central state.

It is not disputed here that growing black pressures were crucial for the establishment of a democratic, post-apartheid South Africa. What is questioned is the claim that the NP was driven to the negotiating table by the uprisings of the mid-1980s. The record does not support the claim that the (increasingly differentiated) black majority had, at that stage, the appetite or capacity to precipitate a civil war against South Africa's still well-organized, heavily armed government. It is also suggested that there has probably been an underestimation of the impact of the growing black skilled and middle classes, whose mere existence was rendering apartheid unworkable and who seemed to prefer a reformist, rather than a revolutionary, strategy and outcome.

Sporadic mass actions intensified this evolutionary process, pushing South Africa toward more thorough deracialization and democratization. Without mass pressure, it is unlikely that *deracialization* would have been accompanied by *democratization*. Instead, there might have been a continuation of the process of "authoritarian reform" leading to a "multiracial autocracy." Instead, mass action helped to secure South Africa's "negotiated revolution."[18]

It is also not disputed here that international influences had significant effects on South Africa. What is questioned is the claim that economic sanctions forced the regime to negotiate. Instead, it is suggested that international influences had mixed effects, both positive and negative, and that they included not only sticks but also carrots in the form of constructive engagement. Apart from these deliberate attempts to end apartheid, South Africa was also influenced by neutral forces affecting all countries. These included the changing global balance of power (following the collapse of the USSR), the closer integration of South Africa into the global economy (intensifying the need for economic efficiency), and the changing international *zeitgeist* (further challenging racism and authoritarianism).

These domestic and international developments undermined the sustainability and legitimacy not only of apartheid, but also of revolutionary violence, pushing both the NP and its main challenger, the ANC, toward negotiation. The fact that South Africa was already moving in this direction—that there were powerful domestic forces for reform, including a reform-minded section of the elite—increased its susceptibility to international influences, as did the desire of both the English and the NP *verligtes* to remain part of the international community and to play a growing role in Africa.

By the mid-1980s, with multiple domestic and international pressures undermining apartheid, the process became *overdetermined*, making it increasingly difficult to distinguish among these forces. I hypothesize that the following sequence led to apartheid's demise by negotiation rather than revolution:

1. The reforms were precipitated by domestic pressures within the oligarchy, of which the most effective came from business and the NP *verligtes*.
2. These pressures were reinforced by domestic agents outside the oligarchy: sporadic mass actions and the activities of trade unions, ANC/UDF, and Black Consciousness/Azapo/National Forum. Further study is needed of the role of blacks functioning "within the system."
3. These domestic pressures, in turn, were reinforced by external factors: the international anti-apartheid campaign, mainly led by the ANC; the stick of sanctions and isolation; and the carrot of constructive engagement.
4. In addition to these deliberate attempts to end apartheid, it was also undermined by "neutral" forces: demographic trends (tilting the population balance in favor of blacks); economic growth (strengthening the black industrial and middle classes, intensifying skill shortages, reducing white fears of black competition); and closer integration into the global economy and culture (intensifying South Africa's exposure to a *zeitgeist* favoring antiracist, democratic norms and reform/negotiation rather than confrontation/revolution).
5. The influence of, not so much ideology, as implicit beliefs about the future: the conviction of blacks that they would eventually prevail, contrasted with the growing belief of the ruling Afrikaners that apartheid was becoming unworkable and indefensible.

Thus apartheid was ended by an (unusual?) combination of reform from above and pressure from below, interacting with and reinforcing each other. Moreover, this domestic process occurred in an international context that, from the mid-1980s, pushed the contending parties toward accommodation, rather than revolution or intensified repression.

This hypothesis accords a crucial role to divisions within the ruling oligarchy and to those who—whatever their reasons and aims—precipitated and helped to sustain the reforms. These reforms were not halted by a counter-revolution (as in Czarist Russia in 1825 and 1905), and the process did not spiral out of control (as in France in 1789 and Russia in 1917) because the bureaucracy and military/security forces remained loyal to the state, and the NP's challengers never became strong enough to dislodge it.

The reforms, which in any other country would be considered significant rather than cosmetic or marginal, facilitated black economic advance and political mobilization and were accompanied by major shifts of opinion among whites, especially the ruling Afrikaners who, hitherto, were heading in the opposite direction, like the Rhodesian whites under Ian Smith. The change of direction began around 1970 when the NP still looked impregnable. Indeed, all analysts agree that the NP's effective clampdown in 1986 demonstrated its continuing capacity and political will to maintain control.

Some insisted that de Klerk must have undergone a sudden "Damascus conversion." Whether or not he underwent a significant emotional/moral experience, his action seemed—to those who believed reforms were underway and as he himself said—a logical evolution of the post-1970 reforms. But de Klerk's timing and boldness were shaped by his own psychology and political calculations, including his loss of support to both Right and Left in the 1989 election. There is, moreover, a finality to the extension of political rights that made his bold action a "leap in the dark." After February 1990, when the banned movements were legalized, the rules of the political game changed. The NP's power to control events declined rapidly, while the ANC consolidated its base and handled the negotiations skillfully.

A central question in this debate is the origin of the reforms, and the political fluidity, that seemed impossible before 1970. If pressures from within the oligarchy, particularly from business, were a major factor driving this process, then the liberal argument is correct. But if the aim of business was to secure a counter-revolution that would perpetuate the apartheid regime, and if they only abandoned this aim under domestic and external pressures, then the revisionists were at least partially correct, that is, in relation to the aims of business, though not to the long-term incompatibility of capitalism and apartheid.

Chapter 5 examines some theoretical issues raised by these contending analyses. Chapter 6 looks to the future, particularly the continuing tensions among liberals, Marxists, and nationalists in post-apartheid South Africa.

CHAPTER 5

THEORY, POLITICS, AND PSYCHOLOGY OF THE DEBATE

Man will become better when we show him what he is like.
—Anton Chekhov

Some disagreements in this debate seem due more to lack of clarity over terminology than to differences over substantive issues. It is impossible to assess whether economic growth, mass action or sanctions eroded or reinforced apartheid without a clear definition of apartheid and of the criteria for assessing whether it is being eroded or reinforced.

Apartheid differed from other twentieth-century systems of discrimination and exploitation by its institutionalization and legalization. Ending this leaves class inequalities that, initially, will remain largely along racial lines. But establishing legal and political equality, and ending explicitly racial restrictions on the vote, mobility and access to jobs and property, mark the end of the institutionalized discrimination that led the international community to label apartheid uniquely offensive. South Africa became, in the words of Neville Alexander (2002), "an ordinary country" with much inequality and racial discrimination that still needs to be redressed.

A useful criterion for testing whether apartheid was being eroded or strengthened is the ANC's list of key apartheid measures, whose abolition it called for in its eight-point program (Walshe 1970, 278). But as these measures were removed, the debate was confused by shifting definitions of apartheid and by the dismissal of these reforms as "cosmetic restructuring" that would strengthen apartheid if capitalism remained. That capitalism differs from apartheid is shown by its existence in countries without apartheid, including South Africa today. It is confusing to lump them together.

Related to this is the definition of 'real reform.' The "clean slate" demanded by Bundy and O'Meara's "irreversible rupture with the past" imply everything must change drastically and quickly. But social change seldom happens this way. To dismiss the scrapping of job bars, pass laws and legal prohibitions against interracial marriage as neo-apartheid restructuring is to engage in verbal gymnastics that reduce words to meaninglessness. I suggest as a definition of real reform changes that undermined South Africa's hierarchical, racial principle, rather than simply extending rights and improving conditions in "separate" spheres (whether or not these were beneficial to those affected).

The term *capitalism* is at the heart of the debate, yet many analysts seem vague about its meaning, sometimes seeming to include any intensifying commercial activity. The classical Marxist and liberal definitions of capitalism include the determination of supply and prices by markets rather than state regulation; a significant degree of private ownership of property; and "free labor" in the sense of freedom from political coercion. Thus, restrictions on mobility (whether "passes" in South Africa, *propiska* in the USSR, or *hukou* in China) are features of a society that is not fully capitalist.

As Glaser observed (2001, ch. 3), anti-capitalism sometimes seems to encompass an antipathy to *modernity*. Some progressives now bracket industrialization and even the rational, scientific basis of knowledge together with the capitalism and globalization they reject. They do this without saying what they mean by these terms and what they envisage as the alternatives and counterfactuals. As Bertrand Russell noted, "Industrialization frees men from the worst forms of servitude, the burden of stupefying labour." And as Keynes noted, before the industrial and preceding agricultural revolution, there had been no great advances in the average standard of living. Since then, living standards, including access to education and health, have risen dramatically despite rapid population growth and growing pressure on resources.

Scholars should make clear, when they object to capitalism, whether they are including modernization and westernization and give some indication of their alternative conceptions of social organization. Knee-jerk, anti-capitalist reactions obscure the fact that there are difficult, universal problems relating to the scarcity of resources, incentives to work, and problems of cooperative production and collective action that any system must deal with, and that economic growth, social cooperation, and political order cannot be taken for granted. Capitalism provides one set of mechanisms for dealing with these problems. Many of these mechanisms are imperfect and unjust, but capitalism has achieved unprecedented levels of production and, despite its deficiencies, the trial-and-error of market mechanisms has proved more efficient and flexible than state planning. Capitalism has also—pressured by organized labor and by competition from the Red Peril—been socially and politically adaptable, inter alia, because it works with (rather than against) the grain of self-interest and facilitates the existence of alternative power bases, which are a necessary, though insufficient, condition for democracy.

Marxists who now accept that market mechanisms, subject to public scrutiny and regulation, can provide useful mechanisms for economic management should qualify their opposition to capitalism accordingly. A more discriminating approach would aid clearer thinking about the problems that all social systems must cope with and provide a better basis for developing realistic policy options, which seem likely to retain at least some features of capitalism.

Notably absent from revisionist writing are some relevant terms and categories such as conservatism and anarchism. Conservative disappeared from neo-Marxist typologies as they lumped together liberals and conservatives. This gives a distorted view of South Africa's intellectual landscape obscuring, *inter alia*, the fact that it was conservatives who produced the "conventional white settler version" of South African history, on which official discourse and teaching primers were based, and liberals who challenged this. Ignoring anarchism sweeps under the carpet the basic problem of politics, which is, as Alexander Herzen said, "Why should anyone obey anyone else?" This problem can become more acute with democratization, rising education levels and modern technology as individuals and groups feel able to do their own thing. Recognition of the basic problem of social order and of differences between conservatives and liberals would provide a more realistic view of the political spectrum and the range of possible principles and policies.

LIBERAL PRINCIPLES AND VALUES[1]

The dismissal of liberals as "untheoretical" (O'Meara 1983, 8), and "unaccustomed to conceptual thinking" (Saunders, see p. 118), with their work "buried under a welter of facts" (Marks 1986, 166), and the conflation of liberals not only with conservatives but with segregationists (Dubow, p. 19f), suggests a need to sketch out some liberal principles and values.

Most liberals are not—as Isaiah Berlin put it in his famous essay (1953)—hedgehogs with one all-encompassing theory. They are usually foxes with many ideas and theories, which they insist must pass the minimal hurdle of empirical testing against the evidence. But this, and the insistence of liberal historians on respect for the bare Rankean facts, does not mean they lack theory—explaining how and why social change happens.

A basic liberal *political principle is the primacy of the individual* as distinct from the group, and the provision for each individual of liberty, civil rights, freedom of speech, movement and the right to engage in political activity. However, this stress on individual rights does not preclude liberals from analyzing social development in terms of class, racial, or other group interests: liberals are not necessarily methodological individualists, though some are, such as Friedrich Hayek. Nor do liberals deny that people have group identities, and multiple ones at that. But they believe the basis for civil and political rights should be individual. The eclectic Amartya Sen (2001) is difficult to classify philosophically, but his belief that "individually self-determined action, resting on individual capabilities, is the key to abolishing personal misery and establishing social justice," fits well with liberal principles.

The tension between individual and group rights is recognized by liberals, as is the dilemma posed by the attractions and dangers of group identities. Berlin recognized that "nationalism was responsible for both magnificent achievements and appalling crimes." The liberal response is to stress the need for constraints on the state and on the claims of all effectively mobilized groups, whether ethnic, religious, business or trade union, and on the importance of establishing and respecting institutions, rules and due process. This need for *constraints on power and respect for the rule of law* is central to liberals, who reject arguments for temporary periods of authoritarianism, whether by the military, proletariat, or religious and other charismatic figures.

Whether or not liberals are teleologists (i.e., believe in the inevitability of certain historical trends), they strongly prefer promoting social change by reformist, constitutional means and do not believe in "the cleansing power of violence." But liberals are not necessarily pacifists and do not rule out recourse to violence (their stance on this under apartheid is discussed in Chapter 6).

Economic liberalism is not only concerned with markets and production but with their relation to political freedom. For liberals, markets are not merely instrumental mechanisms that work better than commandist ways of determining the supply and price of labor, goods and services. Markets and private property also serve a political purpose by providing centers of power independent of the state, thus enabling citizens to finance and control their own churches, research institutes, trade unions, and media (while recognizing that problems can be created by, for example, media monopolies). Many liberals follow Hayek (1944) in regarding the role of markets in promoting freedom as being as important an their role in promoting economic efficiency and material progress.

The basic liberal economic principles are that individuals should be free to engage in legal economic activities, from which they can make profits and accumulate private property, and that production and prices should be determined more by markets than by state direction (while recognizing problems regarding externalities and public goods). Beyond these basic principles, views range from laissez-faire libertarians to social democrats. Laissez-faireists favor a minimal role for the state in regulating the economy, imposing taxes and providing social welfare, on the grounds that intervention by state bureaucrats hinders economic efficiency and undermines political freedom. Social democratic liberals support the policies followed by European social democrats and American New Dealers, including progressive taxes to fund social safety nets and public goods, and state regulation to enable markets to function more efficiently and fairly.

The tension between the desire to allow freedom for economic agents, while curbing the negative effects (diseconomies) of their activities, has long been debated among liberals. The founder of neoclassical economics, Adam Smith, in his *Wealth of Nations*, warned that businessmen "seldom gather together, even for merriment or diversion, but the conversation ends in a conspiracy against the public, or in some contrivance to raise prices."[2] Paul Samuelson advocated antitrust measures to curb the concentration of power in large corporations. Joseph Stiglitz highlighted the problem of imperfect markets and asymmetric information. These debates are subject to swings of the pendulum with wide support for the Beveridge and New Deal proposals of the 1930s and '40s followed by a swing against state regulation and 'welfare dependency' during the 1970s; although this was qualified by Galbraithian concerns about "private greed and affluence amidst public squalor."

Mancur Olson (1965) highlights the capacity of wealthy individuals and big organizations—whether of farmers, manufacturers, workers or professionals—to override the common good. Recently, revulsion at the excesses of crony capitalism (the Enron and other corporate scandals; the massive theft of public property in the Russian privatization; and the inflated salaries and perks corporate managers routinely award themselves) have led to disillusionment among many liberals, and to a growing belief among them that, unless there is improved regulation of markets and corporate governance and a halt to growing inequality, this erosion of the checks and balances on capitalism will undermine its workability and legitimacy.

On social policy, liberals oppose ascriptive hierarchies and advocate meritocracy, but they are divided over the priority to be accorded to negative and positive liberty. Berlin (1958) argued that priority should be given to the absence of repression and harm. But Tawney (1964) believed freedom means "not merely the absence of repression but also the opportunity of self-organisation." The continuing tension between liberty and equality is evident in current debates about affirmative action.

Libertarians like Robert Nozick oppose affirmative action on the grounds that the use of group categories breaches the principle of treating individuals equally, arguing that priority should be given to the protection of individuals and freedom of markets from bureaucratic control. But liberals like John Rawls support affirmative action to facilitate fairer competition and social justice and stress the obstacles to a fair start in life posed by inherited wealth and unequal access to resources such as education and health services.

On international relations, the classic liberal position, set out by Kant, J. S. Mill and President Wilson, is that liberals should work for an orderly international environment with multilateral institutions to keep the peace. Liberals advocate freer trade both to promote material progress and decrease the likelihood of war, based on their belief that democratic societies are less likely to go to war with each other. The divisions among liberals over strategies to reduce global poverty and inequality reflect their differences over domestic policy. Laissez-faireists look to market forces while welfarists argue that markets need to be regulated and that fairer, not just freer, trade is needed. The debate about international policy has been sharpened by the revival of pre-Keynesian unrestricted capitalism with strong tendencies toward monopoly. This trend has been championed by *neoconservatives*, confusingly termed 'neoliberals.' Classic conservative policy is exemplified by the 'realist' theories of Henry Kissinger, who argued that in an anarchic, lawless world, states are bound to give priority to the protection and promotion of their own national interests. Conservative realists believe states must rely on power and are skeptical of international institutions such as the UN, World Bank and Kyoto Treaty that impinge on state sovereignty. By contrast, liberals support strengthening international law and institutions.

From the time of Adam Smith, liberals recognized the *shortcomings of capitalism*, including its stimulation of acquisitiveness and competitiveness—although they regard these traits as having useful as well as negative effects. However, most liberals believe capitalism is better than the alternatives that have yet evolved, particularly in its achievement of high levels of production and its constraining effects on nationalism, racism and patriarchy, due to its stimulation of overlapping interests and the diffusion of power that arises from the growth of interests independent of the state and the family. The outcome of these processes is greater individualism, which creates both the need and the opportunity for people to come together freely. Paradoxically, many who dislike this individualism advocate the human rights approach for which it seems to be a precondition.

The wide spectrum of views among liberals, and the continuing open revision of their theories and policies, was hailed as a strength by Mill who argued that out of "the collision of opinions," truth would emerge and liberty be preserved. But Berlin was more pessimistic, fearing that the yearning for "clean slates," "transformation" and "final solutions" had deep psychological roots and that, instead of convergence around common values, there was more likely to be the persistence of "incommensurable values" and polarization that would prove difficult to manage by agreed procedures and mechanisms rather than the resort to violence. Far from believing in the infallibility of "the liberal project," liberals do not believe in final answers or solutions.

In South Africa, as Hilda Kuper (1979) noted, liberals focused on opposing racism and protecting the liberty of the individual from the state. This stress on individual rights is evident in the writing of mainstream liberals, as well as in the policies of political organizations such as the Liberal Party, Progressive Party and Democratic Party/Alliance (DA).[3]

Recently, there has been a deviation from this by two groups who identify themselves as liberal. Afrikaner *verligtes* who became converts to liberal principles during the 1970s continue to stress group rights, which they insist are important to most people. Giliomee argues that "the hard reality liberals have to face is that people see themselves not just as bearers of individual rights but also as members of a particular community" (2005, 95). The second group is the Africanists, like Barney Pityana, chair of the Human Rights Commission, who said, "We are all liberals now," yet advocates black empowerment policies based on legalized group distinctions.

The tension between individual and group rights is evident in South Africa's liberal constitution, which defines rights in terms of the individual while also referring to groups (chapter 14, clause 235 refers to "any community sharing a common culture and language"). Group rights supporters could perhaps be termed liberal nationalists, who believe people should be viewed not only as individuals, but also as members of a group/nation. Clearly, liberalism is a broad church, but whether people are qualified 'liberal nationalists' or classic individualists, those who do not support individual civil, political and economic rights and curbs on state power, fall outside the bounds of the definition of liberal.

In social policy, South Africa liberals have tended, as Hilda Kuper noted, "towards [support for] the welfare state" rather than laissez-faire policies. However, there were differences between liberals who were primarily concerned with securing civil and political rights and equality before the law for all citizens (exemplified by Molteno's constitution for the Progressive Party) and those according priority to economic discrimination and poverty (MacMillan, van der Horst,

Peter Brown). These twin strands were evident in the policies of Jan Hofmeyr, the only liberal who briefly held some political power and used this during the 1940s both to erode racism and to lay the basis for South Africa's universal welfare provisions. (Recent shifts in the DA's socioeconomic policies are discussed in Chapter 6, as are the liberal strands within the ANC and Black Consciousness movement.)

In view of the revisionists' derogatory remarks about liberal social scientists (Saunders 1988, 194f.), it is worth recording that their work has not been limited to the historians and economists referred to in Chapters 2–4. Noteworthy work has been produced on political theory by du Toit, Degenaar, Simkins and others, including comparative studies of multiethnic and transitional societies and alternative models for South Africa. New techniques for monitoring and analyzing elite and popular opinion were used by Schlemmer, Gagiano, Mattes and Reynolds. Pioneering sociological fieldwork was done by Ellen Hellman, Simon Bekker and Elizabeth Ardington. Useful work was produced on the spatial aspects of apartheid by geographers such as Chris Rogerson and Tony Lemon; on constitutional, family, and human rights law by Tony Matthews, John Dugard, Sandra Burman and Anthea Jeffrey; and on international relations by Graeme Evans, Jack Spence, Greg Mills, and others. Liberal scholars have made significant contributions to the study of South Africa and its place in the world.

THE NEO-MARXIST REVISIONIST MODEL

Some striking features of the neo-Marxist model emerge from Chapters 2–4. First, their *rejection of aspects of classical Marxism that seem to fit South Africa*, in particular, the progressive role of capital in eroding barriers to the mobility of both labor and capital. This progressive role accords with Marx's account of capital's role in eroding feudal-like bonds in Europe and in Asia, where the railways, built by the British state in response to profit-seeking pressures from private capital, helped to integrate India and stimulate industrial development—a view endorsed by Indian historians such as Dharma Kumar (editor of the 1983 *Cambridge Economic History of India*). Marx himself declared: "The bourgeoisie have played a most productive role . . . they have created wonders greater than the pyramids of Egypt."[4]

Another striking feature of the neo-Marxist model is its *retention of features of Marxism that are challenged by South African development*, particularly Marxism's denial of the salience of racism/ethnicity in explaining the divisions between blacks and whites, English and Afrikaners. Underlying this is their insistence that South Africa's evolution was shaped by class and that race and nationalism were mere epiphenomena of capitalism. Thus, neo-Marxists denied that racism divided the working class, insisting that the action of white workers in uniting against, instead of with, blacks was stirred up by capital (see p. 37f). Apart from their unproven assumption that class consciousness is natural, while ethnic consciousness is false or "artificially constructed," this argument conflicts with evidence that mineowners tried to dampen racial conflicts on the mines. It also raises questions about why it was necessary to stir up racial divisions if class divisions already existed, and why there was such resonance to racist propaganda. The neo-Marxist analysis also denies political agency to the well-mobilized white unions, deriving from their theory of the state as "fundamentally and in the final analysis the agent of international monopoly capital"—a theory conflicting with evidence that, on many issues, mining capital did not get its way when opposed by white labor and other local white interests.

In their later work, Wolpe and O'Meara attempted to resolve these contradictions. Neville Alexander salutes O'Meara's "herculean" efforts and Wolpe's "attempt to salvage the pride. . . . and analytical relevance" of the neo-Marxist model (2002, 24, 177). But Alexander confesses he found their efforts unconvincing—a sentiment fully shared by non-Marxists. But at least Wolpe and O'Meara confronted these problems; most revisionists simply ignored them, despite their emphasis on the importance of theory and of "finding in Marxism a powerful tool of analysis."

As noted in Chapter 3, theory loomed large in the neo-Marxists' early work. But with the retreat from their underdevelopment/ immiserization, Althusserian and Poulantzian hypotheses, their attention to theory declined and, apart from fulsome references to Marx in the introductions to their books, there was usually little Marxist analysis in their texts. Later, Frederick Johnstone (1982) acknowledged that much of their work was "only partially or tangentially

Marxist . . . [though] taking the approach of historical materialism and class analysis".

This growing theoretical vacuum was evident in the lack of development of (as distinct from much reference to) the suggestive ideas of Gramsci on the role of institutions and agency, of which South Africa is an interesting case. This is presumably because revisionists did not take seriously the adaptive potential of South Africa's (undoubtedly flawed) institutions and the inevitable need for all societies to build on the institutions they inherit. Also puzzling is the revisionists' lack of reference to contemporary analytical Marxists such as Jon Elster and John Roamer, whose work confirms the possibilities for rigorous, yet nuanced, economic analysis.

Instead, many revisionists have—as noted by Alexander (2002, 26), Smith (1988, ch. 5) and Glaser (2001)—retreated to "passing intellectual fashions" and "abstruse discourse analysis . . . the portmanteau category of 'postmodernism,' which has become a refuge for those who have withdrawn from the battlefield . . . and are seeking ways of getting away from oversimplified, deterministic . . . Marxism."[5] Smith (1988, 185) pointed out that the revisionists' best work was "remarkably free of Marxist analysis or terminology". There is little sign of this in the writing of Charles van Onselen, based on solid empirical research and clear, well-written analysis— rather like the good narrative history for which the supposedly "untheoretical" liberals are derided. Likewise, there is little sign of Marxist theorizing in the best work of, *inter alia*, Bundy, Beinart, Delius, Dubow, and Marks—although this work does not bear out claims of transforming the subject: it builds on what was there and stands alongside contributions by others.

There were Marxists who, using the classical Marxist model, recognized the progressive role of capital in undermining apartheid in late twentieth-century South Africa. But the work of Tickten (1991) and McKinley (1997) was marginalized in the debate—as was work by other Marxists outside the ranks of the revisionist coterie, such as Sender, Fine, Gelb and Saul. Curiously, most of these dissident Marxists remained more hostile to capitalism than those revisionists who shifted towards the liberal analysis and policies—while still straining to distance themselves from liberals. This suggests the Marxist dissidents were, for better or worse, more theoretically engaged and committed.

Grappling with theory is a necessary and difficult part of scholarly activity. But those who use theory to put down others deemed "unaccustomed to conceptual thinking," while making sweeping claims for themselves ("transforming the subject with powerful theoretical tools"), invite scrutiny of their claims. It is paradoxical that the revisionists rejected aspects of Marxism that explain much about the role of capital in South Africa, while retaining features that seem contradicted by the South Africa case. It is also paradoxical that the revisionists, who now refer to themselves as progressives or radicals, still strain to differentiate themselves from liberals, with whom their position is converging. These paradoxes suggest that the reason for their continuing hostile rhetoric is not primarily theoretical or ideological. The extent to which this hostility is rooted in political and psychological factors is discussed later, after examining another striking feature of their model.

Assumptions about Individual and Social Behavior

> *"Naturam expelles furca tamen usque recurret (You can throw out Nature with a pitchfork, but it will always reassert itself)."*
>
> —Horace, Epistles I
>
> *"What will always be discovered by a diligent and impartial enquirer is that wherever human nature is to be found, there is a mixture of vice and virtue, a contest of passion and reason."*
>
> —Dr Samuel Johnson.

The third striking feature of the neo-Marxist analysis is *the lack of universal assumptions that encompass the behavior of all people*: black and white, business and labor, Afrikaners and English-speakers. This seems at least partly due to the neo-Marxist insistence that all human behavior is "socially constructed," rather than shaped by instinct or biology, and that the basis of this construction is class. During the revisionists' recent period of academic hegemony, they energetically enforced a taboo against any questioning of this belief. (Some liberals also subscribe to the belief that all human behavior is socially constructed, though not to the assumption that class forms the basis of this construction.)

This taboo emerged in reaction to pseudoscientific, racist theories that, misusing Darwin, proclaimed the existence of a biologically-based hierarchy among individuals and 'races' (people linked by descent, often evident in physical characteristics). These racist assumptions were used as the basis for eugenic theories that justified dominating, or even eliminating, allegedly inferior or dangerous individuals and groups, most notoriously by the Nazis. Such theories were also to justify apartheid (Thompson 1975, ch. 3; Dubow 1995).

The theories underlying "scientific racism" have been thoroughly discredited, both by their appalling consequences in slavery, the Nazi holocaust and apartheid, and by scientific research, which shows greater intraracial genetic variance (among individuals within the group) than variance among 'races' for characteristics such as intelligence. However, due to the history, the issue of an instinctive or biological dimension to human behavior remains sensitive, especially in countries with a history of institutionalized racism. In South Africa, many reacted against scientific racism by embracing the opposite view—that human behavior is entirely socially constructed and that, in Mao Tse Tung's words, people are "blank slates" on which social engineers can freely paint their designs (Pinker 2002).

Since the mid-twentieth century, the study of human behavior has been transformed by research on the chemistry of the brain and on genetics, linguistics, and psychology. This research is facilitating more rigorous investigation of the extent to which human behavior is socially constructed and/or biologically inherited. There remain fundamentalists on both sides of this debate, but there is a growing consensus that it is not a question of nature or nurture, but of *the extent* to which human behavior is shaped by both and whether the balance between them is shifting with growing human mastery of science and technology.

Thus, while Daniel Dennett (1995) stresses the role of the genetic inheritance in shaping the evolution of all living creatures, he argues that "whereas animals are rigidly controlled by their biology, human behavior is largely determined by culture . . . growing from . . . but also away from a biological base". Adam Kuper (1994), one of the few South African social scientists who has engaged with this work, likewise stresses our dual inheritance of genes and culture while arguing that culture (our capacity to learn) is now outpacing our biological inheritance. But Gary Runciman (1998) points out that, despite this, biological processes do not cease when learning and choice enter. Luigi Cavalli-Sforza (2001) insists we cannot make sense of human history unless we recognize that "human beings are part of the animal continuum . . . enmeshed in the ecosystems of which we are part." Cavalli-Sforza urges historians to make use of, rather than shy away from, the findings of modern genetics, which he put to good use in his study of human migrations.

Nurturists (those who maintain all human behavior is socially constructed) fear that recognition of our genetic inheritance will be misused politically. Stephen Jay Gould warned that socio-biology could be used to bolster beliefs in the superiority of Caucasian males. Nurturists also fear that recognizing the role of instincts, such as aggression and greed, is tantamount to sanctioning them.

But it does not follow from the fact that something *is* so, that it *ought* to be so, or that it cannot be modified. Taking account of the biological dimensions of human behavior does not rule out a moral framework and rules to (dis)encourage certain behavior. The starting point for social science must be the attempt to understand human nature as it is; failure to do so will skew our understanding from the start. Steven Pinker (2002) argues that it is harmful to spread false beliefs, such as that people in pre-state societies were inherently peaceable[6] when recent research shows high levels of violence and homicide in many of these societies. These illusions leave people bewildered by the violence around them and unappreciative of fragile advances, such as the rule of law and democratic governance, that need to be recognized and nurtured, not taken for granted.

The nurturist argument was an advance on beliefs in unchanging, primordial identities—and a counter to the destructive political use to which they were often put. But we need to review the mantra of Leroy Vail (Vail 1989, 7f.) and others that "ethnicity is not a natural cultural residue but a consciously crafted ideological creation". This mantra has become an obstacle to confronting and investigating the powerful psychological resonance of "identity" feelings—whatever their origin and nature. As Niehaus argued (2002, 558f.), it is not evident that 'tribal' and 'national' identities were so readily constructed and manipulated by colonial (and other) regimes, for "it is not always apparent who invents or imagines these communities." The truth is complex, with individuals and groups trying to manipulate and use each other as well as struggling to understand and manage their own feelings and the world around them.

This view receives support from recent studies. Paul Seabright (2004) argues that human evolution bears witness both to widespread fear and suspicion of strangers and to fascination with them, as well as to the capacity to widen the circle of those regarded as having a shared humanity, though this is often a gradual process. Robert Putnam acknowledged that, in his forthcoming Harvard University study, *The Myth of the Melting Pot*, he has found, to his dismay, lower levels of trust in ethnically diverse communities in which, "People hunker down; the effect of diversity is worse than has been imagined. It is not just that we don't trust people who are not like us . . . we don't trust people who do not look like us" (cited *Financial Times*, January 2007).

Implications of Behavioral Assumptions for Analysis and Policy

Recognition of the importance of our primal, often unconscious, drives and emotions—fear, greed, aggression, the craving for status and power, altruism—has implications for analysis and for policy, including understanding the dangers of attempting to change societies rapidly by "wiping the slate clean." As George Eliot wrote in her introduction to *Felix Holt*, "The reason why societies change slowly is because individual men and women cannot have their nature changed by doctrine." The horrific consequences of attempts to do so suggest we are not blank slates that social engineers can wipe clean before imposing their own designs.

Recognizing the role of our primal drives and emotions does not mean denying the influence of structural factors: whether individuals and groups are located in a benign or unfavorable environment and whether they have property, knowledge, and skills. It is to be expected that those with property will seek to protect it; but this does not preclude them from being influenced by enlightened self-interest and altruistic feelings. Likewise, people who lack property, power and status are often eager to acquire them and, whether or not they do, are also likely to be influenced by a mixture of self-interest and altruism.

Taking account of these fundamental dimensions of human behavior makes it unsurprising that relations between blacks and whites in South Africa—whether on the nineteenth-century frontier or in twentieth-century mines, factories and suburbs—were often affected by fear and suspicion of strangers with different customs and characteristics and feelings of kinship with those familiar in language, social customs and physical characteristics. Nor is it unusual for these differences to serve as markers around which people cluster in attempts to secure their interests in a confusing, frightening world.

Further empirical research, unimpeded by dogma, is needed to investigate whether there is an inbuilt tendency toward suspicion of strangers/outsiders, so as to provide more effective ways of coping with and countering this. The fact that many in the ANC now assert their African identity and refer to "our own people" may ease the taboos that inhibit research on relations among South Africa's self-identified 'races'/nationalisms, whose history of both cooperation and conflict offers a rich, challenging field for researchers (who should not, however, await these political signals before open-mindedly investigating these issues).

As shown in Chapters 2–4, the world presented by the revisionists is Manichean, consisting of demons—business, liberals, "conservative" blacks—whose behavior is entirely selfish and malign, and saints—black labor, "progressives" (sometimes white labor and Afrikaner nationalists)—who seem free of self-interest and aggression. These Manichean assumptions led revisionists to deny the well-documented evidence that business wanted to erode apartheid. When this denial became untenable, revisionists dismissed the evidence of business pressures for reform on the grounds that these were motivated by self-interest and undertaken with malign intent. Such reasoning implies that self-interest is not a universal feature of human behavior; treats the behavior of white business as intrinsically different from that of white labor (because class is what counts); and takes no account of the real world tensions between the desire of most people to secure their survival and self-interest while also seeking other social and ethical goals.

This Manichean worldview rode roughshod over the evidence; involved a mode of reasoning innocent of economic logic and human psychology; and lacked a sense of reality—of how people usually behave, how social change occurs, and of the constraints on what is possible. These behavioral assumptions also underlie moral assessments of how people behaved—and should have behaved—under apartheid. And these assessments, in turn, affect current perceptions of, and relations among, people in post-apartheid South Africa.

Demonizing and Romanticizing Political Agents

Curiously, the main objects of recrimination in post-apartheid South Africa have not been the conservatives/racists who planned and enforced apartheid. Their behavior is treated as straightforward and almost taken for granted. The main objects of recrimination are people whose past behavior is regarded as ambiguous or problematic and who are accused of complicity with apartheid.

Charges of being complicit or coopted are hardly special to South Africa. 'Collaborating with the enemy' remains a painful subject in postwar Europe, where (with the exception of West Germany) there has been less progress in confronting the appalling past than in South Africa with its remarkable (though imperfect) Truth and Reconciliation Commission. Nevertheless, charges of complicity cast a shadow that could, in more stressful circumstances, turn into a poisonous cloud.

The OED defines complicity as partnership in wrongdoing. In apartheid South Africa, this could be viewed as operating on at least three levels:

A. people directly involved in planning or implementing state policies;
B. people not directly involved in (A) but engaged in activities that kept the apartheid state functioning;
C. people who opposed apartheid but did not challenge the government in ways that resulted in their being imprisoned, banned, or otherwise punished, so that they were able to lead 'normal,' even comfortable lives.

Category A seems straightforward, yet it raises some tricky questions. Does it include *verligtes* such as Simon Brand and Willie Esterhuyse, who remained in the NP and Broederbond while attempting to shift their policies? (And, if they were complicit, does it follow that all senior ANC politicians and officials are co-responsible for the unnecessary suffering allegedly caused by its policies on Aids and Zimbabwe?)

Category B covers the numerous people whose activities in transport, banking, agriculture and health were essential for the functioning of South Africa's economy and society. Were they all complicit in "propping up the apartheid state"? Does this include blacks who, by the late 1970s, constituted two-thirds of employees in the public sector, as well as the majority of employees in the private sector and who, in both sectors, were moving into more skilled and senior jobs? The revisionist challenge—why business did not bring the apartheid regime to its knees by withholding their services and taxes—also applies to many blacks who, in theory, could have brought the system to a standstill by withholding their labor.

Category C includes people who were not engaged in A or B and who voted, denounced, and even demonstrated against apartheid, but whose actions are judged inadequate because 'they should have done more.' They are like that morally ambiguous Everyman who, while concerned about the suffering around him, fails to act on the demanding injunction of Karl Jaspers that "we are all co-responsible for every wrong and every injustice in the world"—with the implication that these injustices require our full attention and urgent action (Sanders 2002). People connected with South Africa—whether white or black, within the country or abroad—who continued to lead normal, even comfortable lives, fall into this category.

The difficulty of assessing complicity is illustrated by the case of *the South African media under apartheid*. The media's culpability was the subject of a special hearing of the TRC. Until about 1970, the Afrikaans media loyally supported the NP. Thereafter, the *verligte* media became more critical of apartheid, though they continued to support the NP. But the Afrikaans media, whether unquestioningly loyal or increasingly critical, was not the focus of the TRC's attention. This was on the English media, which was denounced for its conduct under apartheid by black journalists led by Thami Mazwai.[7] Their view was reflected in the TRC's findings which concluded:, "The term 'opposition press' ... was a misnomer. ... The English media often adopted a policy of appeasement towards the State. ... in so doing, they helped sustain and prolong ... apartheid" (1998, 4:168f.).

The English media ranged from conservative to liberal. The latter included the *Rand Daily Mail* (and its successor, *Business Day*), the *Evening Post*, *Daily Despatch*, *Sunday Times*, and *Financial Mail*. The record shows that they provided frequent, critical coverage of apartheid, documenting and exposing mass removals, detention without trial, prison conditions, and the murders of Steve Biko, Matthew Goniwe, and others. They also gave frequent, sympathetic coverage to the emerging black trade unions and NGOs.

This coverage was produced under stringent government controls and pressures on editors, journalists, and newspaper proprietors. This pressure drove journalists such as Anthony Delius, Stanley Uys, and Donald Woods out of South Africa. Others—Laurence Gandar, John Sutherland, Tony Heard, Gerald Shaw, Patrick Lawrence, Allister Sparks, Ken Owen—remained but worked under growing pressures, including declining circulations as conservative readers disliked, or were apprehensive, of their confrontationist stance. Falling circulations reduced advertising revenue and led to mounting losses for outspoken papers. Yet, despite financial crises and a decline in resources and in journalistic standards, critical coverage continued. The doggedness of the South African media in keeping racism and human rights abuses on the agenda, and in providing a counter to the government-supporting media, including the state-owned South African Broadcasting Corporation, compares favorably with press coverage in authoritarian states in eastern Europe, Latin America, and elsewhere.

In post-apartheid South Africa, the media operate in a democracy with a bill of rights and independent judiciary to protect them. Yet many journalists are nervous of the ANC's sensitivity to criticism of the errors and corruption that occur under all governments and that it is the media's duty to expose. Black journalists and editors are in the front line of this pressure, which is milder than that endured by the media under the NP. Some, such as William Gumede, Mondli Makhanyi, Sipho Seepe, Aubrey Matshiqi, Karima Brown, and Xolela Mangcu, continue South Africa's tradition of critical, outspoken journalism. But some have been accused by, among others, Archbishop Tutu of sycophancy toward powerful politicians. Tutu's criticisms were denounced by Thami Mazwai (now head of Mafube Publishers) who, while courageous in standing up to the apartheid regime, attacked the *Mail & Guardian* and *Sunday Independent* for revealing the corruption associated with South Africa's controversial arms budget, on the grounds that these disclosures were motivated by a racist, antiblack agenda and were "not in the national interest" (*Mail & Guardian*, April 15–21, 2005). This accusation mirrored those of the compliant NP-supporting press against the "unpatriotic, irresponsible" English media under apartheid.

This is a reminder that, despite their undoubted shortcomings, the liberal English media performed a useful, often courageous, job under apartheid. Nevertheless, they are accused of complicity on the grounds that they "should have done more." If this is the criterion, who will escape whipping for complicity, or at least complacency, in the face of the daily horrors occurring in Bosnia, Lebanon, Zimbabwe, Burma, Chechnya, and Sudan, while most of us continue to lead tolerable, even comfortable lives?[8] Mandela rightly praised the TRC for its path-breaking role "despite its imperfections." These imperfections are very evident in the TRC's sectoral reports on the

Media and Business hearings, on which its findings are unlikely to withstand the test of time (on the Business Sector Hearing, see below, p. 181).

Also relevant in influencing *the conduct of people living under authoritarian regimes* are fears about the security of themselves, their families, and "the groups" to which they and others identify themselves as belonging. These security fears are often stirred up and manipulated; nevertheless, they reflect deep feelings and are not merely surrogates for racism. These fears pose dilemmas for people living under regimes they do not like, especially if they are apprehensive, not just about government retaliation, but also about the possible consequences of overturning the boat in which they find themselves. This dilemma led many people to leave South Africa. This did not necessarily mean they were indifferent to the evils of apartheid—though some were. It often meant they were scared of the risks involved in confronting the NP.

Most critics of apartheid who remained in South Africa refrained from outright confrontation with the NP until the mid-1980s, when they began to believe taking risks might produce results. This behavior has been described as "timid and selfish," but it applied to most people, black and white, Marxist and liberal, rich and poor. This timidity, or prudence, was why many Marxist and liberal academics did not remain in South Africa and confront the NP but left the country—just as many of those engaged in revolutionary activity based themselves outside South Africa. But most people cannot exit from systems they dislike, and the fact that they generally give priority to keeping themselves and their families as safe and comfortable as possible is not *per se* evidence that they do, or do not, want apartheid—nor that they would not behave in the same way under a nonracial or even an inverted racial system.

To argue that the failure of people to confront ruthless governments by withholding their taxes, closing their businesses, and withdrawing their labor is evidence that they "really want" to shore up apartheid (communism, or any other system) reveals a lack of a sense of reality, and of self-awareness about one's own behavior. These accusations also raise questions about the underlying model of how politics works.

The image of totally politicized populations seldom reflects reality. The essence of politics is negotiation and compromise—and the alternative is warfare. The inevitable compromises and ambiguities of everyday life need to be integrated into more realistic models of how people usually behave. Few function as fulltime revolutionaries. Most people, most of the time, are preoccupied, and can barely cope, with their personal lives. This does not preclude them from disliking the system they live under, nor from doing their bit against it on occasion, especially when they think this might not be too risky and might produce results. But opposition is seldom total because people have no option but to function 'within the system': they cannot opt out of the world. Moreover, those who condemn others of complicity are themselves vulnerable to accusations from even purer 'noncollaborationists,' who outflank everyone in their 'more holy and less complicit than thou' stance, which usually condemns them to irrelevance, except in so far as they are as spoilers of what is achievable.

There are people who act as tools of those they purport to oppose, but the terms 'co-opted' and 'collaborator' are too readily used, often with the aim of smearing political rivals or those who choose different tactics. A useful test of whether these alternative tactics amount to co-option is whether personal self-advancement and self-enrichment are involved. If not, it needs to be recognized that challenging and changing policies and systems can take many forms, and it is simplistic to treat all tactical questions as matters of principle. People can appropriate institutions for their own purposes and these, even if self-serving, can have unintended consequences, including the use of these positions for opposition and mobilization. Some subtle ways of expressing opposition can in the long-term be as effective in securing change as the revolutionary actions that are sometimes necessary and feasible. Some revolutionaries perform heroic deeds, but many also want to satisfy their own material and emotional needs, as is evident from their demands for credit and rewards. Meanwhile, supporters of evolutionary change often make useful contributions and personal sacrifices. There is much heroism in the lives of ordinary people who soldier on with the task of meeting their family and community duties.

The only clear distinction it seems possible to make is between this wide range of 'ordinary people' and those who actively support systems such as apartheid, by formulating and enforcing them or resisting their reform and abolition. However, this raises the objection of Mahmoud Mamdani (1996) that, in South Africa, this logic ends up with a small number of perpetrators alongside a much larger number of beneficiaries. There is no easy answer to this moral conundrum. The TRC was surely persuasive in arguing that those who derived privileges and benefits from apartheid—whether or not they wanted these—should now support measures to redress the damage. Affirmative action, the activities of foundations like the Business Trust and, above all, policies that redistribute to the poor, who are overwhelmingly black, are among such measures (discussed in Chapter 6).

The Manichean mirror image of demonizing those so readily deemed guilty of complicity is the *romanticization* of those portrayed as self-sacrificing heroes and angels. Hence, as discussed in chapter 4, the failure to confront the well-documented evidence of the reluctance of 'the masses' to take risks when they have something to lose, particularly when they do not believe their efforts are likely to succeed. Denying this ignores the great difficulties of mobilizing opposition to authoritarian regimes and, hence, the case for taking advantage of relaxations in the political constraints, double-edged though these possibilities often are—for all sides.

The fact that trade unions played an important, constructive role against apartheid—and remain champions of democracy and human rights in South Africa and in neighboring Zimbabwe, Namibia and Swaziland—has led some analysts to ignore less positive aspects of their behavior and policies as they, like everyone else, attempt to protect and promote their own interests.

Historically, trade unions have often been counters to the economic might of capital and political power of the state (although not in the case of unions that are 'sweethearts' of the state, political parties, or employers). Independent unions that represent the interests of their members have contributed to improved wages and working conditions and the establishment of social safety nets.

However, in countries with high unemployment, these benefits are often limited to a small proportion of (unionized) workers, and by raising the costs of employment, the benefits can reduce the growth of formal jobs as well as impede the creation of the informal jobs that, while often low-wage and poorly regulated, provide the first step on the ladder for the unemployed. Where there is an overriding evil—such as apartheid, dictatorship, or child labor—trade union opposition to these evils might outweigh any employment losses. But clearly the short-term interests of relatively privileged union members can serve as an obstacle to job creation.

This is a painful dilemma for Cosatu, which struggled under apartheid to acquire decent working conditions and political rights for its members and now faces the dilemma posed by high and growing unemployment. If Cosatu fails to confront this and to overcome its dismissive, hostile attitude toward what unionists describe as "worthless," low-wage informal jobs, its members will be undercut and its membership will decline. Indeed, this is already happening both absolutely and as a proportion of the working-age population.

Trade unions sometimes act in other unprogressive ways. The oldest (white) unions in South Africa were an example, and they are hardly unique. Racist behavior has appeared in unions elsewhere, as have problems of corruption, bureaucratization (with officials acting in their own rather than members' interests), and strikes that antagonized the public. In France, the powerful police union is an obstacle to much-needed police reform. In the UK, the Prison Officers' Union protects violent warders while the disruption of public services by rail and mine unions swelled public support for Thatcher's curtailment of union rights after her 1979 election.

In South Africa, the prison warders union, Popcru, protects venal officials while the Democratic Teachers Union hinders urgent educational reforms (Lodge 2002, 142). A secure future for unionized workers will depend partly on whether Cosatu takes an enlightened, long-term view of *the self-interest that they, like everyone else, pursue*. Romanticizing the unions will induce complacency and shortsighted policies instead of encouraging them to confront these problems.

Similarly, the argument that trade unions are the main support for democracy, and the companion thesis that the middle class is not, needs qualification.[9] Studies worldwide show a strong correlation between democratization and the emergence of a middle class. This hypothesis even receives some support from voting patterns under apartheid, with qualifications due to racial/ethnic factors.

Under apartheid, the more prosperous constituencies were the most liberal—the white working class the most *verkrampt*. However, this pattern was complicated by ethnic factors: initially, the emerging Afrikaans middle class supported the NP of Malan and Verwoerd. But with economic advance, the more prosperous constituencies became a source of support for the *verligtes*, while the less well-off continued to support the *verkramptes* (see Chapter 3).

Thus, despite the complicating effect of racial/ethnic factors, even South Africa gives support to the hypothesis that prosperous middle classes tend to become sources of support for democratization. The conclusion is, surely, that both the nonracial trade unions, and the white and black middle classes, played a role in promoting democratization and that both are likely to remain crucial for its consolidation. Romanticizing the unions while demonizing the middle class is misleading, and unhelpful for democratization.

But it is not only trade unions that need to be de-romanticized in post-apartheid South Africa: so do 'free markets.' Their advocates need to confront the harsh effects and long-term problems that coexist with capitalism's high levels of production, including:

- growing inequalities within and between countries as corporate executives award themselves huge salaries and perks while undermining the job security and pensions of their employees;
- the lack of social responsibility reflected in inadequate health and safety standards for employees and consumers, poor corporate governance, corruption, and environmental damage;
- the contradiction between business advocacy of "free markets" and "rolling back the state" alongside their demands for subsidies and protection for their own products (demands often supported by their unionized workers, with the costs borne by consumers);
- the contradiction between principles of competitiveness and social justice and the unequal playing field provided by the unearned inheritance of huge fortunes by a tiny minority.

A myth that *is* being deflated in South Africa (and in Northern Ireland, the Middle East, and elsewhere) is the romanticization of revolutionary violence. Scholars, including but not only, the social historians of the Wits History Workshop, are confronting the dark side of revolutionary violence, including its contribution to high crime levels. Their work explores, inter alia, the long-term consequences of undermining the rule of law, for which the NP bears the heaviest, but not the sole, responsibility.[10]

Manichean worldviews lead to disillusionment and despair when the romanticized challengers behave in ways distressingly similar to everyone else. Karl Marx did not indulge in romantic illusions about the supposedly unselfish, democratic instincts or shrewd, sensible judgments of most people. Commenting on the endorsement of Napoleon III's dictatorship in the 1852 French plebiscite, he wrote, "Universal suffrage did not possess the magical power attributed to it [by revolutionaries]. . . . Instead of these imaginary people, the electors revealed the real people"—that is, people who often voted out of selfishness, misguided feelings of patriotism, or mistaken judgements about what would serve their own or the common interest.

POLITICAL AND PSYCHOLOGICAL INFLUENCES ON HISTORIANS

The growing convergence in the analysis and policies of revisionists and liberals poses a paradox: why do revisionists/progressives still strain to differentiate themselves from liberals? It was argued previously that this is difficult to explain in theoretical and ideological terms; to what extent is this due to political and psychological factors?

If historians support the ANC, NP, SACP or DA, is this bound to shape and distort their work? The criterion must be the extent to which the historian strives to select and analyze the evidence evenhandedly; deals fairly with all agents; and avoids toeing any political line. Indications that one is failing to do this is behavior that assumes: "we can't say anything critical about sanctions (armed struggle, business, the unions) or we will lose credibility with" the ANC (business, unions, etc.). Another negative indicator is the portrayal of agents (government, trade unions, business) as invariably good or bad. This is the case whether the predetermined stance is due to calculation (the concern not to lose credibility), to conviction (the desire to express solidarity), or to personal feelings. In practice, theoretical, political, and personal factors often blend into accounts that reveal a pattern of selecting evidence showing (un)favored agents in an invariably bad or good light. The link being identified here is not with theory or ideology but with *political* loyalty or antipathy.

All historians have preferences and biases, but they can choose whether to indulge in or lean against them. A minimal professional requirement is, surely, that they should not ignore, but recognize and record, evidence that does not support their preferences. If historians are to produce accounts that are as evenhanded and truthful as possible, they need to lean consciously against their preferences. In South Africa, conservatives accuse liberals and the Left of systematically portraying whites as aggressors and blacks as angels. Liberals and the Left accuse conservatives of doing it the other way round. Marxists/progressives and nationalists accuse liberals of uncritical pro-Western bias; liberals accuse them of uncritical anti-Western bias. But not all conservatives, liberals, Marxists, and nationalists allow their political preferences to dominate their analyses to the extent of omitting facts and trends that do not fit their ideological frameworks and political preferences (as noted previously in the different cases of van der Merve, Walker, Trapido and Giliomee). The problem of political loyalties is hardly special to South Africa. An example of historians striving to constrain their political and ethical preferences from determining their selection and analysis of material is recent work on Nazi Germany by Ian Kershaw, Richard Evans and Anthony Beevor who, although repelled by Nazism, strive to record and analyze the social circumstances and human behavior that produced the inhuman policies. This involves, inter alia, recognizing German grievances over the 1918 Treaty of Versailles and the brutality on all sides that characterized both world wars. Instead of producing 'patriotic' national histories, these historians force themselves—and us—to look straight at the terrible facts, thus producing more truthful accounts, and achieving deeper understanding of the human nature and social pressures that shape the behavior of all people.

Political influences are likely to be magnified when academics aspire to play a political role themselves. Colin Bundy (2001, 2002) endorsed calls to historians not to be "mere passive spectators [but to] shape history." Bundy maintained that the revisionists had done just this: "Revisionist historical scholarship became the most influential body of work shaping understanding of the South African past [and was not limited to] the academy. . . . In addition to its indisputable scholarly impact, [revisionist] history became the master tool of intellectual resistance to apartheid and that tool was forged and honed in the Institute of Commonwealth Studies seminar. . . . a site of radical, *engagé* scholarship."

The revisionists' other flagship institution, the Witwatersrand History Workshop, also nurtured political ambitions, evident in the complaint by Belinda Bozzoli (1990, 253f.) about "the growing assertiveness among many black intellectuals seeking to capture ideological, cultural and organisational space . . . in precisely the field in which our Workshop was attempting to operate. . . . [Black intellectuals] adopted the role of 'gate-keeper' between ourselves and the audiences we sought." Bozzoli noted that the Workshop "bred a certain amount of resentment among those excluded groups of intellectuals" (referring here not to the routinely excluded white liberals, but to the assertive black intellectuals), but she was convinced that "a culturally informed Marxism disseminated by an independent group of intellectuals is more likely to be accepted by ordinary people than [the views of] nationalist and populist intellectuals who seek to lead them [on the basis of] crude nationalism." Dubow added (2002, 2) that the Wits Workshop "altered the apartheid mindset of the white liberal middle classes, helping them to understand, and engage with, the liberation struggle" (A questionable claim, as liberals were excluded from the Workshop and were, in any case, debating these issues long before its establishment in 1978).

It surely does not make one less of a Marxist, Christian, liberal, or nationalist if one confronts the painful facts about Stalin, the Inquisition, the Americans in Vietnam and Iraq, or the inevitable human flaws in the NP, DA, CPSA, and ANC. Both Karl Marx and Adam Smith were more detached and driven by the desire to understand the intellectual issues than their followers. Marx was as clear about the progressive role capital played in some phases of economic development, as he was critical of its destructive role in others. Smith was as frank in his admiration of the contribution of capitalists to economic development, as he was about their schemes for self-enrichment at the public expense. They strove to understand the world as it is.

PERSONAL AND PSYCHOLOGICAL INFLUENCES ON HISTORIANS

When E. H. Carr (1961) urged that, before studying the work, we should "first study the historian," he was referring to the historian's political views and, presumably, class position. But this surely needs to be widened to include the historian's career interests and other relevant social and psychological factors.

Preferences and biases are often inherited from the family and, if reinforced by the peer group, can become so deeply ingrained that people are unaware of the extent to which we all serve as receptacles for inherited beliefs and animosities. Some scholars are sufficiently self-aware to acknowledge privately that they are not prepared to say anything (un)favorable about Mandela, Buthelezi, de Klerk, or Oppenheimer—or to question the belief that all behavior is socially constructed—as this would adversely affect their professional prospects and relations with colleagues and friends. But most lack such self-awareness.

During the anti-apartheid struggle of the 1970s and '80s, there was an expansion of university posts and research funding on South Africa from UN agencies, foreign governments, and private foundations. The success of the revisionists in securing such funding helped to establish the dominant position that—as noted by Bundy, Saunders, and others—they acquired.[11] This provided them with considerable patronage to dispense: appointments to jobs, research grants and sabbaticals; invitations to serve on boards and attend conferences; publication and reviews of their books.

However, the reasons for keeping in with the dominant revisionist coterie were not merely instrumental, but were strongly reinforced by psychological factors, including the desire to express solidarity with the anti-apartheid struggle and to be regarded as a good, progressive person. This concern was accompanied by reluctance to criticize members of the dominant coterie, even when disagreeing with them. Ken Smith observed (1988, 164) that, while some revisionists seemed uncomfortable with their "theoretical reductionism, [they] avoided confronting them." One might add that these doubters seemed equally uncomfortable with, but unwilling to confront, the revisionists' often vindictive and damaging personal attacks on "the excluded intellectuals."

The advent of post-apartheid South Africa, and the growing convergence of their analysis with that of the liberals, has not reduced the striving of the revisionists to maintain their separate group identity, and it remains standard practice among them to ignore the liberal origins of the allegedly new trends in their work (discussed in the Appendix). This informal blacklisting of anathematized authors remains a plague in South African studies and has spread, as such plagues do, to behavior within, as well as between, groups—behavior from which some liberals are not exempt. The consequent manipulative, talismanic use of referencing raises questions about the value of the Citation Index. (Perhaps academics, like business, lawyers and doctors, need a formal code of conduct and complaints procedure about professional misconduct?) This widespread misuse of referencing reinforces doubts about whether the divisions in the South African debate are due to theoretical and ideological differences rather than to political and personal factors, including the material and psychological benefits of group identity and solidarity.

The revisionists on whom this study has focused are probably no worse than many other academic establishments. They invite scrutiny because of their systematic denigration of others and their sweeping, widely accepted claims of their intellectual and moral superiority and crucial political role ("honing the master tool of intellectual resistance to apartheid"). As noted previously, some revisionists raised suggestive questions and posed challenging hypotheses, but so did other scholars, and the record, including the revisionists' own shifts, suggests that the others were closer to the truth. What the revisionists excelled at was academic entrepreneurship, exemplified by their constant claims for the uniqueness of their own products ('product differentiation') and the assertion of their intellectual property rights, while riding roughshod over those of others.

Whether or not the revisionists comprised a distinctive "school," they identified themselves as such, and were distinguished by their conviction that they comprised an intellectual vanguard, as well as by their unusually effective group mobilization, strengthened by the resources and patronage that became available for scholars and activists working on South Africa. Group mobilization brought the benefits and comforts of solidarity, imparted energy and commitment to their work, and resulted in an enormous output.

But group mobilization holds dangers for intellectuals. Future generations will have to judge whether this period was, as claimed by Etherington (1996) and others, "the golden age of South African history." The revisionist hegemony polarized an already heated, politicized debate; drove people into entrenched positions with a tendency to fudge rather than clarify shifts in their analysis; and discouraged engagement with scholars of opposing views. It was accompanied by what many felt was "a lowering of standards of what counts as evidence and explanation" (Hughes 1977). For those excluded and demonized, the era of revisionist hegemony had baleful, even traumatic, effects, damaging their reputations, careers, and capacity to work. Professional and personal interests and ties seem at least as important as theory and ideology in accounting for the acrimony and deficiencies, as well as the intensity and energy, of the South African debate.

Finally, the categorization of participants in this debate needs reconsideration. As Smith complained, there has been an "artificial division of historians into schools" (1988, 162). This is highlighted by the revisionists' response to criticisms of their misrepresentation and undervaluation of the liberals: they simply coopted a couple of them into the ranks of "radicals" while ignoring their intellectual challenges (see pp. 13, 188, 192 no. 7). But scholars cannot be so readily pigeonholed. As Jeff Peires (1977, 65) wrote, there are good and bad historians in all parts of the political spectrum, as well as many "who do not categorise themselves as liberals or radicals, but simply as historians. . . . Honest and capable academics report the truth as they see it, and some of their findings are 'liberal' and some are 'radical.'"

The fact that many revisionists are now shifting toward the liberal analysis, values and policies, while still striving to maintain their separate group identity, suggests these labels serve as a substitute for analysis and as a political and professional tool for identifying insiders and outsiders. Group mobilization (whether instinctive or socially constructed) tends toward the exclusion and demonization of outsiders. It is, by its nature, antithetical to honest, independent intellectual work.

Chapter 6

How Historians Shape the Future

> *The role of Intellectuals is to open men's eyes —not tear them out.*
>
> —Alexander Herzen

This chapter discusses the influence on post-apartheid South Africa of historical grievances and fears; the role of historians in exacerbating, or explaining and resolving, these feelings; and the call to historians to be politically *engagé*.

Influence of Historical Grievances and Fears on Post-Apartheid South Africa

The debates dominating public and academic discourse in twenty-first–century South Africa are increasingly driven by blacks and are mainly among African nationalists, liberals and a rather different Left, which includes a broad range of (mostly less dogmatic) Marxists. Racial divisions cut across these ideological positions. (Many revisionists/white progressives complain they have been sidelined in this debate, and marginalized by affirmative action, and that their contribution to liberation has not been reciprocated by the ANC.[1])

Resentments of, and against, White Liberals

The tense relationship between the black elite and white liberals is partly due to historical resentments; partly to current rivalries. The historical resentments are summarized in the accusations by Kadar Asmal et al (1997, 69, 120f., 135, 179) that liberals adopted a "holier-than-thou" attitude towards the ANC's resort to violence; engaged in McCarthyite cold war behaviour towards the ANC's alliance partner, the South African Communist Party (SACP); by opposing sanctions, failed to express solidarity with the anti-apartheid struggle; and—most damagingly—"acquiesced in [Botha's] murderous states of emergency. . . . and aggression against neighbouring African states"

Asmal et al. accuse liberals of being "hypocrites. . . . who do not respect the universal standards they proclaim." In publicly declaring how much he "hates liberals,"[2] Asmal's coauthor, Ronald Suresh Roberts, is not alone. Frene Ginwala, former Speaker of South Africa's House of Assembly, reiterates the neo-Marxist allegation that South Africa's liberal tradition was "imbued with racism. . . . its advent on South African soil stopped black economic development." Leading journalist and publisher, Thami Mazwai, declares he "detests liberals" and warns of "a liberal conspiracy" against South Africa's new government—warnings reiterated by, *inter alia*, ANC politicians Jabu Moleketi and Josiah Jeli (2002), who maintain that liberals plan to "delegitimise our government and transformation agenda."[3]

Hostility to those termed 'white liberals' is widespread in both scholarly and public debates. Malegapura Makgoba, Vice-Chancellor of Natal University, declared that "liberal racism originated from Western civilisation. . . . blacks are persecuted in their minds by the 'liberal,' a figure who continues to rouse black anger . . . [and is] the nearer neighbour . . . the one whose influence is hardest to analyse and . . . eradicate" (1998, 265f.). Njabulo Ndebele, Vice-Chancellor of Cape Town University wrote, "English-speaking liberals. . . . are blissfully unaware [of] their complicity in soul-murder, their inability to relinquish control over the values they tacitly pressure others to accept. With their condescending platitudes they have massacred hundreds of thousands of souls. The hegemony of Anglo-South African civility is powerful and not easy to cast off. . . . [Liberals] assume there is a meaningful community where there is only a hate-inducing intimacy." Commenting on the ambivalent feelings about white liberals, Steve Biko—who defined "the liberal establishment" as including "radical and leftist groups"—wrote, "The very political vocabulary blacks use has been inherited from liberals, but blacks now desire to speak for themselves . . . overcoming mental slavery [and ending their] collusion in psychic colonisation. . . . The biggest mistake the black world made was to assume that whoever opposed apartheid was an ally."[4]

There are less psychologically charged criticisms of white liberals. Barney Pityana, chair of the Human Rights Commission, wrote, "We are all liberals now. . . . [but] liberalism is not simply about 'being nice' to others who are less fortunate. . . . Liberalism has to be about restoring the rights of people to determine their own future. . . . Liberal protestations [against affirmative action] on grounds of 'colour-blindness' are a ruse for the maintenance of white privilege." However, Pityana distinguished between liberals who are "an anachronism . . . a conservative and reactionary brand of liberalism and genuine liberals" (*The Star* (Johannesburg), June 25, 2002).

Much recent criticism of liberals focuses on the Democratic Alliance (DA), the successor to the Progressive Party of Suzman and Slabbert, now led by Tony Leon. ANC Cabinet Minister Essop Pahad said, "I don't take Tony Leon to be a liberal . . . the DA's support base it is very far from being liberal." The ANC chief parliamentary whip, Tony Yengeni, described "Leon's brand of rightwing liberalism as the clever way of protecting white privilege and racism. . . . The DA has hijacked the liberal mantle for itself . . . the ANC is the most liberal party in South Africa." In a thoughtful challenge, ANC cabinet minister Pallo Jordan wrote, "It has never been in dispute that the antecedents of the DA come from the liberal tradition . . . [but the DA adopted] the tattered garments of white anxiety. . . . appealing to the worst fears of white voters and becoming rather illiberal. . . . repositioning itself as the party of the property-owning whites. . . . projecting the interests and suspicions of minorities who are unhappy with South Africa's new dispensation . . . they support every device to impede the advancement of the new African propertied classes [misrepresenting] affirmative action and equal opportunities legislation as racial quota systems." Jordan rejects Stanley Uys's prediction that the ANC, if faced with rising discontent, would resort to racial demagogy "as a ruse to . . . [rally] a restive, discontented working class into racial solidarity with wealthier Africans" against whites.[5]

The DA certainly has no exclusive claim to liberal values. The ANC has its own liberal tradition: its former president, Albert Luthuli, said (1962) that liberal values fitted well with the value placed on the individual by the African tradition of *ubuntu*. Oliver Tambo, the ANC's president-in-exile, was a devout Christian and in many ways closer to Swedish Prime Minister Olaf Palme than to the Soviet leaders who provided arms and material support for the ANC. Liberal values are evident in the ANC's role in shaping and respecting South Africa's liberal constitution. The fact that Steve Biko also laid claim to these values is further testimony to the widespread support for them in South Africa.

It is also the case that the DA's social base has changed. It is no longer confined to a small group of English liberals but receives electoral support from some formerly conservative whites, including Afrikaners who never supported the Progressive Party (let alone the earlier, more radical Liberal Party) but are disillusioned with the failure of the demoralized NP to assert itself as an opposition. The DA also receives support from many coloureds and Indians and from a small (and possibly growing) number of Africans: it is thus more diverse than hitherto.

During the 1990s, as Jordan and Pahad noted, the DA's policies shifted to the Right. However, the whole political spectrum then shifted Right, including the ANC and South African Communist Party (SACP). Recently, the spectrum has shifted Left, including the DA, evident in its growing stress on poverty and unemployment; support for a basic income grant; activist policies on HIV/Aids and, recently, the softening of its stance on affirmative action.[6] Paradoxically, these shifts by the DA back toward the welfarist tradition of South African liberals were greeted by the Left with howls of outrage and charges of "opportunism" and "populism."

There are thus many issues involved in the hostility toward what is still referred to as the party of 'white liberals.' This hostility was intensified by the revisionists' damaging misrepresentation of the historical record of liberals, and by the emergence on the international scene of the American neoconservatives, misleadingly termed neoliberals, with whose brush all liberals are being tarred.

Many of the historical charges against South African liberals are incorrect. As shown previously (pp. 60f, 178f), the claim by Asmal et al. that liberals (and business) supported Botha's "murderous" behavior towards his domestic opponents and neighboring countries is false. Asmal et al. also misrepresent the position of liberals on the resort to violence. Many liberals recognized the force of the argument that, after the failure of the passive resistance campaign (in which liberals such as Patrick Duncan participated), and the banning of the ANC and PAC, the NP's political challengers were left with few options. The depth of liberal feeling was indicated by the fact that the first assassination attempt on Verwoerd was by a liberal, David Pratt, and that some liberals joined the underground African Resistance Movement (ARM) at the same time the ANC set up its revolutionary arm, Umkhonto we Sizwe.[7]

When the government exposed the ARM, it was criticized by some liberals, including Paton and Ballinger, on the grounds that its resort to violence contradicted the Liberal Party's principles of constitutionalism and put at risk its legal political activities. But many liberals sympathized with this desperate action, especially as the ARM, like the ANC, tried (unsuccessfully) to avoid damaging civilians. The ARM's activities ended in disaster, as did many actions against the well-organized South African state. But the ARM's treatment was very different: not only did the state prosecutor mock their amateurish efforts, but so did some on the Left who, while treating their own revolutionaries as heroes, sneered at the (hardly unique) occurrence that one of the ARM's arrested members turned state's evidence. ARM members paid a heavy price: John Harris was executed; Eddie Daniels and Hugh Lewin endured lengthy prison sentences; Randolph Vigne, Neville Rubin, and James Currey were among those fleeing into exile to escape arrest.

Also misleading is the allegation that South African liberals were McCarthyite "cold war warriors." McCarthyism was a blot on the record of the United States. But even worse was the often murderous behavior toward liberals and social democrats of the USSR and its international supporters. Their appalling record was exemplified by Lenin's dictum that communists should support the liberals/social democrats with whom they periodically cooperated "as the rope supports the hanged man."[8] Liberals felt this ruthless attitude was reflected in the SACP's willingness to use them, while discrediting and sidelining them and adversely affecting their relations with the ANC, particularly after 1960 when the SACP became the ANC's main channel for arms and finance.

Despite this, South African liberals opposed the NP's persecution of the SACP. Suzman, Paton, Ernie Wentzel, and others raised funds for the defense and support of imprisoned communists, while the liberal universities refused to dismiss banned communists such as Jack Simons. This supportive behavior was not reciprocated. Exiled liberals were frozen out of the Anti-Apartheid Movement, and liberal academics were shabbily treated. The mutual hostility between communists and liberals was thus influenced by cold war rivalries on both sides, and close cooperation between liberals like Paton and ANC leaders like Luthuli ended.

Liberals were divided over sanctions. Peter Brown, Colin and Margaret Legum, and Peter Hain were among their earliest advocates, and Donald Woods among later supporters. But during the 1970s, liberals who believed that economic growth was undermining apartheid, and that opportunities for political opposition were developing within South Africa, became wary of the effects of sanctions and isolation on these new trends.

Similar dilemmas were posed by difficult choices between the symbolic value and practical effect of boycotting Bantu Education schools. Boycotts were powerful signals of opposition to the abhorrent principle of Bantu Education, but they deprived children of their education. Bishops Huddleston and Reeves closed their church schools and went into exile. Archbishop Clayton denounced apartheid but kept his schools open. Faced with what Paton (1974, 233f.) called the "excruciating choice" of whether to treat such issues as matters of principle or tactics, many (though not all) liberals took a pragmatic stance.

On these painful dilemmas, the ANC too had its pragmatists. When the NP removed coloureds from the common role in 1958, replacing them with four white representatives, the noncollaborationist Unity Movement, and some within the ANC, urged a total boycott. But Nelson Mandela opposed this, arguing "The parliamentary forum must be exploited to put forth the case for a democratic and progressive South Africa."[9] Parliament was used in this way not only by liberals like Ballinger, de Beer, and Slabbert, but also by SACP members Sam Kahn and Brian Bunting before their expulsion from parliament. Suzman used her parliamentary position to elicit information about pass law prosecutions, discriminatory expenditure on education and health, and the treatment of political prisoners, for whom her prison visits secured improvements, including access to further education.

But there were limits to the capacity of liberals (and others) "to do more." As Leo Kuper observed (1974, 263), in polarized racial and religious conflicts, liberals are, in the short run, usually ineffective: "They have no mass following . . . no power . . . no skill in, nor inclination for, violence . . . and are easily emasculated by government repression, or liquidated by extremists of both sides". In such situations, their contribution depends on long-term influence on the climate of opinion.

In post-apartheid South Africa, younger liberals in particular aspire to play a more active political role and they resent their continued exclusion from public office, as well as the marginalization and even demonization of the DA, now the main opposition party. An example is the exclusion of the DA from chairing any of the forty parliamentary committees, which are chaired either by members of the ANC or by smaller, less liberal parties such as Inkatha and the NNP (the NP's heir). This behavior contributes toward what is denounced as the DA's tendency to indulge in "constant, hyper-critical" sniping (what Weber termed "negative politics"). It also fans fears that the official parliamentary opposition is being delegitimized—a process that would certainly threaten the consolidation of democracy.

A conundrum represented by and for the DA is that in most transitional democracies, a party with its middle class base and historical record of opposition to authoritarianism and racism is likely to be a contender for power rather than a permanent party of protest. Such middle-class parties often support pro-poor policies for the reasons noted previously: an interest in expanding society's skills and countering social problems such as crime and disease, especially if they have developed a welfarist ethic (the DA's stance on redistribution is discussed later).

This is how the DA thinks it should be viewed, but it is not how other political parties want it to be viewed, as it might then—if the salience of race declines—become a rival for power. That this possibility does not yet seem to be in sight is an indication of the continuing salience of 'race' in South African politics. But it is not only racial issues that remain salient: the Left's hostility to the DA, even (especially?) on issues on which they agree, signals the continuation of (nonracial) ideological and political rivalries. Thus, the competing perspectives and calculations in South African politics revolve round the same interaction between 'race' and class that has been a central theme of South Africa's history over the past few centuries and shows, as yet, little sign of disappearing.

Finally, a seemingly minor complaint that causes intense irritation: Pityana is right to insist that, when living under systems like apartheid, the priority must be to get rid of them. But this is easier said than done and, in the meantime, "behaving decently" can (as George Orwell wrote in his essay on Charles Dickens) make a difference to those directly affected, as well as keeping alive the idea of a humane society. However, this stance can lead to feelings of being morally virtuous and even of being entitled to speak on behalf of the poor and voiceless. That this presumption generates such resentment (especially among those aspiring to play this role themselves?) confirms the importance of psychological, not just material and political, factors in shaping social relations. White liberals (and progressives) often seem oblivious of this. Moreover, while the new combativeness of liberals reflects resentment at the way they have been misrepresented and politically marginalized, it also reflects some of the triumphalism that followed the collapse of the Soviet Union. This has mainly affected conservatives and their successors, the neoconservatives. But some of this has rubbed off on liberals, contributing to overconfidence in their record and policy prescriptions—to which recent international developments are providing a harsh, salutary correction.

AFRIKANERS IN POST-APARTHEID SOUTH AFRICA

The ANC's irritable reaction to English liberals contrasts with its almost velvet-glove treatment of Afrikaners. The ANC stated it was willing to discuss an Afrikaner "homeland"; included the NP in its first Government of National Unity; and in 2004 absorbed into a coalition the remnants of the demoralized NP, which President Mbeki praised for having become "a party of non-racism and democracy" in contrast to the DA, which he described as "the home of the most stubborn representatives of white supremacy" (*ANC Today*, January 18, 2005).

Yet Afrikaners have fears and grievances, including the growing suspicion that President de Klerk "gave away too much" at the constitutional negotiations, particularly in failing to entrench minority rights and guarantees for the Afrikaans language and culture. This complaint comes not only from *verkramptes*, but also from *verligtes* like Giliomee (2003, ch. 17), who fear that de Klerk miscalculated, leaving Afrikaners in a weak position and putting at risk their individual and group interests.

This emerging "stab in the back" legend relates to the period in which de Klerk and the *verligtes* who backed him were fighting a rearguard action against the *verkramptes*. Shortly before the 1994 election, white extremists attacked the convention center where the constitution was being negotiated and attempted a coup in the Bophutatswana Bantustan. During the negotiations, the NP focused on security and economic issues, including guarantees for the predominantly Afrikaans bureaucracy. With hindsight, the *verkramptes*' strength was probably overestimated, but this was where most fears were focused.

Another factor affecting the outcome was the unexpected weakening of the NP's position during the transitional period, 1990–94. Those who had discussions with de Klerk at this time confirm it was *not his intention to give away power, but to share it* (Renwick 1997; Waldmeir 1997). De Klerk and his supporters anticipated that group rights and power sharing would be entrenched in the constitution and that any shift to majority rule would take place gradually. But the NP lost control of the political agenda, partly because it lost the propaganda war over responsibility for the murderous activities of the Third Force. This weakened the NP's authority and strengthened the ANC politically. Some observers also consider the ANC negotiators, especially Cyril Ramaphosa and Thabo Mbeki, outsmarted the NP in the constitutional negotiations.[10]

The NP, including the *verligtes*, also overestimated the extent of black support they and their allies might win in post-apartheid elections. This was based on opinion polls showing that up to 20 percent of Africans, and higher proportions of coloureds and Indians, approved of de Klerk. However, these snapshots of public opinion did not allow for the political dynamics of a rapidly changing situation in which voters would soon be able to choose between the NP and ANC. While more coloureds and Indians supported the NP or DA than many anticipated, the huge African vote came out overwhelmingly for the ANC.

Many Afrikaners also express growing reservations about South Africa's liberal democratic constitution. Giliomee (2000, 95, 101f.,

125f.) argues that the Westminster system on which it is based "works only in racially and ethnically homogeneous societies" and is unsuited to multiethnic countries with a history of conflict. Giliomee maintains that states with large ethnic majorities are at risk of becoming "majoritarian tyrannies," with the minorities permanently excluded from political power. He chides liberals for supporting the constitution, arguing that: "Liberals have too easily assumed . . . support across racial lines for liberalism. . . . [Nineteenth- and twentieth-century] liberals wasted their time, and the country's, with the qualified franchise. . . . and their belief in 'moving forward in faith.'" Instead, they should have thrown their weight behind consociational devices such as compulsory power sharing in multiethnic cabinets, minority vetoes over legislation, and a rotating presidency.

The new South African constitution includes proportional representation, which provides greater representation for minorities, and a Constitutional Court and Bill of Rights, which act as checks on the parliamentary majority. The constitution does not therefore conform to the standard Westminster model. Among the reasons for the NP's failure to secure consociational devices was that these were tainted by their association with 'separate development' institutions, such as the Tricameral Parliament, clearly designed to perpetuate white domination. Another factor, as Landsberg (1994) and Guelke (2005) noted, was the lack of international support for consociational mechanisms. This was partly due to the shift of international support away from de Klerk and toward the ANC during the transitional period, inter alia, because of the allegations that he covertly supported Third Force activities, including the 1992 Boipatong massacre. Whatever the truth of these allegations (see p. 198 no. 17), they weakened de Klerk's authority both domestically and internationally and strengthened the ANC's negotiating position.

The ANC is not unsympathetic to the desire of Afrikaners and other minorities to have their own languages and educational institutions, provided entry to them is nonracial. What is more problematic for those wanting to secure the future of Afrikaans, and other indigenous languages, is the desire of many people to be educated in English, especially at tertiary level. This is because of the utility of a language that is spoken internationally, not because of the influence of English-speaking whites, who remain as excluded from political power as they were under the NP.

Some observers claim Afrikaners are adapting better to post-apartheid South Africa than English-speaking whites. The merging of the NP and ANC points to the further reduction of racist ideology and behavior, as do declining social barriers between white and 'brown' (coloured) Afrikaners. Most Afrikaners stress their deep historical roots in South Africa and their continuing commitment to the country. However, opinion polls do not bear out the claim that they are more accepting of black rule than the English. Schlemmer found that 80 percent of Afrikaners were unhappy about the treatment of their culture in post-apartheid South Africa, compared with 20 percent of the English (Giliomee 2003, 663). Many Afrikaners have joined the ranks of *émigrés* from South Africa—though this outflow seems to be driven more by anxiety about job prospects under affirmative action than by political considerations.

Changes in deeply-rooted attitudes take time to effect, but the accusation that most whites remain deeply, or "subliminally" (unconsciously) racist, and that they even nurse the malign hope that post-apartheid South Africa will fail, is not supported by evidence. The attitude of many whites seems rather to be summed up in ex-President de Klerk's speech (to the South African Business Association in London, 25 January 1999) that, despite many problems: "The new South Africa is by far a better place than the old . . . our negotiated settlement averted a catastrophe. . . . South Africa is becoming a winning nation, destined to play a pivotal role in Africa and an important role internationally."

It is too soon to say whether, from the viewpoint of Afrikaners, de Klerk miscalculated. This judgement will depend partly on assessments about whether he could have got better terms or pursued a better option (such as partition); partly on how race relations evolve. Minorities elsewhere contemplating whether to share, or give up, power will observe the outcome in South Africa closely.

Tensions, and Policy Trends, within the Tripartite Alliance

"South Africa consists of two nations: the one black and poor, the other rich and white"

—President Thabo Mbeki

The aim of our National Democratic Revolution is: " to encourage the emergence of a common South African identity . . . [with] African hegemony in the context of a multi-cultural, non-racial society"

—Nation Formation & Nation-building, 1997
ANC Mafeking Conference document.

The major political debate and power struggle, is now within the Tripartite Alliance of ANC, Cosatu and SACP. The main divisions are between African nationalists/Africanists, the Left and various, less effectively mobilized, liberals and pragmatists. Africanists and the Left are the pace-setters within the ANC, and each have their own distinctive version of the fear (parallel to that expressed by Afrikaners) that "our leaders have sold us out."

Tensions between Africanists and the Left have long historical roots. In 1959, the ANC, committed to nonracialism, expelled the Africanists, leading to the formation of the PAC under Robert Sobukwe. This was followed by subsequent expulsions and breakaways. However, under President Mbeki, many former PAC/Black Consciousness activists have been incorporated into influential positions within the ANC, and are among those who complain that nothing has changed: the ANC is in office but not in power and "the transition is incomplete." Most Africanists are not anti-capitalist: they urge support for black business and are the driving force behind the ANC's Black Economic Empowerment (BEE) policy. But Africanists are impatient with the pace of change; the continuing degree of social stratification along racial lines; and of what they believe is continued control by whites, whom Mbeki himself describes as "that elite which is [still] setting the political agenda." According to this view, whites have lost nothing, made no sacrifices, and paid no price for apartheid.

Africanists also accuse whites of remaining deeply, even if unconsciously ("subliminally") racist; of lacking faith in the capacity of a black government; and of hoping that blacks will fail, with South

Africa becoming "another African basket case," thus proving the superiority of white rule. Africanists fear inferior Bantu Education has set them up—"booby-trapped us"—for failure, and view white complaints about "lowering standards" as a smokescreen for perpetuating their own privileges, pointing to the mediocre standards of many whites who previously monopolized senior positions from which able blacks were excluded but are now moving into (Maphai and Gottschalk 2003; Ramphele 1998).

The Left has different concerns, accusing ANC leaders of abandoning their socialist principles under pressure from 'global capital' and the World Bank, and of "swallowing the whole neo-liberal agenda." Initially, these accusations were publicly expressed by a small group whom the ANC termed "ultra-leftists." But recently, similar criticisms have been openly made by Cosatu and the SACP who, in 2006, issued major policy documents challenging ANC's cautious macro-economic strategy and calling for more expansionary policies and an end to "capitalist accumulation" including by the black bourgeoisie.[11]

The Left is uncomfortable with BEE, which conflicts with its non-racial principles, and particularly with the focus on nurturing a small, rich black elite. The Left attributes this to the influence of business (and liberals) whom they accuse of wanting to create a black elite to serve as their allies against the masses. At the same time, Africanists accuse business and liberals of opposing affirmative action. As discussed later, many liberals oppose, or have reservations about, BEE for the same reason as the Left: that it conflicts with their nonracial principles.

Another concern of the Left (and of liberals) is of authoritarian trends or, at least, a "hollowing out" of democracy. Not only Cosatu, with its established democratic credentials, but also the formerly Stalinist SACP—now evolving into a Gramscian (Euro-communist) party—want the consolidation of South Africa's new democracy and complain about the centralization of power in the Presidency; the sidelining of parliament, aided by the 'closed list' electoral system, which facilitates the removal or 'redeployment' of MPs who do not toe the party line; the bullying and cowing of the media; and the staffing of the judiciary, SABC and other independent institutions with compliant political appointees.[12]

The ANC and Business

The Left's view of the ANC as selling out its socialist principles to, and being locked in a "cosy" relationship with (global and domestic) capital, and the depiction of business (and liberals) as promoters of BEE, is misleading and ignores the complex relations between capital and the ANC and the continuing salience of racial divisions.

Despite ANC's close relationship with the SACP, and support for the USSR during the Cold War, its driving force was nationalism and the desire to be liberated from apartheid. As noted previously, Western reluctance to take a tougher line against the apartheid regime earlier contributed to ANC's close relationship with the SACP. The ANC's 1956 commitment to nationalization of "the mineral wealth . . . banks and monopoly industry" coexisted with its stated desire to nurture an African business class (a "patriotic bourgeoisie"). Even during the cold war, there were disputes over these conflicting commitments, with Thabo Mbeki among those insisting: "The ANC is not a socialist party. It has never pretended to be one. . . . and it will not become one . . . for the purpose of pleasing its 'Left' critics" (John Saul 1984, 20).

However, ANC's departure from its commitment to nationalization does not necessarily imply a "cosy" relationship with South Africa's established (English, Afrikaans and foreign) capital. Nor does its aim of nurturing an African bourgeoisie necessarily imply—in a political system based on universal suffrage—ignoring the interests of the mass of voters. ANC's history and broad base point to a mixed economy and attempt to balance the interests and claims of competing constituencies and conflicting principles. Portraying the South African government as "in the pocket" of international capital—or of Africanists, Cosatu, SACP—impedes understanding of the political economy dynamics and realistic policy options.

The ANC wants to show that an African government can nurture, and certainly not damage, its inheritance of Africa's most developed economy and infrastructure. It also believes (as do most contemporary governments) that cooperation with private capital is one of the requirements for this aim. But South Africa's government also wants to show that Africans are in control of the polity; that it can deliver its dual promises of nurturing an African bourgeoisie and raising mass living standards; and that it will secure for South Africa a leading role in Africa and the wider world.

Securing these aims involves not only wooing investors, in fierce competition with other countries, but also imposing on them its own priorities, including affirmative action in employment; an increasing share of African ownership of the private sector; and the retention of a large state sector. These priorities impinge heavily on business and there is uncertainty on all sides as to how far and fast they will be pursued.

This uncertainty makes for a tense relationship with business, evident in periodic outbursts—not only by Cosatu, which regularly accuses business of "investment strikes"—but also by Mbeki and senior cabinet ministers, who have reacted sharply to even mild criticisms of policy and sober assessments of economic prospects by, inter alia, Tony Traher of Anglo American and Pieter Cox of Sasol, who were accused of being unpatriotic and damaging South Africa's interests. Meanwhile, pharmaceutical companies were accused of spreading diseases such as AIDS to increase drug sales.

The muted, nervous reaction of business to these attacks prompted Helen Suzman and Tony Leon to accuse business of being craven and obsequious towards the ANC. Shubane and Mackay depict business as ANC's "uncritical and silent partner" (1999). Giliomee (2005) complains that Afrikaans companies are so anxious to appease the ANC that they have become reluctant to support Afrikaans cultural institutions. Simkins (Giliomee and Simkins 1999, 339) paints a more complex picture, portraying big business as willing to "sponsor the enrichment of a small African elite" and acquiescing in costly, highly regulated affirmative action labor legislation that only large companies can cope with, but which will damage small-medium firms.

Business, as usual, prefers to avoid conflicts with a government that (like the NP) exercises considerable powers and prerogatives affecting its operations. Nevertheless, there has been (private and public) business criticism of state policies on, inter alia, Zimbabwe and Aids, as well as on the high crime rate and problems in service delivery and administration (Gumede 2005, 172, 218). These criticisms are denounced by many in the ANC as racially motivated and unpatriotic. Business support for political parties is a particularly sensitive issue. In December 2003, James Motlatsi and Bobby Godsell of AngloGold Ashanti (of the Oppenheimer group) felt constrained to issue a public statement setting out their view that: an effectively functioning democracy is "good for society and good for business. . . . [Multiparty democracy] cannot operate effectively without funds for political parties. . . . Our shareholders, employees and customers have different political allegiances . . . [therefore we shall] promote political competition and public debate. . . . " by providing support for a variety of viewpoints. Despite ANC's protests, Anglogold divided its large donation into equal parts for the governing and main opposition parties (ANC and DA), with smaller shares for other parties.

These sensitivities suggest ANC's relations with *white* business are not as cozy as some believe. However, close, amiable relations exist with the black, particularly African, businesspeople that ANC is nurturing via contracts, mining licenses, and financial support. Mbeki and other ministers encourage and woo the Black Management Forum and salute the emergence of black multimillionaires such as Saki Macozoma, Reuel Xhoza, Patrice Motsepe, Tokyo Sexwale and Cyril Ramaphosa, some of whom are likely contenders in the competition to succeed Mbeki as President in 2009.

Clearly, relations between the ANC and capital are not simply about class, but are permeated by the issue of 'race,' which affects the attitude of capital—and everyone else—to the difficult, sensitive issue of black economic empowerment in a situation in which the black majority now has political power, while the white minority still dominates the commanding heights of the private economy. The black share of ownership is estimated at about 5 percent of listed companies, though blacks increasingly dominate the large state sector, including numerous parastatals. Whites also predominate in professional, managerial and office jobs, though blacks are advancing rapidly in both state and private sectors.

The Race-Class, and the State-Market, Debates

Many would agree with Mbeki's depiction of South Africa as consisting of "two nations: one black and poor, the other rich and white" and on the need for the post-apartheid government to redress this. The policy issues are whether to adopt class-based or race-based strategies, and the extent to which use should be made of market mechanisms or state intervention.

Class-based policies would include higher taxes on the rich, and redistribution towards the poor via increased social spending, as well as the transfer of assets such as land and housing. Race-based polices require affirmative action, specifically targeted at blacks which, obviously, requires categorizing people into groups and thus re-racializing policy. (A subsidiary question is whether affirmative action will be confined to the majority Africans, or include coloureds and Asians.) The case for a class-based strategy is that, as Africans constitute the overwhelming majority of the poor, they would be the main beneficiaries of redistributive class measures, which have the added advantage of not re-racializing policy. It is also argued that this strategy would be more efficient economically, being more likely to stimulate large-scale job creation and a wider domestic market. Support is given to this view by the rapid growth of the black middle class (small-medium business, professionals, skilled workers) outside the parameters of BEE, due to economic growth and the ending of apartheid, which improved their access to training, contracts, financial credit etc.

The argument for *race-based measures* specifically targeted at Africans (and coloureds and Asians?) is that it is not just a question of reducing poverty by job creation and social expenditure, but also of changing the racially skewed ownership of assets (land, business, housing), as well as the occupational structure, in which professional and managerial jobs are still dominated by whites. These (artificially created) structures will tend to be perpetuated by inheritance, superior white education and home nurturing, and informal networks. Correcting these entrenched socioeconomic structures—creating a level playing field—requires direct state intervention, including positive discrimination in favor of blacks.

The argument for affirmative action does not rest only on the moral case for correcting unjust, deliberately distorted socioeconomic structures, but also on prudential grounds. Vincent Maphai (2003) argues that affirmative action should be assessed not simply on the basis of principles, but on utilitarian grounds, and that affirmative action for blacks, like proportional representation for whites, is a confidence-building measure aimed at reducing historical resentments and fears, thus contributing to social and political stability.

There is intense debate throughout South African society about both the principle and the implementation of affirmative action, particularly about the ANC's version of this in BEE, which focuses on the transfer of equity ownership to blacks and the promotion of black managers and professionals. Many white businesses supported measures to promote black managers and increase black equity ownership, partly influenced by their experience of the mellowing effects of prosperity on Afrikaners. But they, and many others, have become concerned about the way BEE has been implemented, leading, to the rapid growth of a small group of very rich, politically well-connected, beneficiaries. It has also led to the displacement, through early retirement or blocked advance, of experienced white managers, administrators, and professionals, especially in the public sector. Anglogold Ashanti recently set out its concern about these trends, stating that Anglo American companies had been actively training and promoting blacks since the mid-1970s (before the job color bar was legally abolished) and would continue to do so, but that they would neither make token appointments of blacks in front offices, nor practice reverse discrimination against white males, whom not only the state sector, but many private companies, now refuse to engage, or even elbow out of jobs.

The outcome of BEE has been widely attacked. William Gumede (2005, 223) expressed the "huge disappointment" of disillusioned black intellectuals with BEE's delivery of large benefits to the few, alongside continued mass poverty. Desmond Tutu (in his 2004 Mandela Foundation lecture) deplored the new elite's "scramble onto the gravy train," warning that ANC was creating a generation of sycophantic yes-men, concerned to enrich themselves and indifferent to the needs of the poor. Cosatu leaders denounced the "incestuous relationship between black business and politicians as a dangerous cancer eating into the body of our democracy" and expressed concern that BEE was also causing "a massive crisis in our public service" (*Financial Times*, April 18, 2006).

Surveys by Schlemmer (1998, 361) suggest that black workers agree with Cosatu's critical stance towards BEE, which receives more support from the black elite—each correctly perceiving who the beneficiaries are. There are frequent attacks on "fat cats" in correspondence columns in the media, web sites and talk shows, such as a letter warning: "Those black folks enriching themselves with the spoils of our democracy will one day answer through a second revolution against capitalists" (*Financial Times*, April 18, 2006). President Mbeki himself chided those "using positions of state power for personal enrichment."

Whatever one's view of the principle of affirmative action, this outcome is an extreme version of what often happens to such programs in practice: their benefits are seized by the relatively well-off and those with political connections. This was anticipated, and formed the basis for reservations about the policy by, *inter alia*, Khehla Shubane (1995) and Kenneth Hughes (1993). However, it is the stated aim of ANC policy that transformation should include, not only the reduction of discrimination and poverty, but also the advance of blacks, especially Africans, into visible positions at the commanding heights of the economy, in both state and private sectors. Mbeki often said it was BEE's aim to encourage the growth of an African elite, "a patriotic national bourgeoisie," whose members would be the equals of whites; provide role models for blacks; and ensure that blacks were visible among the richest, most successful South Africans—and this is happening.

A major issue in the debate about BEE is its effect on economic efficiency and growth. Mamphela Ramphele (1998), one of the founders of Black Consciousness and a leading advocate of the principle of black empowerment, recognizes "the tension between excellence and equity," and urges blacks to confront the implications of South Africa's acute skill shortage for its growth rate, international competitiveness and administrative capacity. Ramphele argues that the "denialism" by many blacks about South Africa's skill shortage stems from their vulnerability to the racial myth of white superiority, and their fear that recognizing the need for white skills will be "interpreted as proof of our intellectual inferiority and unreadiness to govern." Ramphele urges blacks to be "courageous enough to accept criticism . . . [and to] swallow the bitter pill that . . . white males . . . represent the fulcrum around which the country's future intellectual capital must be mobilised [We need to recognise white males as] national resources . . . that represent the research capacity South Africa desperately needs and encourage them to take their responsibilities seriously and [help nurture] . . . the next generation of South African researchers." Political analyst and businessman, Moeletsi Mbeki, recently reiterated his earlier warning about the likely economic distortions and costs of BEE, which would "create an artificial scarcity [of skilled and professional blacks] and a massive salary premium for its beneficiaries" (cited http://everfasternews.com, October 7, 2006).

Thus, the ANC is confronting the same Becker-type choices and calculations about the trade-off between economic efficiency and racial preferences that the NP faced during the 1970s (see p. 55). The ANC will be under similarly conflicting pressures from uncompetitive employers and workers who want protection and those who give priority to efficiency and faster growth. Once again, these pressures are coming not only from the private, but also from the state, sector. Managers of state departments and parastatals are warning of the costs, and the adverse implications for South Africa's international competitiveness and administrative capacity, of "the purging of qualified, experienced white managers and the rapid promotion of inexperienced BEE candidates." That these problems are being taken seriously by ministers and technocrats is evident in the lament of Reserve Bank governor, Tito Mboweni, that when the Bank trains black staff, they soon leave for more highly paid jobs in the private sector. Mboweni now holds onto his long-serving Afrikaner technocrats because "they stay and do the work."[13] And, as in the past, these concerns about rising costs are reinforced by international competition and by a *zeitgeist* hostile to racially-based policies.

There is, surely, a strong case for affirmative action along the lines argued by Maphai and Ramphele, especially correcting for disadvantaged and disrupted family backgrounds and schooling. But some variants are indefensible on both ethical and prudential grounds. The first is giving preference to foreign blacks (from Africa or Asia) over indigenous whites, who are more familiar with, and committed to, the country. The second is the proposal for "demographic representivity": proportionate racial representation in all spheres: education, politics, business, the professions, sports teams—a requirement that ignores the varied spectrum of talents and tastes among the population, itself changing in composition since abolition of the bans on racial inter-racial sex and marriage.

These racist variants of BEE are fuelled by historical grievances and resentments that have surfaced in the affirmative action debate, and the feeling among many, though by no means all, blacks that even liberal/progressive whites do not understand the depth of, not just material, but also psychological injury inflicted by apartheid. Ramphele insists the past cannot simply be wiped out. Maphai deplores the tendency of whites to be "non-reflective" about the past and to brush aside the historical legacy.

It is true, as Africanists stress, that most whites remain economically well off. Yet, much has changed for them. They have, as Maphai recognized (2003), "lost their privileged status," including their exclusive control of political power and its associated advantages: preferential access to the best jobs, education and social resources. It is valid to question whether anyone should have such privileges (which the black elite is now acquiring). But everyone experiences the removal of privileges to which they are accustomed as a loss. The negotiated settlement was an act of faith—a leap in the dark—with risks as great as the major extensions of political rights in nineteenth century Europe and elsewhere. Whites reject claims that apartheid was equivalent to Nazism, pointing out that, over the twentieth century, the South African population increased from 5m to 43m, with the proportion of Africans rising from 68 to 80 percent, and with rising levels of literacy, skills and (until the Aids epidemic) life expectancy. Moreover, the white oligarchy did not simply plunder, but helped to develop, the country. They also, eventually, recognized the evils of apartheid and, despite the risks to themselves, renounced it, albeit under growing though not decisive pressures.[14]

What most whites, including many who now term themselves liberals, are reluctant to confront is that they remain a privileged economic minority amidst continuing black poverty and racial inequality. Many whites are also reluctant to signal unreservedly their recognition of the terrible costs apartheid inflicted on blacks—including the aspiring elite—and the advantages it accorded to whites, whether or not they wanted these.

The feeling of whites that they are denied recognition for their contribution to building South Africa—and of liberals/progressives that they are denied credit for their opposition to apartheid—has presumably contributed to their lack of response to Archbishop Tutu's pleas for more generous support for reparations for the victims of gross abuses under apartheid (the relatively small number of 22,000 cases documented by the TRC) and their lack of a sense of urgency about the need for redistribution. Valid concerns about BEE's delivery of large benefits to the few would carry more weight if its critics supported widely-based redistribution. But whites also need to recognize that there was severe discrimination against the black elite and that they too have legitimate claims.

These heated exchanges underline the importance of, not only conflicts over economic interests and political power, but of psychological factors, including different historical perspectives. This dimension, and the wide range of views among blacks on the race/national question, is illuminated by the exchanges between Malegapuru Makgoba, Vice-Chancellor of Natal University and Marcus Ramogale, V-C of Venda University. Makgoba compared the "dethroned white male" to dethroned, resentful baboons and urged whites to subordinate themselves to, and acquire the culture of, the newly dominant Africans. In response, Ramogale, while welcoming the Africanism that debunks racial domination, urged "the now powerful African elite to find termination to the endless human history of conquest, domination and enforced mimicry.... [and develop] a political philosophy of equality and diversity" (*Mail & Guardian*, March–April, 2005). Mamphela Ramphele (2001), former vice-chancellor of Cape Town University, warned that: "solidarity networks bedevil South African politics.... and create tensions between loyalty to the nation and to one's own group, however defined."

The importance of the psychologcial dimension was highlighted by reactions to Coetzee's novel, *Disgrace*. Its depiction of black-white relations in post-apartheid South Africa evoked a sharp response from President Mbeki against what was perceived as a portrayal of blacks as desiring vengeance against, or at least domination and Africanization of, whites. Some observers interpret Mbeki's controversial policies on Aids and Zimbabwe largely in psychological terms, arguing that the former was driven by his reaction against alleged Western misconceptions of African sexual behavior and the latter by his reaction against Western preoccupation with the rights of a few white farmers and indifference to the fate of the more numerous blacks whose land they had originally seized.[15] James Myburgh (2003) challenges Tom Lodge's view of Mbeki as a pragmatist and moderate, seeing Mbeki as an ideologue—"a Leninist of a special type"—who, while no longer a socialist, remains committed to the revolutionary transformation of South Africa, including the centralization of power in the ANC and "Africanisation of ownership and control of wealth, including land.... a racial rather than a socialist transformation."

Mbeki's reactions reflect the deep, widespread resentment of many Africans against white racism and European cultural arrogance. But Mbeki's record also reflects other tendencies, evident in his respect for South Africa's liberal democratic constitution, including acceptance of the two-term limit on his Presidency and Constitutional Court rulings against his government; the launching of corruption charges against leading ANC figures (many securely-established Western governments recoil from similar action); his insistence on disciplined economic management and his public recognition of, and struggle to deal with, severe problems of administrative capacity and delivery.

THE STATE-MARKET DEBATE

While the debate about race-versus-class based policies reflects the continuing effects of inherited socio-economic structures and psychological scars, the *state-versus-market debate* is less psychologically charged, but pervaded by inherited ideological hang-ups on all sides. The Left's accusation that ANC leaders buckled into pressure from global capital, the World Bank, etc. and "swallowed the whole neo-liberal agenda" reflects their tendency to deny autonomy to political agents whose behavior does not conform to their Marxist model (see p. 35 on their interpretation of the role of white labor on the gold mines). As noted by Sampson (1999, 435) and others, ANC leaders were greatly influenced by warnings from the leaders of Mozambique, Tanzania, India and China—on the basis of their own experience and mistakes—against the dangers of 'macro-economic populism,' including the expansionary economic policies and nationalization advocated by the Left.[16]

The ANC selected some of what are termed 'neo-liberal' policies, striving for low budget deficits and low inflation, and liberalizing many import tariffs. Whether or not one agrees with the criticism that it should have tolerated somewhat higher inflation in the interests of faster growth, and lowered tariffs more slowly to protect manufacturing jobs, disciplined macro-economic management does not per se imply adherence to 'conservative' economic policies, as is evident from many of their other policies. These include the huge increase in social spending. In 2005, almost a quarter of South Africans (about 12m out of 45m) received welfare support (pensions, child benefit, disability grants), which amounted to 3 per cent of GDP.[17] Spending has also increased on health, education, housing and sanitation. The ANC's flagship policy of affirmative action/BEE (which covers gender and disability as well as race) is not a 'free market' but a highly interventionist policy. Other departures from the standard neo-liberal package include South Africa's cautious privatization, which has left much of the huge state sector in place; its slow dismantling of exchange controls, which helped keep the economy stable during the international currency upheavals of late 1990s; and its refusal to introduce the more flexible labor policies urged by many economists and businessmen. Thus South Africa selected those elements of 'neo-liberalism' that suited it, and the disciplined macro-economic policy pursued by its economic managers, Tito Mboweni, Trevor Manuel and Alex Erwin, provided the framework for steady, now rising, economic growth.

However, this rising growth is largely driven by high commodity prices, which are notoriously volatile and—while they last—reduce the competitiveness of manufacturing and agriculture. Most seriously, South Africa has not addressed the deep structural weaknesses accounting for continued, widespread poverty and inequality. This is rooted in high unemployment: the rate is around 30 percent on the narrow definition of those actively seeking work; 40 percent of those wanting work, but discouraged from seeking it. Poverty is worst in rural areas, where 70 percent of the poor live, though they are fleeing to the cities, exacerbating social problems in crowded slums and the high crime rate.

Inequality remains extreme. Apartheid South Africa was rated the world's most unequal country. There is debate about whether the Gini coefficient (measuring inequality) has worsened, but it is agreed that post-apartheid South Africa remains among the world's most unequal countries. Increased social expenditure ameliorates poverty, especially as research suggests this expenditure has been well-focused on the poor (Simkins 2005; Gelb 2004). But this huge program will become fiscally unsustainable if not supported by the creation of productive jobs on a large scale, even if these jobs are, initially, low-paid.

Unemployment is the biggest challenge facing South Africa. But while it is *the most important problem, it is not, for politicians, the most urgent*, because of the inability of the disparate, unorganized poor to apply effective political pressures. There is an economic, as well as moral and political, case for the kind of affirmative action that supports economic growth by empowering blacks, via improved access to education, health, housing and support for small-medium enterprises in both rural and urban areas. BEE is a distraction from, and may even impede the task of tackling, large-scale job creation by undermining investor confidence, exacerbating the skill shortage, and weakening administrative capacity.

To sum up the debate: Africanists are justified in insisting on the need for significant changes in South Africa's racial occupational and ownership structures. But they need to recognize that, whatever strategy is adopted, sustainable results cannot be produced quickly.

As Robin Cohen warned (1986), ending apartheid (and, one might add, introducing affirmative action) cannot quickly change deeply rooted social structures: this takes time. Attempts to force rapid transformation are likely to impede this process by slowing economic growth. BEE also does not address, and even makes it more difficult to confront, mass poverty rooted in high unemployment.

The Left correctly identifies poverty and inequality as the central problem. But its diagnosis of the problem is monocausal and simplistic and its policy prescriptions unconvincing and even alarming. The Left has no alternative that rivals the (imperfect) record of market mechanisms and private ownership in providing economic incentives, high levels of production and rising living standards. Instead, the record of cooperative and communal systems of socialist production, and/or of reliance on highly expansionary macro-economic policies, has been dismal.

Liberal economic policies and mechanisms have a better record of success and can be more readily combined with forms of redistribution that avoid economic dislocation and social upheaval. This is linked to the stress liberals place on rules, institutions and democratic procedures, and on working with, rather than against, the grain of human nature. However, redistribution is not an inevitable concomitant of liberal policies which can, in their *laissez faire* forms, be accompanied by continued, even growing inequality, particularly if they fail to address highly skewed historical inheritances, whether of skills or of assets such as land and businesses. The DA's *laissez faire* position on property rights—in a situation in which whites, comprising 11 percent of the population, still own over 80 percent of its farmland, alongside acute land hunger among Africans—is indefensible and politically unsustainable. The DA rightly says lessons must be learnt from the disaster in Zimbabwe. This includes lessons for itself, on issues such as land distribution and tax levels. It is surely worthwhile for the rich in South Africa to pay a medium-term price for long-term social and political stability.

However, it is by no means only, or even mainly, the DA that is an obstacle to reform in vital areas such as land and agriculture. It is puzzling that the ANC, like so many African (though not Asian) governments, avoids the issue of agrarian reform. This seems, *prima facia*, one of the obvious ways of reducing unemployment and generating livelihoods, providing it includes redistribution of land and supporting services to small-medium farmers, whose activities are very labor intensive.

Ironically, in 1993, the World Bank—routinely accused by the Left of opposing pro-poor policies—urged redistribution of 30 percent of white farmland to blacks, together with mechanisms, such as progressive land taxes, vouchers and support services for new farmers, financed by a budget which though large, was much smaller than South Africa's huge, controversial defense budget.[18] But since 1994, little land has been redistributed, despite widespread land hunger and growing demands from rural communities. In 2005, the government issued a revised version of the 30 percent redistribution plan; but this now aims to promote—not labor-intensive small-medium farmers—but large-scale, capital-intensive black farmers, who will be the equals of white farmers and will use mechanized technology, rather than labor.

Such 'modern' technology is favored by influential voices on both Left and Right, who dismiss labor-intensive production as inferior and second-best, and want South Africa to become a high-tech, high-wage, capital-intensive economy. They also insist that small-medium farmers cannot succeed in Africa, unlike those in Asia (and earlier in Europe). Indeed, they fear land reform will damage South Africa's successful large-scale farming. By contrast, the World Bank argued that well-planned redistribution, combined with support services for new producers, need not threaten South Africa's successful agriculture, pointing out that almost 80 percent of production comes from 20 percent of farmers, and that many marginal white farmers are willing to sell.

Clearly, the main constraint is not the acquisition of land, but how it is acquired and who the beneficiaries will be, as well as disagreements about the workability of what seems an obvious, well-tried strategy. But, whatever one's view of agrarian reform as a component in reducing unemployment, the obstacle has not, in this case, been the World Bank and global capital. The choice was, and remains, South Africa's. The bitter, still unresolved debate over this issue illustrates the importance not just of interests and power, but also of ideology and mindsets, and the deep disagreements, and uncertainties, on all sides, about how to tackle these difficult, basic problems.

No individual or group has a solution; indeed, there is no single, final solution. Learning from history, instead of repeating past blunders, and trying to understand and explain historical grievances and fears, instead of stirring them up, will help to avoid the Zimbabwean route.

POLICY OPTIONS

Redress for poor blacks (the vast majority) seems fairly straightforward—which is not to say easy. It requires labor-intensive economic growth, reinforced by social safety nets, education and health services, and rural and urban infrastructure (housing, clean water), with financing provided by taxes on richer citizens and, hopefully, from economic growth.

Redress for the emerging middle-upper class blacks is more complex because the evolution of these classes is usually gradual and incremental, as they build up their skills, know-how and capital. In South Africa, this process was deliberately blocked by apartheid until the 1970s. The aspiring members of these classes are now both impatient and politically mobilized.

A class-based policy, reinforced by elements of affirmative action—in education, promotion of small-medium (rural and urban) enterprises—would, surely, be preferable, on moral, economic and long-term political grounds, to continued support for BEE millionaires and the rapid promotion of inexperienced managers and professionals. Such a strategy would depend on the willingness to adopt enlightened, long-term policies by:

1. The very rich, mainly but no longer only white, who would need to pay higher taxes and facilitate some redistribution of assets, including land: South Africa's inheritance and capital gains taxes remain low by international standards;
2. Unionized, formal sector workers (African, coloured and white) would need to accept the relaxation of minimum wages, and hiring/firing regulations, essential for the growth of labor-intensive small-medium enterprises and public works programs, if jobs are to be generated on a large scale and the rural influx to urban areas slowed;
3. The black elite would have to be willing to slow the pace of their dash to catch up with whites.

Some argue that South African politics would work better, and its democracy be more firmly consolidated, if the Tripartite Alliance split, leading to more class-based political divisions, including a non-racial party of the Left that would give priority to the needs of the poor. Gumede and Friedman cite the emergence of growing demonstrations by the landless, unemployed and workers against failures in the delivery of basic services as signs of growing social movements that will provide mass support for a party of the Left. However, apart from their emotional ties and overlapping memberships, Cosatu is constrained from breaking away from ANC by the strong support for the ANC among its large membership. The SACP, with its small membership, depends for its large parliamentary representation on being included in the ANC candidate list (SACP members account for 73 of the ANC's 297 MPs.[19])

Against the argument for a breakaway party of the Left, it is argued that ANC dominance has: provided political stability and "prevented debilitating conflict over policy"; enabled the government to take a long-term view and eschew "short-term populist" economic policies; and that, single-party dominance, while dangerous for democracy, "may help to integrate ethnically diverse societies" (Butler 2005). It could also be argued that it would be good for the political process if the DA split into its libertarian and social democratic wings, which would similarly encourage more class and issue based politics. The counter-argument is that, as politics still functions largely along racial lines, this would merely weaken South Africa's small but vigorous opposition.

Failure to take redistribution seriously and to make the shift towards a more class-based strategy is likely to intensify the risk of mass unrest over lack of jobs, land and services, as well as the drain of scarce skills as the minorities emigrate, worsening South Africa's capacity problems and international competitiveness. The resulting problems would increase the likelihood of the white and black elites blaming each other and engaging in a populist contest for mass support. This would obviously threaten economic growth, political stability and the consolidation of democracy.

However, if this negative spiral is set in train, post-apartheid South Africa would hardly be the first country to choose a self-destructive strategy. The NP came close to making such a choice, and history records at least as many failed as successful states. The historical record also suggests that the expulsion or exodus of skilled minorities may be a factor in economic decline: Muslims and Jews from 15th century Spain, Huguenots from seventeenth-century France and, in the twentieth century, Asians from Uganda;

Lebanese and groups of 'foreign' Africans from various West African states.

To conclude: in its consolidation of democracy South Africa seems, thus far, closer to the successful democratic transitions in Chile, Poland, Ghana, Hungary and Czech Republic than to the dubious cases of "managed democracy" in Russia and Uganda. Accusations of hollowing out democracy should be taken seriously, but centralization and the concentration of power in the executive are hardly special to South Africa. The claim that South Africa has become a "majoritarian tyranny" is not supported by evidence that its government treats individuals and groups tyrannically. Clearly, a policy that made the minorities feel accepted as full citizens, and gave them such credit as they deserve for their contribution to building the country and, later, to ending the apartheid system that disfigured it, would increase their commitment and counter any perverse desires to see their own country become another 'African basket-case.'[20]

Managing this process, and balancing the understandably impatient demands from blacks, and the insecurities of nervous whites, will place tremendous demands on political, business and trade union leadership—and on the researchers and advisors who must provide them with the honest, reliable information and analysis required for intelligent, long-term policy-making

THE CALL TO HISTORIANS TO BE POLITICALLY ENGAGÉ

"In the lecture rooms of the university no other virtue holds but plain intellectual integrity"

—Max Weber

There is an obvious tension between Weber's injunction and the demand of Sartre, Chomsky, and others, that intellectuals must be politically *engagé*. The *debate about South African sanctions* provides an example of the effects of such politicization on scholarly work.

As noted previously (p. xxx), despite claims that economic sanctions delivered the *coup d'grace* to apartheid, there has been little research on their actual impact. Among the reasons for this is the difficulty of assessing the effects of sanctions, including differentiating these effects from factors, such as trends in international trade and capital movements, that also affect the economy of South Africa (or other targeted country). The most rigorous way of measuring the impact of sanctions is by using a General Equilibrium Model (GEM), which tracks both the direct effects of specific sanctions and their ripple effects throughout the economy. A GEM was available for South Africa, but was used by few researchers. Moreover, surprisingly little attention was paid to their findings, or to the few rigorous case-studies of the impact of sanctions on specific economic sectors.[21]

Whether the reason for this lack of interest was that participants in the debate did not like the findings of these studies, or were uninterested in the actual effects of sanctions, these studies confirmed the well-known lessons from earlier cases: viz, that the targeted country does not respond passively, but engages in sanctions-busting and actively searches for substitutes for sanctioned products.

These studies also confirmed that sanctions frequently have unintended, sometimes perverse, effects. These were evident in South Africa's vigorous response to trade sanctions, which resulted in an *increase* in its exports (see p. 93). The widespread belief that financial sanctions were more effective may be true, but has not yet been established. Such an analysis will need to differentiate their effects from those of "normal" market forces, such as the flight of foreign capital in reaction to the mid-1980s domestic unrest and to Botha's disastrous Rubicon speech and intensified regional destabilization policy. This research will also need to take account of the fact that the limited sanctions on South Africa were only imposed for a few years and that, despite being under sanctions, South Africa was more successful than many other countries in reducing its foreign debt. This is not to dismiss the possible importance of financial sanctions but to note the lack of evidence for sweeping claims about their efficacy.

There has, likewise, been little research on the political effects of South African sanctions. The evidence available is ambiguous and does not bear out claims of widespread support among blacks for sanctions that might damage the economy, particularly their own jobs. Nor does the evidence support claims that sanctions were decisive in persuading whites to abandon apartheid (see p. 93).

In view of the resources allocated to the South African sanctions issue by the UN, individual governments and foundations, and the fact that South Africa remained unusually open to researchers, it is surprising that so little effort was made to study their effects. The reasons for the paucity—and the sidelining—of rigorous research appear to be both political and psychological, and are linked to the unintended effects sanctions can have.

These unintended effects include the "collateral" damage sanctions often inflict on third parties, and the perverse political reactions they often provoke from their targets. The contradictory political effects of sanctions on South Africa, contributing to the white backlashes in the elections of 1966, 1977, 1987, and 1989, were discussed previously (p. 71). Here we shall briefly review the debate about the economic effects of sanctions, which became the subject of intense propaganda warfare.

Sanctioned governments invariably attempt to shift the costs away from themselves and their supporters towards third parties. In South Africa, the debate centered on (i) who was likely to bear the costs of any slowdown in economic growth and (ii) the backwash effects of sanctions on neighboring African countries. Supporters of sanctions argued they were having (or would have) a major impact on the South African economy but would *not* lead to job losses for black workers. Opponents of sanctions produced the mirror image of this contradictory argument, maintaining sanctions would have little effect on the economy but *would* lead to job losses for blacks. Such arguments are exercises in *propaganda warfare, not serious analysis*.

The needs of propaganda also shaped the debate about the impact of sanctions on neighboring African countries. Little rigorous work has been done on this but it seems that South African sanctions led to some gains for neighboring countries, as firms relocated their South African operations to them and they received additional aid. But neighboring countries endured losses when South Africa retaliated against them for their alleged support for sanctions and/or the armed struggle. However, the huge, ever-growing estimates of the costs inflicted by South Africa on its neighbors aroused skepticism. More sober, evidence-based estimates would have made it clearer what was happening, and provided a better guide for policy-makers on how to avoid actions that might lead to damaging South African retaliation, or take appropriate measures to protect them. But the issue became too politically polarized to permit a reasoned, evidence-based debate. If economic sanctions had been imposed for more than a few years, their adverse effects on neighboring countries would probably have been even worse.

An overlooked aspect of sanctions is their effect on long-term economic and political developments. If sanctions and isolation are in place for long—as in Iraq, USSR, Burma, North Korea, Cuba and Iran—they are likely to cause structural shifts in the economy, and also political changes, such as increased authoritarianism, justified by national security imperatives.[22] In South Africa, the mere threat of sanctions led the NP to take pre-emptive measures, setting up huge import-substitution industries for armaments, oil, diesel engines and computers. The costs of these economic distortions might well be preferable to the alternative of military conflict, but these long-term economic and political effects need to be recognized.

Sanctions cannot, of course, be measured solely in terms of their effects on erring governments. They serve symbolic purposes, as a signal of international values and norms. Sanctions campaigns can also, as Archbishop Tutu argued, provide a political alternative for activists who might otherwise resort to violence. These considerations need to be given due weight. But this does not absolve analysts from keeping their thinking straight about the effects of sanctions, rather than acting as cheerleaders for, or against, them.

Finally, analysts need to be aware of the multiple interests generated by sanctions campaigns, which usually take on a life of their own, serving not only as symbols of great moral issues, but generating lobbies that can lose sight of the main aim of changing the political behavior of the targeted country. Thus, the anti-apartheid campaign was not only a symbol of antiracism and anticolonialism; it became involved with the political agendas of foreign governments and NGOs. In Africa, North America, Europe and Australia, governments and NGOs claimed: "We ended apartheid: we did it with our sanctions." In the United States, the 1986 Anti-Apartheid Act was identified as the key event, not only by activists such as Randall Robinson of Transafrica, but also by academic analysts. Similar claims were made in other countries, with people pointing to their official sanctions, unofficial boycotts and demos as key turning points. Churches, trade unions, and universities identified their particular actions as crucial in securing the demise of apartheid and were eager that the key role of Denmark, Canada, the United States, and various NGOS be recorded. [23]

These activities might well be a justifiable source of satisfaction for those involved, but the claims arising from them cannot be accepted at face value by analysts. International solidarity with the opposition in 1930s Spain and, more recently, in Tibet and Burma, did not secure their aims. The job of analysts is to seek to understand the actual impact of these activities on the course of events, not to be swept along by the claims of the numerous agents involved in these campaigns, who are partly driven by their own interests and agendas.

Notwithstanding the sweeping, unsubstantiated claims about the success of South African sanctions, lessons about the risks and complications of sanctions have been learned and, following a period of increasing resort to sanctions worldwide, especially by the United States, there is growing concern about their unintended effects. This had led to rethinking about the utility, and ethics, particularly of comprehensive sanctions. These doubts are not based solely on the long-held skepticism about the efficacy of sanctions,[24] but also on the argument that they are not a benign, "velvet glove" alternative to war.

Cortwright and Lopez (1995, 102–3) argue that economic sanctions need to be recognized as a form of warfare and one that, in the case of comprehensive sanctions, aims directly at inflicting damage on civilians. They also point out that the aim of "bringing to its knees" the targeted economy is likely to affect most severely those outside governing circles, as rulers have more capacity to shield themselves and their supporters, while shifting the costs to others. These ethical conundrums do not mean economic sanctions should not be used. It means their consequences should be recognized; their costs, benefits and risks weighed; and preemptive measures considered, so that informed decisions can be taken about imposing them.

The unrigorous, cursory nature of the debate about South African sanctions needs to be recognized by those who wish to understand their impact on South Africa, and to draw lessons for their application elsewhere; so does the fact that economic sanctions against South Africa were not really put to the test, as few were applied, and these for only a brief period.[25] Bearing these qualifications in mind, the South African case suggests that:

1. Sanctions can help to establish international rules and norms and send a warning message to regimes breaching these.

2. It is useful to deploy carrots and sticks: isolation by some, constructive engagement by others; quiet diplomacy alongside public denunciation. But this combination is difficult, as both engagers and threateners need to be convincing, and this often leads to misunderstanding and recriminations between them.
3. The difficulty of anticipating and assessing the effects of sanctions requires the imposers to watch for, and react flexibly to, unintended, negative, effects.
4. South Africa's receptivity to external influences (including, but not only, sanctions) was enhanced by the presence of reformers within the ruling elite, and the close interaction of outsiders with a wide variety of domestic groups favoring (moderate or radical) reform both within and outside the oligarchy.

In the present stage of our knowledge, conclusions about South African sanctions remain ambiguous; but the Southern African region offers some clearer, though little noticed, lessons about sanctions: those threatened or imposed by South Africa on Lesotho and Rhodesia, two small, landlocked countries, adjacent to, and heavily dependent on, South Africa. These cases confirm that sanctions are most likely to be effective when imposed by relatively large, strong states on smaller, weaker and, especially, dependent states. These contrasting cases suggest that each case of sanctions is different, and that account must be taken of the specific economic and political conditions of the target country, and of its neighbors, who play a crucial role both in implementing—and evading—sanctions, and in experiencing their effects.

The propaganda warfare that invariably accompanies sanctions underlines *the need to separate research from advocacy*. If the international community is to have a better basis for policy-making, research departments in the UN and elsewhere charged with assessing their economic and political effects, and monitoring their implementation, need to be independent of governments and lobbyists. Their role should be to analyse and set out the policy options as impartially as possible.

The consequences of failure to do this are evident in the current cases of Iraq and climate change. On the latter, experts testifying before the U.S. Congress confirmed that they were not only pressured to produce evidence supporting the policies of the Bush administration, but that they themselves began, often unconsciously, to shift their analyses in anticipation of these pressures. As Rick Plitz of the US Climate Change Science program explained: "A kind of anticipatory self-censorship sets in" (*Guardian* (London), January 31, 2007).

In the case of South Africa, if the neo-Marxist revisionist model of a non-reforming—indeed unreformable—South Africa had prevailed, the imposition of comprehensive sanctions and intensified revolutionary activity might well have been attempted. The likely consequences would have been a devastating civil war, possibly ending in partition, as well as even greater destruction of neighboring countries. South Africa's negotiated settlement was imperfect but, surely, preferable to war, especially as it established rules and procedures for securing further non-violent changes.

A rigorous, evenhanded approach does not require historians and social scientists to be neutral. But politically driven accounts mislead policy-makers, while simplified, Manichean world views lead to disillusionment and despair when the romanticized challengers acquire power and behave in ways distressingly similar to their predecessors. *Being engagé is not enough*—indeed, it often serves as an obstacle to the reliable information and straight thinking that will better serve the long-term interests of individual countries, and the international community, than propaganda warfare, however well-intentioned.

The Role of Historians in Post-Apartheid South Africa

To conclude, by returning to our starting-point: what does this study suggest about the possibility, and social relevance, of historical truth? All social scientists have the problem of distinguishing "facts" from interpretation, and of developing awareness of the influence on their work of their ideologies and values, as well as their professional and personal interests, ties, and emotions. Historians have the added difficulty that, while many propositions of history are falsifiable—in this sense it is scientific—these propositions cannot be proved, because they cannot be replicated and tested. Nevertheless, examining our historical evolution at different times, places and circumstances—and drawing on the increasing knowledge and insights provided by biology, neuroscience, and psychology—historians can eliminate some hypotheses and propose alternatives, based on the discernment of regularities, patterns and analogies.

This still leaves wide areas of uncertainty, and this increases the temptation to resort to extreme relativism, which provides an easy rationalization for those with a weak case—"my interpretation is as good as anyone else's." But, as Carr (1961, 21) put it: "It does not follow that, because a mountain takes on different shapes from different angles, it has no shape at all, or an infinity of shapes." Postmodernists have highlighted the inevitably partial, biased, and simplified nature of our representations of social reality. But the limits of their extreme relativism have been incisively exposed by, among others, Richard Evans (1997), particularly in the case of the holocaust deniers.

The fact that we lack absolutely certain grounds for our interpretations does not mean there are no standards for evaluating them. A valuable tool is the falsifiability principle of Popper (1959): that the test of whether an interpretation is plausible is that it is, in principle, testable; that it has not yet been falsified; and that, if subsequently contradicted by evidence or logic, it will be rejected. The respect of historians for the truth is demonstrated by their willingness to amend beliefs that conflict with the evidence, or are internally illogical, and to recognize the strengths of those they disagree with and the weaknesses of those with whom they sympathize.

But we have to accept that final, definitive versions of the past are not possible, and that history will remain in a continuous process of revision. Rather than encouraging illusory beliefs in definitive versions, historians should make their readers and students aware of *the inevitability of a range of interpretations*, some of which come closer to the truth than others because, inter alia, they are supported by evidence and reason and pass the falsifiability test. In situations of extreme political polarization, historians are at increased risk of being swayed by calls to show solidarity with good causes, and by their own ideological, emotional and instrumental desires to do so. Being self-aware and open about our ideological and political commitments helps to counter their distorting effects upon our work. The danger signal is not so much having links with particular organizations, as being concerned to avoid interpretations they dislike. Similarly, the need for greater self-awareness about the temptations and inhibitions of professional and personal links, whether related to career prospects or to keeping in with—or distancing oneself from—particular individuals, coteries or 'schools.'

Yet, despite the intensity of these problems in South Africa, this study shows *an expanding area of agreement about facts and trends even among those who strain to obscure this and to differentiate themselves from others.* The reintroduction of academic niceties such as refraining from boastful, self-referential cronyism (encouraged by misuse of the Citation Index) and behaving in a collegial, evenhanded way in acknowledgements and referencing, would help to expand these areas of consensus. It would also encourage an approach that seeks to understand and explain rather than blame and moralize. The argument that it is sometimes justified, for political reasons, to simplify, obfuscate, and adopt extreme positions merely perpetuates the distortions and misunderstandings that fuel the cynicism of a more educated public about the manipulation of information, not only by advertisers and politicians, but also by the media and academics.

Society supports academics with scarce resources, and the privilege of academic freedom and autonomy, in the expectation that (as with the judiciary) this will enable them to pursue the truth as impartially as possible. Historians cannot do this unless they strive, in their professional work, to distance themselves from their political, ideological and personal interests and preferences. Indulging these undermines their independence and capacity to think straight. It also militates against their distinctive task, which is to strive for a detached, long-term perspective that not only illuminates the evolution of particular societies and periods, but does so in a context that addresses the universal questions of who and what we are and how human societies have evolved in such varied forms.

Striving for a detached, evenhanded approach is likely to produce more sober, balanced accounts of our past evolution and deflate utopian expectations that end in disillusionment, cynicism and despair. Rather than indulging in manipulative, politicized analyses, historians should accept as sufficient the responsibility laid on intellectuals by de Tocqueville that their ideas "form an atmosphere breathed in by governors and governed . . . from which both unwittingly derive the principles of their actions." Chekhov predicted that "man will become better when he knows himself better." It is the calling of historians to contribute to this knowledge—no more, but no less either.

Appendices to Chapter 3

Appendix 1 responds in more detail to some challenges to the liberal analysis.
Appendix 2 responds to the charge that liberal historians made unacknowledged use of the research of the neo-Marxist revisionists.

Appendix 1: A More Detailed Response to Some Challenges to the Liberal Analysis

Some challenges to the liberal analysis require a more detailed response than provided in Chapter 3. First, the claim that, until the end, business supported major pillars of apartheid, such as influx control, decentralization and Botha's "security state system." Second, theoretical and methodological issues, including the charge that liberals present an overly homogeneous view of business interests.

Deborah Posel was (like Legassick) unusual in engaging directly with her liberal contemporaries. Posel argued (1991, 14, 258, 267) that, notwithstanding vocal business criticism of the controls over African mobility, in practice, the implementation of influx control was "closely aligned with business interests . . . and the majority of employers in industrial and commercial firms . . . had vested interests in the influx control legislation" which provided them with cheap, docile workers—as shown by the fact that business protests were "out of step with their daily economic behaviour": that is, they continued to use the system by employing workers provided by the official Labor Bureau. Posel maintains that business wanted the adaptation, not abolition, of influx control, and that the liberal critique of NP policy "fails to recognise that satisfying . . . [the needs of business] was one of the principal purposes of the influx control policy of the Native Affairs Department (NAD)."

Posel does not allow for the fact that people usually continue to operate within the confines of legal and politicalsystems they are trying to change. Employers were obliged to secure labor via the official channels: penalties were imposed on employers and employees who tried to bypass the system.[1] Posel is also mistaken in believing that liberals did not realize it was NAD's intention to provide a smooth supply of labor for industry. They understood this very well but rejected NAD's plan as unworkable and as denying freedom of choice. The experience of South African employers bore out the liberal argument that the allocation of labor by bureaucrats, rather than markets, is invariably inefficient, costly and oppressive: hence their growing pressures against it.

Posel does not provide evidence to support her contention that—notwithstanding the growing calls by business for the relaxation, and then the abolition of, influx control—the majority of urban employers 'really' wanted to retain them, with minor adjustments. Without such evidence, it is unjustified to focus on a minority of cases (which should certainly be noted) while ignoring the well-documented evidence of the increasingly vocal pressures from business to end the controls.

Similarly, the claim by Terreblanche (1997, 13) and others that business "enthusiastically" supported and made "huge profits" from the separate development policy is not supported by the evidence. There were some cases, mostly of Afrikaner and foreign (particularly Taiwanese) capital, induced by large state subsidies to decentralize their factories to the Bantustans. The existence of this minority is noteworthy; but this does not justify ignoring the opposition of the majority! The 1967 Physical Planning Act was introduced precisely because business would not decentralize voluntarily.

In opposing the Physical Planning Act, Oppenheimer argued that it was economically unviable to decentralize labor-intensive manufacturing to the Bantustans and that 'separate development' would never be politically acceptable to blacks. His stance was supported by Assocom and FCI, who urged that the allocation of capital and labor be left to the market, rather than to government direction and that South Africa's economy should not be fragmented by setting up independent Bantustans. Trevor Bell's study of *Industrial Decentralisation in South Africa* showed that most businessmen refused to decentralize and that the policy failed.[2]

The NP was angered by business opposition to this crucial economic pillar of separate development. Oppenheimer was denounced as unpatriotic, and the Minister of Planning threatened that, unless he cooperated in implementing the policy, "[t] he government will approach his requests for African labour differently from [those of other companies].... Each Oppenheimer application ... will be closely scrutinised. I will not allow Oppenheimer and the Progressive Party to destroy our policy" (Lipton 1985, 34, 154). Leading Afrikaans businessman Andries Wassenaar confirms in his book, *The Assault on Private Enterprise* (1977), that the NP set up state corporations as "a bulwark against the Anglo American Corporation."

Initially the Afrikaanse Handelsinstituut (AHI) supported decentralization. But as the policy was enforced and its costs became clear, the AHI joined English business in opposing its economic (though not initially its political) aspects. What the revisionists did not understand was that the Physical Planning Act was not a paper tiger. The NP made serious efforts to enforce its aims of reducing African numbers and keeping them out of skilled jobs in 'white' areas—as was confirmed by the official 1958 Viljoen Commission, the 1971 White Paper on decentralization, and numerous official statements. The 1979 Riekert Commission expressed alarm at the adverse impact of this policy on economic growth and urged repeal of the decentralization sections of the Physical Planning Act (Lipton 1985, 77). The NP only retreated from this policy after an intense struggle with business.

When some revisionists came to accept, tacitly, that business did not support the economic aspects of separate development, they shifted their argument to its *political dimensions*, particularly business attitudes toward the Bantustans and the Tricameral Constitution. These measures raised the dilemma of the "ethnic trap:" whether to use their unintended, double-edged possibilities as ways of undermining apartheid.

As discussed (in chapter 4), the ANC was among those who occasionally supported using these possibilities. But this question became very polarized over the 1983 Tricameral Constitution, which set up separate representative councils for coloureds and Indians within a constitutional system loaded in favor of whites and, initially, still excluding Africans. The Tricameral precipitated the formation in August 1983 of the United Democratic Front (UDF), which became the most effective mass movement in South African history.

The UDF argued that establishing new political institutions along racial lines would set politics in a mold that entrenched the NP's divide-and-rule policy. This assessment was shared by the Progressive Party and by businessmen, like Oppenheimer and Tony Bloom, all of whom opposed the Tricameral. However, the Tricameral received qualified support from Assocom and FCI on the grounds that it was "the first step" toward granting representation in the central parliament to coloureds and Indians, particularly after the NP accepted the principle that Africans too should be included[3]. Assocom combined this qualified support with a statement calling, in 1983, for "a common citizenship and labour mobility" for all South Africans, including Africans, while the FCI's Business Charter called for legal equality and universal suffrage.[4] They were thus applying to the extension of political rights the piecemeal, incremental strategy that was eroding socioeconomic apartheid and opening up political space in South Africa. This does not mean their assessment was correct. But it suggests that their record, including their 1983 statements of political principle, supports their claim that they viewed the Tricameral as a first step toward establishing common (rather than separate ethnic) political institutions.

The final position to which the revisionists retreated in claiming that capitalism and apartheid were inextricably linked was their argument that there was *"an effective political alliance between business and the military"* in planning and implementing Botha's Total Strategy and its associated "security state system." The latter referred to the State Security Council and network of regional and local branches of the National Security Management System (NSMS), to which Botha began to shift political power.[5] The State Security Council became important, but the NSMS was only activated in 1986, when Botha's securocrats were given increased powers not only over security but also over the delivery of essential services, such as water and electricity, which the NP planned to direct toward its potential black allies.

The evidence of business support for this system rests on claims that: during the mid-1980s unrest, "capital supported crackdowns" against activists and protestors; some businesspeople sat on the committees attempting to deliver more effective services to the black townships; business was involved in South Africa's defense industries; business support for reform was prompted by, and remained an integral part of, Botha's counter-revolutionary strategy to strengthen the apartheid regime against its domestic and external challengers.

In assessing business attitudes toward the unrest, particularly the uprisings of the mid-1980s, a distinction needs to be drawn between concerns about the general maintenance of law and order and support for the State Security System used by Botha and his coterie, not only against their anti-apartheid challengers but also to sideline their rivals within the NP, such as Connie Mulder (Botha's rival for the NP leadership) and van den Berghe (head of Vorster's Bureau of State Security). Business was not much interested in NP infighting, but it was concerned with order and security. The assumption of the revisionists that business believed the NP was the only guarantor of order and that a black government would be unable or unwilling to provide this is discussed in chapter 3.

Business concern about the delivery of more effective services to black 'townships' was neither new nor an indication that they shared the NP's aim of using this to buy black political allies. The delivery of services concerns all citizens, including employers, under any government, and business had already set up the well-financed Urban Foundation in 1976 as part of a private initiative to improve the appalling services and housing in black urban areas.

South Africa's defense industries were mainly in the state sector grouped around Armscor, which subcontracted to private companies. These were mostly Afrikaans but, during the 1980s, the NP attempted to draw in English capital and succeeded in the case of Barlow Rand and Anglo-Vaal. However, most English (and foreign) firms did not follow suit.

Companies in the arms business are usually motivated more by profit than by ideology, as can be seen from their propensity to sell to all sides if they can. This morally reprehensible practice is not special to the private sector. Since 1994, South African arms sales have become one of its largest manufacturing exports and were, reportedly, sold to all sides in Sudan, Angola, and DRC—conduct hardly unusual among arms manufacturers and traders (Barber 2004, 105). The justified exposure and criticism of (private or state) arms traders should not be confused with analysis of their aims, which are not necessarily to advance any ideology or prop up any regime but to make money.

More pertinently, the maintenance of the apartheid regime did not rest solely, or even primarily, on arms but depended on many industries, such as iron and steel, transport, agriculture and the payment by citizens of their taxes. This is reflected in the revisionists' question as to why, if business wanted to end apartheid, they did not stop paying their taxes. But this question could equally be asked of workers in the defense, mining and transport industries who could bring the economy and administration to a halt by staging a general strike. That they did not do so is hardly evidence that they favored the survival of the apartheid regime. This raises, yet again, the issue of the revisionists' underlying behavioral assumptions: how they think business, workers and 'ordinary' citizens usually behave under authoritarian regimes whose policies they oppose (discussed in Chapter 5).

It is unclear what the NSMS reveals about the interests of business and about South Africa's political economy dynamics. Apart from the aims of centralizing control over all aspects of security, and attempting to manipulate the delivery of services for political purposes, the NSMS seemed mainly related to internal NP struggles, fitting into the category of kremlinological infighting within the political/bureaucratic elite to which most revisionists mistakenly attributed the (truly significant) verligte-verkrampte dispute.

The most systematic attempt to explore the functioning of the NSMS was made by Chris Alden (1996, 258) who pointed out that it was activated very late, only in 1986, and concluded that it explained little about South Africa's political economy dynamics.[6] Alden also pointed to considerable hostility toward the NSMS within the NP itself. Senior cabinet minister, Chris Heunis, complained: "it is not the [role] . . . of the security forces to take over state activities." The shallow roots and narrow support base of the NSMS seem confirmed by the rapidity and ease with which it was shut down by Botha's successor, de Klerk, who was not a member of the inner securocrat circle.

Thus far, little evidence has been produced to support the claim of "a political alliance between business and the military" and of business support for a Pinochet-style military dictatorship. Even before business protests at the arrests and detentions in 1985–86, English business organizations protested against "the sweeping . . . and arbitrary" powers for ministers, including detention of trade unionists and exclusion of the right of appeal to the courts (see p. 60f).

Despite the continual, bitter clashes between the NP and business, revisionists persisted in bracketing them together. But they had different agendas, which overlapped in some respects but not in others.[7] The evidence does not support revisionist claims that, because business supported genuine reforms such as the abolition of controls over mobility—which the ANC itself called for—they must therefore have supported Botha's "Total Strategy" and "security state system." This claim is called into question by business attacks on apartheid over some decades; by their growing calls for a new political dispensation; and by their active support for constitutional negotiations rather than a deracialized military dictatorship.

Yet, the belief that business supported apartheid until the bitter end remains widespread, both in the scholarly literature and in public discourse. This was evident at the TRC hearings, where Terreblanche and others reiterated the early, hard-line neo-Marxist argument about business support for apartheid (see p. 53).[8] As Antjie Krogh noted (1998, 240), at the TRC's Business Sector Hearing, "the tone was set" by Terreblanche's testimony, and the TRC's official Findings (4:58–59) reiterated Terreblanche's claim that business supported Botha's Total Strategy and opposed black trade unions, while making no reference to the role of business in pressing for reform. Among the many who 'reproduce' this myth are Asmal et al. who, in their widely cited study of *Reconciliation Through Truth* (1997, 69, 120f., 135, 179), claim that business never protested against apartheid; that Oppenheimer "never subscribed to the view that apartheid was morally wrong"; and that business and the Progressive Party were "co-responsible" with Botha for destabilizing neighboring African countries.

THEORETICAL AND METHODOLOGICAL ISSUES

William Freund charges liberals with having an overly homogeneous view of business, arguing that there must have been subgroups that continued to benefit from, and support, apartheid. In particular, Freund (1987) argues that my book, *Capitalism & Apartheid*, relied too heavily on public statements by businessmen and their organizations. Kenneth Hughes (in correspondence with me) drew attention to the related problem of collective action: the difficulty of mobilizing numerous and competing businesses for effective political action.

These issues about the *diversity of business interests and difficulties of collective action* are central to any analysis of the business role.

However, the liberal analysis was not solely based on the public statements of businessmen and their organizations. Bell, Schlemmer, myself, and others conducted intensive fieldwork during the 1970s and early 1980s in mines, factories, and offices throughout South Africa. This fieldwork provided evidence of the ferment on the shop floor, as employers pressured white workers to agree to black job advance and training, and to accept changes in the occupational structure, that were often taking place ahead of changes in the law. The existence of these trends was confirmed, not only in interviews with black and white workers and their unions, but also with officials in the Departments of Economics, Planning and Labor, including the regional Labor Bureau. Some of these officials were conniving at, and attempting to manage, what they viewed as an inevitable process of black advance. But, whether or not they favored this advance, they confirmed the existence of growing pressures from employers for these and other reforms.

This process remained politically sensitive until the 1979 amendment to the Industrial Conciliation Act. And it became sensitive again after the 1982 verkrampte backlash, which ended in the breakaway from the NP of the Treurnicht's Conservative Party, supported by major white unions (see p. 70f). Hence, while researchers could cite their findings, it was seldom possible to provide details of the workplaces, businessmen and officials involved because of the constraints placed on our observations and interviews, which were usually off-the-record. However, this fieldwork confirmed the public statements of business and informed our analyses of what was happening on the shop floor.

Freund's criticism that *Capitalism & Apartheid* portrays capital as homogeneous is puzzling, because I resorted to the awkward device of analyzing the interests of capital by sector in order to highlight the differences between agricultural capital (compatible with apartheid until the late 1960s, partly because farmers ignored the job bar and employed blacks in skilled jobs), mining capital (which found the job bar costly but supported measures to reduce the cost of unskilled labor until 1973, when the gold price rose), and manufacturing and commercial capital, long opposed to many apartheid policies. But while emphasizing these sectoral differences, I also argued that, from the late 1960s (when there emerged both a shortage of skilled, and surplus of unskilled, labor), there was an increasing convergence of views among employers about the growing costs of apartheid. *Capitalism & Apartheid* also stressed the differences between English and Afrikaans capital, with the latter initially concentrated in agriculture and then, in their growing mining and manufacturing interests, dependent on state support. This analysis does not, surely, portray South African capital as homogeneous.

The difficulties of collective action raised by Hughes are not special to business. As Mancur Olson (1965) showed, collective action is even more difficult for mass organizations like trade unions and political parties, because of the "free rider" problem: the difficulty of securing subscriptions and support from large numbers of people who, even if they benefit from an organization's efforts, try to "free ride" on the subscriptions of signed-up members. Hence, despite intense competition within business, collective action is often less difficult for them, especially in sectors dominated by a few large businesses—as was the case in much of the South African private sector. In addition, these pressures from private capital were strengthened by growing opposition to apartheid labor policies from managers in the large state sector, who had more influence over the NP.

Nevertheless, Freund and Hughes are right to highlight the problem of collective action, which is often taken for granted. In South Africa, as elsewhere, the mobilization of business, and others, against apartheid was a difficult, lengthy process. But it was eventually successful, especially after verligte Afrikaners became convinced that apartheid was both unworkable and wrong.

APPENDIX 2: RESPONDING TO ALLEGATIONS OF PROFESSIONAL MISCONDUCT

Hans Erik Stolten (2002) challenged liberals, including myself, to reply to the neo-Marxist allegations about our professional misconduct. I welcome Stolten's action in openly placing on the agenda damaging allegations that circulated widely in academic circles but seldom appeared in print.

The first challenge is that the work of contemporary liberals, particularly my book *Capitalism & Apartheid* (*C&A*), draws heavily on but fails to refer to the work of the neo-Marxist revisionists. This charge is set out concisely by Stanley Greenberg (1987a, 78–82), who writes: "Lipton's work . . . is curiously out of touch with the scholarship on South Africa. . . . She manages not to engage the work of others . . . barely any of the Marxist scholarship of the last decade receives mention. . . . While Lipton seems to engage the Marxist critique of South African capitalism, she does so only through phantom authors and argument . . . [and] vague positions attributed to nobody in particular." Greenberg states that among relevant sources I fail to refer to are radical journals, such as the *South African Labour Bulletin* and *Journal of Southern African Studies*, and his book, *Race & State in Capitalist Development*.

These charges are false: *C&A* contains numerous references to Greenberg (see *C&A* 5, 190, 417, 437, 442, 443, and 445). These references are not confined to footnotes but include discussion of his arguments within the text. Chapter 1 of *C&A* sets out the Blumer/Greenberg argument as one of the four main positions in the debate. Chapter 5 sets out the reasons for rejecting their thesis that capitalists readily adapted to apartheid.

Also incorrect is Greenberg's claim that I did not refer to the work of *non*-Marxist scholars such as Lodge, Giliomee, du Toit, and Yudelman. *C&A* contains references to all except one of these authors (see *C&A* 329, 411, 417, 418, 440, 449, 450, 452, and 456). I did not refer to Yudelman's book, which was published in 1984—after *C&A* had been sent to the press.

Greenberg also charges that, apart from my failure to cite these major secondary works, I make little use of primary sources except for confidential, unattributed interviews: "Lipton's analysis depends for its interpretation of recent events on interviews. . . . Yet nowhere does she indicate anything about these interviews: how many, with whom, or their structural positions. . . . [The fact that] these interviews were off-the-record and unattributable is no excuse for her indifference to standards of evidence."

C&A contains over one thousand citations of sources to the text and tables. Thirty of these—less than 3 percent—refer to my interviews; and many interviewees are identified by their names or positions. However, these interviews were conducted during a tense political period when books were banned, critical researchers harassed, and many found it prudent to leave South Africa. The resulting constraint on revealing the identity of interviewees was later attested to by Greenberg himself (1987b, xiii) when he wrote: "To ensure the anonymity of those interviewed . . . I have been purposely vague . . . and not given the dates of interviews . . . to cover my tracks." Quite so!

The footnotes also confirm that *C&A* was heavily based on primary sources, including official statistics, commission reports, parliamentary debates, published and unpublished reports and memoranda of organizations of employers, workers, NGOs, and the media. Secondary sources included a wide range of earlier and contemporary scholars, including the scholars and journals that Greenberg—inexplicably—claims I do not refer to.

Despite the readily refutable nature of the allegations by Greenberg and others, the mud has stuck. This is evident in the credibility given to them by respected radical scholars such as Freund and Stolten, who grind no personal axes and strive to rise above partisanship. Thus Stolten (2002) recorded the widely repeated allegation that "among the work of Marxists whom Lipton strives to avoid is Dan O'Meara, of whose well known work Lipton was apparently not aware [though she] kept building on his well-founded research."

C&A refers to O'Meara on pages 268, 370, 438, 449, and 458. And these references are not confined to footnotes: on page 370 it is stated: "O'Meara is one of the few Marxists who confronted the problem of Afrikaner nationalism treating it, like white racism, as functional for the interests of capital."

Likewise, Freund (in an otherwise constructively challenging review) is presumably influenced by these allegations when he regrets that *C&A* does not refer to the work of Bozzoli—to whom there are references on pages 161, 435, 438, and 449. Freund also chides me for not referring to books published in 1983, 1984 and 1985 and even to a book that was forthcoming! Freund regrets (1987, 84f.): "It is peculiar that Lipton does not engage with more recent writers [and] . . . fails to point out the significance within South Africa's intellectual history of the 1970s revisionist work . . . which produced material on which Lipton and others can stand and more forward. 1970s revisionism need not be rejected but rather used critically."

These accusations, reiterated by Saunders and numerous others, are false. As shown in Chapter 3 of this book, liberals responded directly and quickly to the neo-Marxist revisionists. It was they who conducted the written debate as though we did not exist, while their verbal denunciations on university campuses—occasionally surfacing in publications such as those by Greenberg, Freund, Saunders, and Stolten—reveal their keen awareness of our work. Often, it is unclear whether we are accused of failing to read their work; of using it without attribution; or of disagreeing with and challenging it.

People are prone to suspect others of sins they are themselves inclined to. An examination of the work of Greenberg, O'Meara, Mike Morris, and others who made similar accusations suggests that it is indeed they who seem to be "striving to avoid" references to the liberals, including my work, which has been the main target of their attacks.

In his early work, Greenberg (1980) was a leading exponent of the thesis that apartheid was compatible with capitalist economic growth. He later confirmed (1987a, xv) that it was his aim: "to demonstrate that economic growth in divided societies, such as South Africa . . . would exacerbate racial and ethnic tensions, not, as conventionally supposed, supersede them." Greenberg's later work retains elements of this initial thesis but gradually shifts toward stressing the unworkability of the labor control system and the growing conflicts between business and the NP (1987b, 77, 86f., 161–69). This aspect of Greenberg's analysis is strikingly similar to the arguments about the opposition of business to the Physical Planning Act and the role of the labor control bureaucracy in Bell (1973) and Lipton (1974b; 1979; 1980; 1985), including our pattern of interviewing officials in both the official Labor Bureau and private mining company recruitment agencies. Despite this shift, there is no reference to Bell or Lipton in Greenberg's later publications. Instead, his influential 1987 review denigrated my research and damaged my reputation by accusing me of plagiarism!

This pattern of shifting from the revisionist to the liberal interpretation (without any acknowledgment) is even more marked in O'Meara. As suggested by the title of his later book, *Forty Years Lost*, O'Meara (37) came to view the NP's 1948 victory as having: "set South Africa on a very different course" (37). This contrasts with his earlier emphasis on the "common ground" between the policies of the pre-1948 UP and NP (1983, 235; 1975, 150f.). There is a similar shift in O'Meara's analysis (1996, 175f.) of the 1960s, with his recognition that, during this period, there were "regular demands from big business for the easing of apartheid restrictions [although] . . . they were unsuccessful in their pleas." He lists the Physical Planning Act and job bars (much emphasized in *C&A*) as "particularly criticised by all elements of organised business."

O'Meara's recognition of these early business pressures for reform led, logically, to the abandonment of his earlier insistence that business pressures for reform "only began in 1979," and then only as part of a last-ditch business-military strategy to salvage the apartheid regime. O'Meara's new account of the post-1970 period closely mirrors the analysis of *C&A* (1996, 101, 188, 195). Examples include: how the growing protests by Assocom and FCI led to clashes with Vorster who, O'Meara now writes (1996, 195f.), "lashed out at those demanding coherent, effective reform . . . and denounced the Assocom memorandum proposing a programme of reform. . . . By 1977, it was strikingly clear that capital's demand for purposeful, effective reforms would never be met by the Vorster government."

In contrast to O'Meara's earlier claim that Botha's Total Strategy was "vigorously," "strongly," and "crucial[ly]" supported by, respectively, Assocom, FCI and Oppenheimer (Davies, O'Meara, and Dlamini 1984, 65, 69, 108, 111), O'Meara's later version (1996, 331f.) recognizes business alarm at Botha's domestic repression and his aggressive policies toward neighboring African states, and the deteriorating relations between business and Botha. Ditto, O'Meara's newly awakened recognition of the rising economic costs of apartheid (due to skill shortages, limited domestic market, etc.) and of the "improved productivity" cases for raising wages and for recognising trade unions which, he now writes, can provide business with: "an institutionalised form of collective bargaining and reduced industrial conflict" (1996, 172, 186, 309, 331f.).

O'Meara's later work also identifies white trade unions and the bureaucracy—rather than capital—as the main supports for apartheid, and recognizes that Afrikaans business was "more circumspect" in criticizing the NP than English business, of whom O'Meara even uses my much derided term, "progressive capital," as he does my reference to the NP's 'Afrikaner's First' policy (1996, 331).

Despite this striking shift toward the analysis of *C&A*, there is only one (derogatory) reference to it in *Forty Years Lost* (in a footnote on page 422 of the Appendix) and no reference at all in his other work to Bromberger, Bell or Lipton, although his denunciations of our work at university seminars confirm his keen awareness of it. Yet it is we who are accused of "quietly shifting" toward the analysis of O'Meara and other revisionists while "striving to avoid" any references to them!

The shift in the analysis of some revisionists shows a commendable respect for the evidence. What is not commendable is the way they are doing this, usually without acknowledgement and, instead, with continued denigration of the scholars whose analysis they are increasingly coming to share. Example include O'Meara's continued insistence that liberals treat Afrikaners "as a breed apart;" that they depict "the apartheid state as driven simply by Afrikaner nationalist ideology;" and that he alone has "grappled with [basic issues] on which virtually all the then existing analyses of Afrikaner nationalism were silent" (1996, 10, 11, 427).

The resulting confusion and obfuscation presumably explains why many of those who continue to cite O'Meara (the most widely-cited revisionist on the post-1948 period) do not appear to have noticed the transformation of his analysis but continue to repeat his earlier thesis of "the effective alliance between capital and the military" and his late dating of the emergence of business pressures for "reform."

Recently, frontal attacks on liberal and other historians have declined. But the sidelining and airbrushing of them from the historiography continues—as do the revisionist claims that they "transformed" South African history. This is evident in the complacent comment of Worden (1994, 1f.) that a couple of decades later "some of the dogmatism of the early revisionists has been tempered" alongside his reiteration of the claim that they "transformed our understanding of the South African past; [the impact of our] revolution" remains decisive.

This pervasive tendency remains evident in the recently published *South Africa's 1940s* (2005), edited by Dubow and Jeeves. This book heralds a welcome shift toward recognizing the significance of the wartime reforms. But the claim (248) that it provides "new perspectives" and "evidence of . . . the more diverse . . . possibilities than the summary accounts which see the 1940s as leading [straight to] apartheid" is unaccompanied by any recognition of the longstanding liberal interpretations of this period, which did precisely that. Instead, in an Afterword to the book, Shula Marks writes (278) that O'Meara's *Forty Years Lost* "was surely correct in arguing that the 1948 election set South Africa on a course very different from the one it could have taken, had the Smuts government clung to power." Moreover, while there are approving references to Marquard and Roux, the former is described (11) as "from the political Left" and the latter as "an independent-minded Marxist." If this insistent, indeed obsessive, political categorization of scholars continues, it should be noted that Marquard and Roux were founder members of the Liberal Party and that Roux broke from the Communist Party in 1936 (in protest against its Stalinist conduct) before publication of his acclaimed book, *Time Longer than Rope*.

The examples cited previously are not exhaustive. There are other cases of sidelining and misrepresentation, *inter alia*, on agrarian history, where the "excluded intellectuals" (on this term, see p. 132) are, again, not only liberals but often 'nationalist' historians and social scientists, as well as scholars who do not fit readily into the rigid ideological categories in which this debate continues to be cast. Historians will hardly inspire confidence in their capacity to unravel the distant, poorly documented past when they give such questionable, contentious accounts of the historiography of the recent, well-documented record of their own profession.

Notes

Chapter 1

1. These conflicting interpretations were largely along Marxist-Liberal lines but, as discussed later, there were dissenting voices within both camps, as well as challenges to the neo-Marxists' distinctive version of Marxism.

Chapter 2

1. This book focuses on a selection of the work that neo-Marxists themselves identified as challenging "the conventional liberal version" and forming the basis for their own transformation of SA history. I do not attempt to assess their work on other areas, such as African kingdoms during the precolonial and colonial periods, or gender.
2. On Philip, see Ross 1986 and Babrow 1962.
3. Robertson was conservative rather than liberal in his political views, but the issue is whether earlier historians paid attention to the economic dimensions of apartheid. Those who did so were mainly liberals, but included 'conservatives,' such as Goodfellow (1931, 72f.) who did not question the morality or efficiency of a policy that he recognized was driven by the aim of appropriating black land and labor.
4. Magubane (2002) makes a more justifiable criticism of the *Oxford History*—the editors' decision to exclude from the South African edition Leo Kuper's chapter on "African Nationalism in South Africa" to pre-empt what "legal opinion" advised was likely to be censorship of the whole volume by the SA government.
5. The security fears of whites were real, but their apologists ignored the fact that, when people are deprived of their land, they are likely to retaliate, that is, attempt to recover their lost property!
6. There is no reference to this early liberal challenge in the historiographical surveys by Marks, who writes (1981, 299): "Afrikaner 'nationalist' historians had their counterpart amongst certain English speaking historians whose main concern [was] . . . to defend the actions

of white settlers. . . . More important still in imposing a straitjacket on SA historiography . . . was the intellectual hegemony of the liberal tradition over scholars attempting to present an alternative." Bozzoli (1990, 237) claims that it was revisionists who exposed "the elaborate myths of origin and national progress and redemption, such as the Afrikaner epic of the Great Trek. . . . [and countered the distortions and myths] of official Afrikaner historiography."

7. Following these critiques, Marks (1986, 176) referred to "the need to discriminate between 'liberal' historians of the 1920s and 1930s like MacMillan and de Kiewiet, whose work can still provide inspiration for younger researchers . . . and their successors, writing under the influence of modernisation theory, neo-classical economics, and the Cold War." Marks then recategorized MacMillan as a "radical"—a designation subsequently adopted by Saunders (1988, 131), who added Roux to the list of radicals; by Dubow, who added Burger (Marquard's pseudonym); and by others, including Bozzoli and Delius (1990). Yet MacMillan and de Kiewiet were recognized by all, including initially neo-Marxists, as founders of SA liberal history, while Roux and Burger/Marquard were founder members of the SA Liberal Party.

8. Quotes from Alexander 2002, 20f. and Glaser 2001, ch. 1. Similar endorsements include Saunders 1988, 172ff.; Worden 1994, 67; and Smith 1988, 98f., 175.

9. My early research (Babrow 1962) made much use of van der Merve, whose structuralist analysis differed markedly from the "patriotic" histories of most of his Afrikaner colleagues. The conservative Eric Walker, too, did not allow his sympathy for English settlers to prevent him from amending later editions of his *History of South Africa* (1957) to take account of the new, critical research of MacMillan, Marais, and van der Merve. The issue of how historians handle evidence conflicting with their political loyalties is discussed later.

10. Statement by Anna Steenkamp on the eve of Great Trek in 1836 (Babrow 1962).

11. On this episode, see MacMillan 1929 and Peires 1989.

12. See also Davenport 1966, 113f.

13. This view was also expounded by the nonrevisionist Paul Rich (1984, 1993).

14. On this, see Roux 1948 and Simons 1969.

15. For example, Saunders 1988, 159; and Alexander 2002, 17.

16. According to Rich (1993, 69), Brookes attributed his earlier support for segregation to his sympathy for the Afrikaners in their struggle against the British.

17. Smith 1988, 200; Glaser 2001, 25.

18. Lewsen (1972) records Hoernle's complaint that Cape liberalism was not as color-blind in practice as in theory. Davenport (1966) points to

the social exclusiveness of many Cape liberals. Leo Kuper (1974) regrets the complacent, condescending attitude of some liberals.
19. The quotation comes from Adam Smith's *The Nature and Causes of the Wealth of Nations.*
20. Lodge's account draws on Plaatje's 1930 *Mhudi: an epic of South African native life a hundred years ago* and his *Native Life in South Africa* and Molema's 1920 *The Bantu past and present.* See also B. Willan, *Sol Plaatje: A Biography.* Ravan. 1984.
21. In the Monty Python film, *Life of Brian*, the question is posed about the Roman colonization of Britain: "What did the Romans ever do for us—apart from introducing education, medicine, public health, order, sanitation, irrigation, a fresh water system, and wine?"
22. Another demythologizer is Albert Grundlingh, "Reframing remembrance: Politics of the centenary commemoration of the SA War of 1899–1902," in Stolten 2002.

Chapter 3

1. Davies 1979, 2 and O'Meara 1979, 258f.
2. Saunders (1988, 165, 186f., 195) wrote, "Liberals conspicuously refrained from responding in print to the revisionist challenge. . . . As empiricists [liberals] were unaccustomed to think conceptually [but] when they did learn of the new arguments, they accepted many of them, realising the value of a political economy approach." For similar claims of "liberals quietly taking on board," the new revisionist research, see Worden (1994), Maylam (2001, 178), and Alexander (2002, 25). The phrase "striving to avoid" is from O'Meara (cited in Stolten 2002). These claims are discussed later in the Appendix.
3. Among those Marks (1986) lists as "revolutionising the conventional liberal paradigm" are Legassick, Johnstone, Trapido, Wolpe, Bundy, "later joined by" O'Meara, Davies, Kaplan, Morris, Bozzoli, and Keegan.
4. Davies argues that the racial division of labor "accorded with the requirements of capitalist production, which deliberately divided the working class along racial lines and assigned to white labour its privileged place." Greenberg (1980, 386f.) refers to mineowners' "willingness to honor the racial canons . . . [so they] created new and more elaborate institutions of control and repression. . . . and insisted race lines be drawn more sharply, thus dividing the working class and labor market."
5. This analysis is based on Lipton 1980 and 1985, ch. 5. For a somewhat different analysis of state-mining relations, see Yudelman 1984.

6. O'Meara dismissed the demand of the white Mine Workers Union (MWU) for the job bar on the grounds that MWU was "in no sense . . . an organisation fostering its members' interests" (1983, 89f.). Davies et al. (1976) argue that white workers were "dominated by a racist and parliamentary cretinist [sic] ideology, still in the position of a supportative class." (Some might think these "cretins" did rather well for themselves!) Davies also maintains that, "The petty bourgeoisie is not one of the fundamental classes of capitalist social formation and . . . as Poulantzas argued, has nowhere ever been politically dominant and [should be viewed as] . . . the allied and supportive classes of the politically dominant capitalist class" (1979, 336).
7. Wolpe's hypothesis was among the subjects of sharp public exchanges between liberals and neo-Marxists at the 1976 SALDRU conference at the University of Cape Town. Published challenges to Wolpe include Lipton 1977, 82f.; Knight and Lenta 1980; Bromberger and Hughes 1987.
8. By 1970, only 20 percent of black miners were South African. This remained the case until 1973 when, after the rise in the gold price, mine wages rose sharply. The response was dramatic: by 1982, the proportion of black South African miners had increased to almost 60 percent (Lipton 1985, ch. 5 and Table 8).
9. This point was, however, well understood by the Marxist, Giovanni Arrighi (1967), who argued that possession of land increased black bargaining power, while loss of land lowered black opportunity cost and wages.
10. Among many examples of this is the claim by Beinart and Dubow (1995:14) that the retreat from Wolpe's hypothesis was due to Hindson (1987) and Posel (1991) whom, they claim, "detected" that state policy aimed to drive a wedge between African urban 'insiders' and rural migrant 'outsiders.' However, the detection of this strategy, and the terms insiders and outsiders, are due to Francis Wilson (1975), and the concept to even earlier work by Muriel Horrell and Ellen Hellman, in numerous SAIRR publications, on the significant legal distinction between Africans with Section 10 urban rights and those denied these rights.
11. 'Pass laws' or influx controls were serf-like restrictions on the movement of Africans, particularly from rural to urban areas.
12. This account of reformist trends is based on Lipton 1985, 20–22, 150, 193–94, 272–81. See also Hancock 1968, ch. 27; Ballinger 1969, ch. 9; Paton 1971; Davenport 1977, 238f.; and Lewsen 1987.
13. Roux 1948, ch. 26; Simons 1969, 572f.; and O'Meara 1975.
14. Lipton 1985, 143; and Horwitz 1957, 11. Business criticisms and pressures were recorded by the official 1958 Viljoen Commission.
15. Lipton 1985, 301; and Davis and Fine 1985.

16. The revisionists' recent "reevaluation" of this period is discussed in the Appendix.
17. These concessions included another attempt to erode the mining job bar. This was halted by the white Mine Workers Union, which thereafter supported the HNP (Lipton 1985, 117).
18. This summary is based on Lipton 1985, ch. 2, ch. 3; post-1984 measures are from the Epilogue to the 1986 edition.
19. Among others who subscribed to this analysis were Trapido 1971; and Johnstone 1970.
20. See also Kantor and Kenny 1976; and Jill Nattrass 1977.
21. The neo-Marxist claim that South Africa's growth and profit rates were exceptionally high was later challenged by Terence Moll 1990; and Nicoli Nattrass 1990.
22. Legassick (1976) and Legassick and Innes (1977) did not acknowledge any useful contribution by liberals, but Legassick occasionally engaged with liberals, rather than freezing them, them out of the debate. By contrast, there is no reference to the liberal contribution to the post-1970 debate in the historiographical surveys by Marks (1981 and1986). The assertion by Saunders (1988) that "liberals conspicuously refrained from responding in print to the revisionist challenge" is contradicted by the publications cited in this chapter (and in the Appendix), including my exchanges with Legassick and Innes in *African Affairs* during 1976, 1977, and 1979.
23. Among the many citing 1979 as the date when "the reform era begins" are Beinart and Dubow (1995, 19) and Bozzoli and Delius (1990, 27).
24. Terreblanche 1977.
25. O'Dowd's analysis was further developed during the 1970s and 1980s by Bell, Bromberger, Lipton, and others. The argument here is based on Lipton 1985.
26. In Assocom's memorandum, "Views on the Republic of South Africa Constitution Bill" and FCI's Business Charter (Lipton 1985, 179, 254, 383). Steyn cited SAIRR *Survey*, 1981.
27. O'Meara modified his previous strong claims about the influence of the unions, recognizing that "while relatively weak until the end of the 1970s, [they] managed to survive" (1996, 179).
28. As noted previously, this is section is, unless otherwise indicated, based on Lipton 1985. In this case, see Lipton 1985, 130f., 167, 172–75.
29. African unionization was supported by the (white, coloured, and Indian) unions affiliated to the rival labor federation, TUCSA.
30. Asmal accused not only business, but also the Progressive Party, of being "co-responsible" for Botha's attacks against neighboring countries.
31. On these contacts, see Mandela 1994; Sampson 1999; Sparks 1994; and Waldmeir 1997.

32. These shifts in opinion were charted by, inter alia, Schlemmer, Hanf (1981) and others.
33. Smith 1988, 183; and Saunders 1988, 188.
34. This analysis of the NP's electoral base is based on Lipton (1985), but does not differ much from the analyses in Salomon, Sadie, Welsh, Adam/Giliomee and the later O'Meara (1996).
35. Lipton 1985, 307, 174; and Adam and Giliomee 1979, 174. There is wide agreement on these data, first highlighted by Salomon and Sadie. Ownership shares are based on companies listed on the stock exchange and exclude the public sector, dominated by Afrikaners, as well as most agriculture, also Afrikaner dominated.
36. Lipton 1985, 50; and SAIRR *Survey* 1979, 73.
37. SAIRR *Survey* 1986, I:138.
38. I am indebted to Kenneth Hughes for a useful discussion on this and many other issues.
39. A proponent of this view was Kepple-Jones 1957.
40. The NP, CP and Progressives won, respectively, 48, 30 and 21 percent of the votes. There was also a verligte breakaway from the NP when Wynand Malan, Dennis Worrall, and others left to join the Progressive Party, renamed the Democratic Party (later Democratic Alliance) (Lipton 1990, 37f.; Lemon 1987).
41. O'Meara (1983, 9f, 260f.) rejected Bunting's claim that the NP had links with the Nazis and did not respond to Bunting's charge of extreme racism among Afrikaners. On this debate, see also Christoph Marx (2002); Furlong (2003); Giliomee (2003, 441f.).
42. Giliomee 1992, 170f.; Wilkins and Strydom 1978, ch. 11; Serfontein 1970, ch. 11; Nolutshungu 1971; and O'Meara 1996, 78f.
43. A liberal whose view is close to Nolutshungu's and Giliomee's is Philip Mayer (1975), who wrote, "The stigmata of racial discrimination go even deeper than those of class." Mayer believed economic concessions alone would not secure long-term black political support, although he believed they would legitimate the capitalist system, towards which Mayer did not find hostility among either black workers or elites. But he believed blacks would only accord legitimacy to a system "in which they have a meaningful share of decision-making."
44. In my interviews with black trade unionists, academics and businesspeople, and in exchanges at seminars and conferences at which early versions of this book were presented at the Centre for Development and Enterprise in Johannesburg in 1998, Sussex University in 2000, and the Nordiska Afrikainstitutet in Copenhagen in 2002.

Chapter 4

1. Quoted in, respectively, Maphai 1999; Lodge 1991a, 190; Barber 2004, 34; and McKinley 1997,100. See also Barrell 1990; and Ellis and Sechaba 1992.
2. Bozzoli's case study (1990, ch. 4) of Alexander township stresses the local origins of growing militancy and the ANC's attempt to catch up with and co-opt this. Johnson (1977) argues that the revival of black political activity from the mid-1970s owed little to the exiled ANC and PAC, which, he maintains, had "virtually ceased to exist inside SA." On the 1976 and 1985 uprisings, see also Gunnarson 2002; Hirson 1979; Kane-Berman 1978; and Murray 1987.
3. In the 1988 elections, there were voter turnouts of 45 percent, 35 percent and 25 percent among registered coloured, Asian, and African voters respectively. Registration levels were low, but turnout was higher than in the 1984 elections.
4. At a time of rapid population growth, *the number of police* rose from 11,655 in 1940 to 28,007 in 1960 to 35,635 in 1975 and to 48,921 in 1986. The proportion of blacks in the police was almost 50 percent throughout. *Numbers in the army* (permanent force, not including reservists) rose from 5,322 in 1940 to 17,951 in 1960 and to 30,719 in 1975. The army was engaged in defending the border (or invading neighbors) but supported the police during emergencies, as in Soweto in 1976 and during the mid-1980s unrest (Seegers 1996, 88, 146, 178f.; Brewer 1994).
5. The number of political detainees rose from 453 in 1983 to 29,132 in 1986 (Seegers 1996, 246).
6. A small proportion of white conscripts refused to serve in the armed forces (Nathan 1989).
7. On this, see Waldmeir 1997, 81f., 147f.; Slabbert 2006, 32f.; Guelke 1999, 57; Sparks 1994, 62f., 122f.; and Sampson 1999, 425f.
8. Doxey, M. 1980; Barber and Spicer 1979; Mayall 1984; Blumenfeld 1984; Moorsom 1986; Segal 1964; Hanlon and Omond 1987; and Legum 1964.
9. In 1985–86, the following official sanctions were imposed on South Africa. The EU imposed a "more rigorously controlled" arms and oil embargo and voluntary ban on new investment in, and imports from, South Africa of iron, steel, and krugerrands. The United States imposed bans on exports of nuclear technology, computers, new investment, and loans to the South African government and on imports of gold coins, agricultural products, some minerals, and direct air links. Japan imposed bans on direct investment in South Africa and on computer sales to the South African police and military (Lipton 1990, 1988).

10. On disinvestment, see Ovenden and Cole 1989; Coker 1987; McGrath and Jenkins 1985; Hauck and Kibbe 1989; and on this and other aspects of sanctions, Crawford and Klotz 1999.
11. An indication of this was the shift in the position of U.S. Senator Richard Lugar, an influential supporter of the 1985–86 sanctions who, after the 1987 backlash in South Africa, expressed doubts about their efficacy. This was among the reasons why few further sanctions were imposed.
12. These interviews were conducted during my 1970s and '80s fieldwork. In post-1994 interviews, some of the black businessmen interviewed earlier said their contribution to black advance had been ignored; they had been victimized as sellouts during the 1980s; and in post-apartheid South Africa, they were not receiving the opportunities merited by their entrepreneurial experience, as BEE favored the politically well-connected.
13. On the Africanists, see Biko 1979; Thoalane 1974; Gerhart 1978; and Nolutshungu 1982.
14. Mandela 1994, 401; Sampson 1999, 313f.; and Gumede 2005, 25.
15. Among the few who explored this were John Brewer 1986; Craig Charney 1995; and Anthony Marx 1992.
16. These contacts included secret meetings at Mells Park in the UK from 1987 to 1990 between senior NP and ANC representatives; the discussions between the imprisoned Mandela and NP ministers, including Kobie Coetzee and President Botha; and the 1987–89 conferences in Dakar between Afrikaner intellectuals and the exiled ANC, organized by IDASA, an NGO founded by Slabbert and Boraine with funding from George Soros's Open Society Institute. See Waldmeir 1997; Sampson 1999; Sparks 1994; and Slabbert 2006.
17. A shadow has been cast over de Kerk's reputation by some serious accusations. The claim that he refused to apologize for apartheid is incorrect: his apology to the TRC on May 14, 1997, is documented in Giliomee 2003, 651. The second accusation is that de Klerk connived at the murderous Third Force activities during the transitional period, 1990–94, including the 1992 Boipatong massacre. As Guelke (1999 and 2005) points out, this accusation was so damaging that de Klerk appointed the Goldstone Commission to investigate the charges. Goldstone concluded, there was no evidence to support them. The TRC (vol. 2:642ff.) later agreed there was "little evidence of a centrally directed . . . Third Force [although there seemed to be] an informal network . . . involving senior security officers who engaged in unlawful activity." The TRC also noted that "de Klerk's capacity to intervene was limited . . . he lacked a security force background . . . and had the difficult task of ensuring that the security forces . . . continued to support the transition, and did not turn towards a military . . . solution."

Other assessments include Suzman's view (*Optima*, May 2004) that de Klerk, unlike Vorster and Botha, was reluctant to shed blood, and

Giliomee's view (2003, 637f.) that de Klerk: "lacked the ruthlessness that characterises most great leaders in turbulent times. He was not prepared to walk over corpses . . . and had no stomach for a show of force." This was also the view of General Meiring, who complained to de Klerk, "You never used your strong base to negotiate from . . . you never used the military power available" to strengthen your negotiating position. The security/defense forces resented de Klerk's dismantling of Botha's National Security Management System, sidelining of the State Security Council, drastic cuts in military expenditure, and 1992 purge of twenty-three senior military officers. However, Pigou and Bell (2001) believe de Klerk could not have been as ignorant as suggested by his insistence that he did not know what was going on, and they accuse him of being "fundamentally dishonest." Mandela too distrusted de Klerk but believed there would have been "a destructive civil war . . . had it not been for de Klerk's daring far-sightedness." The third accusation, that de Klerk "betrayed Afrikaners" by failing to entrench minority rights at the constitutional negotiations, is discussed in Chapter 6.
18. These terms come from Lipton 1974a; and Adam, Slabbert, and Moodley 1997.

CHAPTER 5

1. I am indebted for discussions on liberalism to Francis Antonie, Jos Gerson, and Michael Lipton, and also to Glaser 2001; Simkins 1986; Butler, Elphick, and Welsh 1987; and Lipton and Simkins 1993.
2. Adam Smith's denunciation of the "monopolistic spirit" was not restricted to businesspeople, but also applied to trade unions, professional organizations, etc.
3. On South African liberal thought, see Simkins 1986; 1987, ch 12; Hughes 1993; and Maphai 1999.
4. I am indebted to Kenneth Hughes for the quote from Marx.
5. Bozzoli and Delius said their Wits Workshop broke away from "the functionalist and reductionist" analysis of the early neo-Marxists in order to develop a "more nuanced, culturally sensitive approach" (1990, 23). What they did not break away from was the habit of claiming they had transformed South African history.
6. For example, Alexander's statement (2002, ch. 1) that people "are not given to making war" in a context implying warfare is due to modern developments such as capitalism and globalization.
7. Cited by Anton Harber, *Sunday Times*, Johannesburg, May 1, 2005. See also Sparks 2003, ch. 5 and ch. 8; and the Stanley Uys/James Myburgh web site: http://ever-fasternews.com.

8. In his story, *Gooseberries*, Chekhov wrote, "There ought to be someone with a little hammer outside the door of every contented, happy person, tapping away to remind him that there are unhappy people in the world . . . that sooner or later life will show its claws."
9. This romanticizing tendency is evident in the otherwise good work of Friedman and Chipkin 2001.
10. See Bozzoli 2004; R. Wilson 2001; and Kynoch 2005. Among the most penetrating studies of the dark side of revolutionary violence are Fyodor Dostoevsky, *The Possessed* and Joseph Conrad, *Under Western Eyes* and *The Secret Agent*.
11. Murray (1988) referred to the revisionists' "dominant and . . . ascendant hegemony," while Etherington (1996) termed this period, "the golden age of South African history."

Chapter 6

1. On these complaints, see Bundy 2002; and Suttner; *Mail & Guardian* (Johannesburg) 2005 (my thanks to James Myburgh for this reference).
2. Suresh in *Sunday Times* (Johannesburg) October 1, 1995.
3. Ginwala cited Johnson and Welsh 1998, 192. Mazwai cited Patrick Laurence 1988 (53).
4. Biko cited by President Mbeki in his website, *ANC Today*, January 28, 2005. Ndebele cited Sanders 2002, 194f.
5. Pahad and Yengeni in *Financial Times* (London) August 24, 1999. Jordan in *Sunday Independent* (Johannesburg) April 29, 2001.
6. See Leon's speech at the Johannesburg Stock Exchange, June 1, 2006.
7. The ARM and Umkhonto did not join up because of reservations on both sides, particularly by Slovo of the SACP and Duncan of the LP. But liberals remained close to SWAPO in Namibia and to the Swaziland Progressive Party. See Vigne 1997.
8. V.I. Lenin, *Left-wing Communism, an infantile disorder*. 1935. Coop Publishing Society of Foreign Workers, Moscow, p 84. In this passage, Lenin urged the British Communist Party, during the 1920s, to cooperate with Labour Party ministers, Snowden and Henderson, holding up as a model the way in which the Bolsheviks used, then destroyed, their liberals and Mensheviks. The demonization of liberals in Russia had earlier origins in the unholy alliance between the Left and the Slavophiles, for whom, as Ivan Turgenev lamented, "the word 'liberal' has entered the scatological vocabulary." This demonization reduced the prospects for the emergence of a more humane, democratic society in Russia. On the SACP, see Roux 1948; Simons 1969; Adam 1993.

Turgenev is cited in the Introduction to Tom Stoppard, *The Shores of Utopia*. National Theatre, London, 2004
9. Patrick Laurence, *Focus* 2004, no 35. Mandela, *Long Walk to Freedom*, 1994.
10. Slabbert 2006; Guelke 1999; Adam 1993; Friedman 1993; and Sparks 1994.
11. McKinley 1997; and Bond 2000. Others termed 'ultra-Leftists' include Cosatu leaders Willie Madisha and Zwelinzima Vavi.
12. Gumede 2005, and the regular articles by Seepe, Welsh and others in *Focus*, *Guardian & Mail* and the Uys/Myburgh web site: http://www.ever-fasternews.com.
13. Mboweni cited *ever-fasternews.com* 8 October, 2006. Similar statements were made by Deputy President, Mlambo-Ngcuka (*African Business*, January 2006) and Minister of Public Enterprises, Alex Erwin (*Mail & Guardian*, May 15–21, 2005).
14. On Nazism accusations see Asmal et al, and the response by Adam et al. (1997, ch. 2).
15. Gumede 2005. On Zimbabwe, see also Ian Taylor and Paul Williams 2002; Stephen Chan 2006; Jack Spence 2006.
16. For a selection from the debate on these competing strategies see Peter Moll et al (1991); Lipton and Simkins 1993; Macroeconomic Research Group (1993); Joffe et al. (1994).
17. Gelb 2004; Van den Berg 2001; and Nattrass and Seekings 2002.
18. World Bank (1994). For differing assessments of the World Bank proposals, see Gavin Williams (1993); van Zyl et al. (1996); and Michael Lipton et al. (1996).
19. Data from Jeremy Cronin, SACP Deputy General Secretary, *Focus*, 2006, no. 43.
20. On the greater propensity to pay their taxes by those who identify themselves with 'the nation' see Lieberman 2002. For a parallel discussion of the relationship between labor productivity and feelings of national identity, see David Dickinson 2001.
21. The few attempts to use a GEM include Spandau 1979; Kaempfer and Lowenberg 1986; and Becker and Pollard 1990. Other systematic attempts to analyse the impact of sanctions include Khan 1989; Lundahl 1992; and Bell 1990.
22. Iraq provides a textbook case of how, even when sanctions succeed in inflicting economic damage, they do not necessarily have their intended political effects. On this see Toby Dodge (2007).
23. This draws on my interviews conducted in these countries between 1985–89.
24. The 1990 edition of Hufbauer and Schott reduce their earlier assessment of (what they define as) successful sanctions from one-third to

one-quarter of all cases. See also the useful study by Crawford and Klotz (1999).
25. Towards the end of the SA sanctions period, more targeted measures, such as bans on travel and freezing the foreign assets of the ruling elite, began to be used. These offer a useful alternative to the sledgehammer of comprehensive sanctions, although they depend upon the ruling elite's wish and freedom to travel, have foreign bank accounts, educate their children abroad, etc.

Appendices to Chapter 3

1. Posel's belief that big urban capital was more progressive than small-medium capital is also questionable. Assocom, which represented small-medium companies, was the most active in pressing for reform. This is because it was even more onerous for small-medium companies to comply with the bureaucratic red tape, high labour turnover, and police harassment of their employees connected with the labour control system. On this see Lipton 1980 and 1985.
2. See also Lipton 1985, 77ff.; and Bromberger and Hughes 1987, 222f.
3. This assessment was strengthened by the statement of Chris Heunis, the Minister of Constitutional Affairs, who said the Tricameral was a transitional institution that "does not address the problem of black constitutional development . . . [but is part of] an evolutionary constitutional path . . . not a final solution" (Alden 1996, 140).
4. In Assocom's memorandum, "Views on the Republic of SA Constitution Bill." FCI's Business Charter. (Lipton 1985, 179, 254, 383).
5. The idea of the "security state" originated with Glenn Moss (1980) and was "elaborated by revisionists into their theoretical construction of the security state." See also Nathan 1989; Frankel, Pines, and Swilling 1988; Pottinger 1988; and M. Swilling (1988). I am indebted to Daryl Glaser for a useful discussion on this and for his book, *Politics & Society in SA*: an excellent contribution to the debate despite his tendency to take the neo-Marxists at their own inflated valuation.
6. In his later work O'Meara came to share the view of those who stressed the NSMS's role in "freez[ing] Botha's conservative opponents" out of power and in recognizing that it was "not fully activated and . . . did not emerge at centre stage" until 1986 (1996, 282ff.).
7. See also Alf Stadler 1987.
8. Similar testimony was given by Cosatu. By contrast, the ANC, while critical of business, recognized that: "some important business organisations opposed some of the laws introduced by successive apartheid governments."

REFERENCE LIST

ABBREVIATIONS

CPS   Centre for Policy Studies, Johannesburg
IRRC   Investor Responsibility Research Centre, Washington, DC
JDS   Journal of Development Studies
JSAS   Journal of Southern African Studies
OUP   Oxford University Press
SAIRR South African Institute of Race Relations
SAJE   South African Journal of Economics

REFERENCES

Adam, Heribert. 1971. *Modernizing racial domination*. Berkeley: California University Press.
Adam, Heribert, and H. Giliomee. 1979. *Rise and crisis of Afrikaner power*. Cape Town: David Philip.
Adam, Heribert, and K. Moodley. 1993. *Negotiated revolution*. Johannesburg: Jonathan Ball.
Adam, Heribert, F. Van zyl Slabbert, and K. Moodley. 1997. *Comrades in business*. Cape Town: Tafelberg.
Adler, Glenn, J. Maller, and E. Webster. 1992. Unions, direct action and transition in South Africa. In *Peace, politics and violence in the new South Africa*, ed. Norman Etherington. London: Hans Zell.
Alden, Chris. 1996. *Apartheid's last stand*. Basingstoke, UK: Macmillan.
Alexander, Neville. 2002. *An ordinary country*. Pietermaritzburg, South Africa: Natal University Press.
Arrighi, Giovanni. 1967. *The political economy of Rhodesia*. The Hague: Mouton.
Asmal, Kadar, L. Kadar, and R. S. Roberts. 1997. *Reconciliation through truth*. Cape Town: David Philip.

Atmore, Anthony, and S. Marks. 1974. The imperial factor in South Africa in the nineteenth century. *Journal of Imperial and Commonwealth History* 3 (1): 105–39.
Atmore, Anthony, and N. Westlake. 1972. A liberal dilemma. *Race* 14 (2): 107–36.
Babrow, Merle. 1962. A critical assessment of George McCall Theal. Master's thesis, University of Cape Town.
Baker, Pauline. 1989. The United States and South Africa. New York: Ford Foundation South Africa Update Series.
Ballinger, Margaret. 1969. *From union to apartheid*. Folkstone: Bailey Bros.
Barber, James. 2004. *Mandela's world*. London: James Currey.
Barber, James, and M. Spicer. 1979. Sanctions against South Africa: Options for the West. *International Affairs* 55 (3): 385–401.
Barrell, Howard. 1990. *ANC's armed struggle*. London: Penguin.
Becker, Charles, and P. Pollard. 1990. *The impact of sanctions on South Africa*. Washington, DC: IRRC.
Becker, Gary. 1957. *The economics of discrimination*. Chicago: University of Chicago Press.
Beinart, William, and S. Dubow. 1995. *Segregation and apartheid in twentieth century South Africa*. London: Routledge.
Bell, Trevor. 1973. *Industrial decentralisation in South Africa*. Cape Town: OUP.
———. 1990. *The impact of sanctions on the South African motor vehicle industry*. Washington, DC: IRRC.
Berlin, Isaiah. 1953. *The hedgehog and the fox*. London: Weidenfeld and Nicholson.
———. 1958. *Two concepts of liberty*. Oxford: Clarendon.
Bernstein, Ann, and Berger, P. 1998. Business and democracy. London: Pinter.
Biko, Steve. 1979. *I write what I like*. London: Heinemann.
Blumenfeld, Jesmond. 1984. *Economic sanctions against South Africa: Would they work?* Uckfield, UK: Brunel University.
Blumer, Herbert. 1965. Industrialisation and race relations. In *Industrialisation and race relations*, ed. Guy Hunter. London: OUP.
Bond, Patrick. 2000. *Elite transition*. London: Pluto.
Bozzoli, Belinda, and P. Delius. 1990. Radical history and South African society. In *Radical History Review* 46 (7): 13–45.
———. 2004. *Theatres of struggle and the end of apartheid*. Johannesburg: Wits University Press.
Brewer, John. 1986. *After Soweto*. Oxford: Clarendon.
———. 1994. *Black and blue: Policing in South Africa*. Oxford: Clarendon.
Bromberger, Norman. 1974. Economic growth and political change in South Africa. In *South Africa: Economic growth and political change*, ed. Adrian Leftwich. London: Allison and Busby.

Bromberger, Norman, and T. Bell. 1972. South Africa in a comparative study of industrialization. London: Seminar Papers of Institute of Commonwealth Studies.
Bromberger, Norman, and K. Hughes. 1987. Capitalism and underdevelopment in South Africa. In *Democratic liberalism in South Africa*, ed. Jeffrey Butler, R. Elphick, and D. Welsh. Cape Town: David Philip
Bundy, Colin. 2001. Newsletter of the Institute of Commonwealth Studies. London.
———. 2007. New nation, new history? In *History making and present day politics in South Africa*, ed. Hans Erik Stolten. Available at http://jakobsgaardstolten.dk. Forthcoming in 2007 by Nordiska Afrikainsinstitute, Uppsala.
Bunting, Brian. 1964. *The rise of the South African Reich*. Harmondsworth, UK: Penguin.
Butler, Anthony. 2005. How democratic is the ANC? *JSAS* 31 (4): 719–36.
Butler, Jeffrey, R. Elphick, and D. Welsh, eds. 1987. *Democratic liberalism in South Africa*. Cape Town: David Philip.
Carr, E. H. 1961. *What is history?* London: MacMillan.
Cavalli-Sforza, Luigi. 2001. *Genes, peoples and languages*. London: Penguin.
Charney, Craig. 1995. *Voices of a new democracy*. Johannesburg: CPS.
Coetzee, J. M. 2002. *Stranger shores*. London: Vintage.
Cohen, Robin. 1986. *Endgame*. London: James Currey.
Coker, Christopher. 1987. *Disinvestment and the post-apartheid economy*. London: London School of Economics.
Cortwright, D., and G. A. Lopez. 1995. *Economic sanctions: Panacea or peacebuilding in a post–cold war world*. Boulder, CO: Westview.
Cox, Michael, ed. 1998. *Rethinking the Soviet collapse*. London: Pinter.
Crawford, Neta, and A. Klotz. 1999. *How sanctions work: Lessons from South Africa*. Basingstoke, UK: Macmillan.
Crocker, Chet. 1992. *High noon in Southern Africa*. New York: Norton.
Danziger, Kurt. 1971. Modernisation and the legitimation of social power. In *Sociological Perspectives*, ed. H. Adam. London: OUP.
Davenport, Rodney. 1966. *Afrikanerbond*. Cape Town: OUP.
———. 1977. *A modern history of South Africa*. Johannesburg: MacMillan.
Davies, R. H. 1979. *Capital, the state and white labour in South Africa*. Brighton: Harvester.
Davies, R. H., D. Kaplan, M. Morris, and D. O'Meara. 1976. Class struggle and periodisation of the state. *Review of African Political Economy* 3 (7): 4–30.
Davies, R. H., D. O'Meara, and S. Dlamini. 1984. *The struggle for South Africa*. London: Zed Books.
Davis, Dennis, and Robert Fine. 1985. Political strategies and the state. *JSAS* 12 (1): 25–48.

De Kiewiet, C. W. 1929. *British colonial policy and the South African republics*. London: Longmans.
———. 1941. *History of South Africa: Social and economic*. London: OUP.
———. 1957. *The anatomy of South African misery*. London, OUP.
Dennett, Daniel. 1995. *Darwin's dangerous idea*. London: Penguin.
Dickenson, David. 2001. National identity and economic development. PhD thesis, Cambridge University.
Dodge, Toby. 2007. The causes of U.S. failure in Iraq. *Survival* 49 (1): x–xx.
Doxey, G. V. 1961. *The industrial colour bar in South Africa*. Cape Town: OUP.
Doxey, Margaret. 1980. *Economic sanctions and international enforcement*. London: Chatham House.
Dubow, Saul. 1989. *Racial segregation and the origins of apartheid*. London: MacMillan.
———. 1995. *Illicit union: Scientific racism in modern South Africa*. Cambridge: CambridgeUniversity Press.
———. 2002. South Africa and South Africans. In *History making and present day politics in South Africa*, ed. Hans Erik Stolten. Available at http://jakobsgaardstolten.dk. Forthcoming in 2007 by Nordiska Afrikainsinstitute, Uppsala.
Dubow, Saul, and A. Jeeves. 2005. *South Africa's 1940s*. Cape Town. Double Story.
du Plessis, E. P. 1964. *'n Volk Staan Op*. Cape Town: Human and Rousseau.
Du Toit, Andre. 1975. Ideological change, Afrikaner nationalism, and pragmatic racial domination in South Africa. In *Change in contemporary South Africa*, ed. L. Thompson and J. Butler. Berkeley: University of California Press.
Du Toit, Andre, and H. Giliomee. 1983. *Afrikaner political thought*. Cape Town: David Philip.
Ellis, Stephen, and T. Sechaba. 1992. *Comrades against apartheid*. London: James Currey.
Elphick, Richard, and H. Giliomee. 1988. *The shaping of South African society, 1652–1840*. Middletown, CT: Wesleyan University.
Etherington, Norman, ed. 1992. *Peace, politics and violence in the new South Africa*. London: Hans Zell.
———. 1996. Post-modernism and South African history. *Southern African Review of Books* 44 (July–August): n.p.
Evans, Richard. 1997. *In defence of history*. London: Granta.
Frankel, Philip, M. Pines, and M. Swilling, eds. 1988. *State, resistance and change in South Africa*. Johannesburg: Southern Books.
Frankel, S. H. 1930. Problems of economic inequality. In *Coming of age*. Ed. E. Brookes. Cape Town: M. Miller.
———. 1938. *Capital investment in Africa*. London: OUP.

Freund, William. 1987. Defending South African capitalism. *Transformation* 4:84–97.
Friedman, Steven. 1987. *Building tomorrow today*. Johannesburg: Ravan.
———, ed. 1993. *The long journey: South Africa's quest for a negotiated settlement*. Johannesburg: CPS.
Friedman, Steven, and I. Chipkin. 2001. *A poor voice? The politics of inequality in South Africa*. Johannesburg: CPS.
Furlong, P. J. 1991. *Between crown and swastika*. Johannesburg: Wits University Press.
Gelb, Stephen. 2004. The South African economy, 1994–2004, and inequality in South Africa. Available at http://www.the-edge.org.za.
Gerhart, Gail. 1978. *Black power in South Africa*. Berkeley: University of California.
Giliomee, Hermann. 1992a. Broedertwis. In *Peace, politics and violence in the new South Africa*, ed. Norman Etherington. London: Hans Zell.
———. 1992b. The last trek. In *Peace, politics and violence in the new South Africa*, ed. Norman Etherington. London: Hans Zell..
———. 2000. Manipulating the past. In *Political Correctness in South Africa*. Johannesburg: SAIRR.
———. 2003. *The Afrikaners*. Charlottesville: University of Virginia.
———. 2005. White led opposition parties and minorities under South Africa's "liberal" dominant party system. Available at http://www.everfasternews.com/index.
Giliomee, Hermann, and C. Simkins. 1999. *The awkward embrace*. Cape Town: Tafelberg.
Glaser, Daryl. 2001. *Politics and society in South Africa*. London: Sage.
Goodfellow, D. M. 1931. *Economic history of South Africa*. London: Routledge.
Greenberg, Stanley. 1980. *Race and state in capitalist development*. New Haven, CT: Yale University Press.
———. 1985. Managing influx control from the rural end. In *Up against the fences*, ed. H. Giliomee and L. Schlemmer. Cape Town: David Philip.
———. 1987a. Failing capitalism. *Social Dynamics* 13 (2): 78–82.
———. 1987b. *Legitimating the illegitimate*. Berkeley: University of California.
Guelke, Adrian. 1993. Sport and the end of apartheid. In *The changing politics of sport*, ed. L. Allison. Manchester: Manchester University Press.
———. 1999. *South Africa in transition*. London: Tauris.
———. 2005. *Rethinking the rise and fall of apartheid*. Basingstoke, UK: Palgrave Macmillan.
Gumede, William. 2005. *Thabo Mbeki and the battle for the soul of the ANC*. Johannesburg: Zebra.
Gunnarson, Gorm. 2007. The tricameral boycott of 1984 and the democratisation of South Africa. In *History making and present day politics in*

South Africa, ed. Hans Erik Stolten. Available at http://jakobsgaardstolten.dk.

Hancock, Keith. 1968. *Smuts*. Vol. 2. London: Cambridge University Press.

Hanf, Theodor. 1981. *South Africa: Prospects of peaceful change*. London: Rex Collings.

Hanlon, Joseph, and R. Omond. 1987. *Sanctions handbook*. London: Penguin.

Hauck, David, and J. Kibbe. 1989. *Leaving South Africa*. Washington, DC: IRRC.

Hayek, Friedrich. 1944. *The road to serfdom*. Chicago: Chicago University Press.

Hepple, Alex. 1967. *Verwoerd*. London: Penguin.

Hindson, Doug. 1987. *Pass controls and the urban African proletariat*. Johannesburg: Ravan.

Hirson, Baruch. 1979. *Year of fire, year of ash*. London: Zed.

Hofmeyr, Jan. 1990. *A survey of white South African attitudes towards sanctions*. Washington, DC: IRRC.

Horwitz, Ralph. 1957. *Expand or explode*. Cape Town: Business Bookman.

———. 1967. *The political economy of South Africa*. London: Weidenfeld and Nicholson.

Hufbauer G., and J. Schott. 1990. *Economic sanctions reconsidered*. Washington DC: Institute for International Economics.

Hughes, Kenneth. 1977. Challenges from the past. *Social Dynamics* 3:1–6.

———. 1993. The dispute about the market and state. In *State and market in post-apartheid South Africa*, ed. Merle Lipton and Charles Simkins. Johannesburg: Wits University Press.

Hutt, W. H. 1964. *The economics of the colour bar*. London: Deutsch.

James, Wilmot, and L. van de Vijver, eds. 1996. *After the Truth & Reconciliation Commission*. Cape Town: David Philip.

Joffe, Avril, R. Kaplinsky, and D. Lewis. 1994. *South Africa and the world economy in the 1990s*. Cape Town: David Philip.

Johnson, R. W. 1977. *How long will South Africa survive?* London: MacMillan.

Johnson, R. W., and D. Welsh, eds. 1998. *Ironic victory*. Cape Town: OUP.

Johnstone, Frederick. 1970. White prosperity and white supremacy in South Africa." *African Affairs* 69 (275): 124–40.

———. 1976. *Race, class and gold*. London: Routledge.

———. 1982. Most painful to our hearts. *Canadian Journal of African Studies* 16 (7): 5–26.

Kaempfer, William, and A. Lowenberg. 1986. A model of the political economy of international investment sanctions: The case of South Africa. *Kyklos* 39 (3): 377–96.

Kane-Berman, John. 1978. *Soweto: Black revolt, White reaction*. Johannesburg: Ravan.

———. 1990. *The silent revolution*. Johannesburg: SAIRR.
Kantor, Brian, and H. Kenny. 1976. The poverty of neo-Marxism: The South Africa case. *JSAS* 3 (1): 20–40.
Keegan, Tim. 1996. *Colonial South Africa and origins of the racial order*. Cape Town: David Philip.
Khan, Haider Ali. 1989. *The political economy of sanctions against South Africa*. Boulder, CO: Lynne Reiner.
Knight, J. B., and G. Lenta. 1980. Has capitalism underdeveloped the labour reserves of South Africa?. *Oxford Bulletin of Economics and Statistics* 42:169.
Krikler, Jeremy. 2005. *White rising: The 1922 insurrection and racial killing in South Africa*. Manchester: Manchester University Press.
Krogh, Antjie. 1998. *Country of my skull*. Johannesburg: Random House.
Kuper, Adam. 1994. *The chosen primate*. Cambridge, MA: Harvard University.
———. 2003. Review of Africanising anthropology. *African Affairs* 102: 163–64.
Kuper, Hilda. 1979. Commitments: The liberal scholar in South Africa. In *The liberal dilemma in South Africa*, ed. Pierre van den Berghe. London: Croom Helm.
Kuper, Leo. 1974. *Race, class and power*. London: Duckworth.
Kynoch, Gary. 2005. Crime, conflict and politics in transition-era South Africa. *African Affairs* 104 (416): 493–514.
Landsberg, Chris. 1993. Directing from the stalls? In *The long journey: South Africa's quest for a negotiated settlement*, ed. Steven Friedman. Johannesburg: CPS.
Lapchick, Richard. 1975. *The politics of race and international sport*. Westport, CT: Greenwood.
Laurence, Patrick. 1998. Liberalism and politics. In *Ironic victory*, ed. R. W. Johnson and D. Welsh. Cape Town: OUP.
Leftwich, Adrian, ed. 1974. *South Africa: Economic growth and political change*. London: Allison and Busby.
Legassick, Martin. 1973. The making of South African native policy. In *The political economy of Africa*, ed. R. Harris. Boston.
———. 1976. Race, industrialisation and social change in South Africa. *African Affairs* 75:224–39.
———. 1980. Frontier tradition in South African historiography. In *Economy and society in pre-industrial South Africa*, ed. Shula Marks and A. Atmore. London: Longman
———. 2002. *Armed struggle and democracy*. Uppsala: Nordiska Afrikainsinstitute.
Legassick, Martin, and D. Innes. 1977. Capital restructuring and apartheid. *African Affairs* 76 (305): 437–82.

Legum, Colin, and Margaret Legum. 1964. *South Africa: Crisis for the West.* London: Pall Mall.
Lemon, Anthony. 1987. *Apartheid in transition.* Aldershot, UK: Gower.
Lewsen, Phyllis. 1971. Cape liberal tradition: Myth or reality? *Race* 13 (1): 65–80.
———. 1982. *John X. Merriman.* New Haven, CT: Yale University Press.
———. 1987. Liberals in politics and administration. In *Democratic liberalism in South Africa*, ed. Jeffrey Butler, R. Elphick, and D. Welsh. Cape Town: David Philip.
Lieberman, Evan. 2002. How South African citizens evaluate their economic obligations to the state. *JDS* 38 (3): 37–62.
Lipton, Merle. 1974a. South Africa: Authoritarian reform? *World Today* 30 (6): 247–58.
———. 1974b. White farming: A case-study of change in South Africa. *Journal of Commonwealth and Comparative Politics* 12 (1): 32–48.
———. 1976. British investment in South Africa: Is constructive engagement possible? *South African Labour Bulletin* 3 (4): 10–48.
———. 1977. South Africa: Two agricultures? In *Farm labour in South Africa*, ed. F. Wilson. Cape Town: David Philip.
———. 1979. The debate about South Africa: NeoMarxists and neoliberals. *African Affairs* 78 (310): 57–80.
———. 1980. Men of two worlds. *Optima* 29 (2): 72–197.
———. 1985. *Capitalism and apartheid: South Africa, 1910–1984.* Aldershot, UK: Gower/Temple Smith. Reprinted with epilogue, Aldershot, UK: Wildwood, 1986.
———. 1988. *Sanctions and South Africa: The dynamics of economic isolation.* London: Economist Intelligence Unit.
———. 1990. *The challenge of sanctions.* London: Centre for the Study of the South African Economy and International Finance, London School of Economics.
Lipton, Merle, and Charles Simkins, eds. 1993. *State and market in post-apartheid South Africa.* Johannesburg: Wits University Press.
Lipton, Michael, Merle Lipton, Mike de Klerk, and Frank Ellis, eds. 1996. *Land, labour and livelihoods in rural South Africa.* 2 vols. Durban: Indicator Press.
Lodge, Tom. 1983. *Black politics in South Africa since 1945.* Johannesburg: Ravan.
———. 1991a. *All, here and now: Black politics in South Africa.* New York: Ford Foundation Update Series.
———. 1991b. The ANC and its historiographical traditions. In *History from South Africa*, ed. J. Brown. Philadelphia: Temple.
———. 2002. *Politics in South Africa: From Mandela to Mbeki.* London: Currey.

Lonsdale, John. 1983. From colony to industrial state: South African historiography as seen from England. *Social Dynamics* 9 (1): 67–83.
Lundahl, Mats. 1992. *Apartheid in theory and practice*. Boulder, CO: Westview.
Luthuli, Albert. 1962. *Let my people go*. London: Collins.
Macroeconomic Research Group (Merg). 1993. Making democracy work. Cape Town: OUP.
MacCrone, I. D. 1937. *Race attitudes in South Africa*. London: OUP.
MacMillan, W. M. 1927. *The Cape colour question*. London: Faber and Gwyer.
———. 1929. *Bantu, Boer and Briton*. London: Faber and Gwyer.
Magubane, Bernard. 1979. *The political economy of race and class in South Africa*. New York: Monthly Review Press.
———. 2002. Whose memory, whose history. In *History making and present day politics in South Africa*, ed. Hans Erik Stolten. Available at http://jakobsgaardstolten.dk. Forthcoming in 2007 by Nordiska Afrikainsinstitute, Uppsala.
Makgoba, Malegapura. 1998. Oppositions, difficulties and tensions between liberalism and African thought. In *Ironic victory*, ed. R. W. Johnson and D. Welsh. Cape Town: OUP.
Mamdani, Magmoud. 1996. Reconciliation without justice. In *After the Truth & Reconciliation Commission*, ed. Wilmot James and L. van de Vijver. Cape Town: David Philip.
Mandela, Nelson. 1994. *Long walk to freedom*. London: Abacus.
Maphai, Vincent. 1999. The new South Africa: A season for power sharing. In *Democratization in Africa*, ed. Larry Diamond. Baltimore: Johns Hopkins University Press.
———. 2003. Race and the politics of transition: Confusing political imperatives with moral rights. Unpublished paper.
Maphai, Vincent, and Keith Gottschalk. 2003. Parties, politics and the future of democracy. *Development Update* 4 (3): 52–74.
Marais, Hein. 1998. *South Africa: Limits to change*. Cape Town: Zed Books.
Marks, Shula. 1981. Towards a peoples history of South Africa. In *Peoples history and socialist theory*, ed. R. Samuel. London: Routledge.
———. 1986. Historiography of South Africa. In *African historiographies*, ed. B. Jewsiewicki. London: Cambridge University Press.
Marks, Shula, and A. Atmore, eds. 1980. *Economy and society in pre-industrial South Africa*. London: Longman.
Marks, Shula, and R. Rathbone, eds. 1982. *Industrialisation and social change in South Africa*. London: Longman.
Marks, Shula, and S. Trapido. 1987. *The politics of race, class and nationalism in twentieth-century South Africa*. London: Longman.
Marx, Anthony. 1992. *Lessons of the struggle*. London: OUP.

Marx, Christoph. 2004. The Ossewabrandwag as a mass movement. *JSAS* 20 (2): n.p.
Mayall, James. 1984. The sanctions problem in international economic relations. *International Affairs* 60 (4): 631–42.
Mayer, Philip. 1975. Class, status and ethnicity. In *Change in contemporary South Africa*, ed. L. M. Thompson and J. Butler. Berkeley: University of California Press.
Maylam, Paul. 2001. *South Africa's racial past*. Aldershot, UK: Ashgate.
McCracken, L. 1967. *The Cape Parliament, 1854–1910*. Oxford: Clarendon.
McGrath, Michael, and C. Jenkins. 1985. *Economic implications of disinvestments for the South African economy*. Durban: Natal University.
McKinley, Dale. 1997. *The ANC and the liberation struggle*. London: Pluto.
Meli, Francis. 1988. *South Africa belongs to us: a history of the ANC*. Harare: Zimbabwe Publishing House.
Moleketi, Jabu, and Josiah Jele. 2002. *Strategies in the struggle for the victory of the national democratic revolution*. African National Congress. Johannesburg.
Moll, Terence. 1990. From booster to brake: Apartheid and economic growth in comparative perspective. In *Political economy of South Africa*, ed. N. Nattrass and E. Ardington. Cape Town: OUP.
Moll, Peter, N. Nattrass, and L. Loots. 1991. *Redistribution: How can it work in South Africa?* Cape Town: David Philip.
Moorsom, Richard. 1986. *The scope for sanctions*. London: Catholic Institute for International Relations.
Moss, Glenn. 1980. Total strategy. *Work in Progress* 1:1–12.
Murray, Martin. 1987. *South Africa: Time of agony, time of destiny*. London: Verso.
———. 1988. The triumph of Marxist approaches in South African social and labour history. *Journal of African and Asian Studies* 23 (1): 79–101.
Myburgh, James, and Stanley Uys. 2003. *Thabo Mbeki's presidency*. London: distributed by stanleyuys@googlemail.com.
Nathan, Laurie. 1989. Marching to a different beat. In *War and society: The militarisation of South Africa*, ed. L. Nathan and J. Cock. Cape Town: David Philip.
Nattrass, Jill. 1977. Narrowing wage differentials. *SAJE* 45:408–45.
Nattrass, Nicoli, and Jeremy Seekings. 2002. Class, distribution and redistribution in post-apartheid South Africa. *Transformation* 50:1–30.
Ndlovu, Sifso. 2006. The ANC's use of history as a weapon of the struggle for liberation. In *The road to democracy*. Pretoria: South African Democracy Education Trust.
Neumark, S. D. 1957. *Economic influences on the South African frontier*. Berkeley: Stanford University.

Niehaus, Isak. 2002. Ethnicities and the boundaries of belonging. *African Affairs* 101:557–83.
Nolutshungu, Sam. 1971. Issues of the Afrikaner enlightenment. *African Affairs* 70:23–36.
———. 1972. Party system, electoral cleavage and performance. *African Review* 2 (4): 449–65.
———. 1982. *Changing South Africa*. Cape Town: David Philip.
O'Dowd, Michael. 1974. South Africa in the light of the stages of economic growth. In *South Africa: Economic growth and political change*, ed. Adrian Leftwich. London: Allison and Busby.
Olson, Mancur. 1965. *The logic of collective action*. Boston: Harvard University Press.
O'Meara, Dan. 1975. The 1946 African mine-workers strike. *Journal of Commonwealth and Comparative Politics* 13:2.
———. 1979. Review of Davenport. *Utafiti* 4:258–61.
———. 1983. *Volkskapitalisme*. Johannesburg: Ravan.
———. 1996. *Forty lost years*. Johannesburg: Ravan.
Orkin, Mark. 1986. *What Black South Africans really think*. Johannesburg: Ravan.
Ovenden, Keith, and T. Cole. 1989. *Apartheid and international finance*. London: Penguin.
Paton, Alan. 1971. *Hofmeyr*. Abridged edition. Cape Town: OUP.
———. 1974. *Apartheid and the archbishop*. London: Jonathan Cape.
Peires, Jeff. 1977. On the burden of the present. *Social Dynamics* 3:63–67.
———. 1989. *The dead will arise*. London: James Currey.
Philip, John. 1828. *Researches in South Africa*. London: Duncan.
Pigou, Piers, and T. Bell. 2001. *Unfinished business: South Africa, apartheid and the truth*. London: Duncan.
Pinker, Steven. 2002. *Blank slate: The modern denial of human behaviour*. London: Allen Lane.
Plaut, Martin. 1991. Debates in a shark tank: The politics of South Africa's non-racial unions. Seminar paper of the Institute of Commonwealth Studies, London.
Pottinger, Brian. 1988. *The imperial presidency: P. W. Botha*. Johannesburg: Southern Books.
Popper, Karl. 1959. *The logic of scientific discovery*. London: Hutchinson.
Posel, Deborah. 1991. *The making of apartheid*. London: OUP.
Ramphele, Mamphela. 1998. *Transforming South African higher education: The tension between excellence and equity*. Cape Town: Institute of Social Studies, University of Cape Town.
———. 2001. Citizenship challenges for South Africa. *Daedalus* 130 (1): 1–18.
Renwick, Robin. 1997. *Unconventional diplomacy in Southern Africa*. Basingstoke, UK: Macmillan.

Reyburn, H. A. 1934–35. Studies in Cape frontier history. *The Critic*, October 1934; January and April 1935.

Rich, Paul. 1984. *White power and the liberal conscience*. Johannesburg: Ravan.

———. 1993. *Hope and despair: English-speaking intellectuals and South African politics*. London: British Academic Press.

Roberts, M., and A. Trollip. 1947. *The South African opposition*. London: Longman.

Robertson, H. M. 1934. 150 years of economic contact between black and white. *SAJE* 2–3, Parts 1 and 11: n.p.

Ross, Andrew. 1986. *John Philip: Missions, race and politics in South Africa*. Aberdeen: Aberdeen University.

Roux, Edward. 1948. *Time longer than rope*. London: Gollancz.

Runciman, Gary. 1998. *The social animal*. London: HarperCollins.

Sachs, E. S. 1957. *Rebels daughters*. London: MacGibbon and Kee.

Sadie, Jan. 1968. The economic factor in Afrikaner society. *Stats* (December): n.p.

———. 1970. Population and economic development in South Africa. *SAJE* 38: n.p.

South African Institute of Race Relations. n.d. Annual surveys. Johannesburg: SAIRR.

Salomon, Lawrence. 1964. The economic background to Afrikaner nationalism. In *Boston University papers in African history*, ed. J. Butler. Boston University.

Sampson, Anthony. 1999. *Mandela*. London: HarperCollins.

Sanders, Mark. 2002. *Complicities: The intellectual and apartheid*. London: Duke University.

Saul, John. 2004. The hares, the hounds and the ANC. *Third World Quarterly* 25 (1): 1–12.

Saunders, Chris. 1988. *Making of the South African past*. Cape Town: David Philip.

Schlemmer, Lawrence. 1980. Change in South Africa. In *The apartheid regime*, ed. R. Price and C. Rosberg. Berkeley: University of California.

———. 1986. *Black opinion on disinvestment*. Durban: Natal University.

———. 1998. Liberalism, democracy, race relations and the rising black middle class. In *Ironic victory*, ed. R. W. Johnson and D. Welsh. Cape Town: OUP.

Seabright, Paul. 2004. *The company of strangers: A natural history of economic life*. Princeton, NJ: Princeton University Press.

Seegers, Annette. 1996. *The military in the making of modern South Africa*. London: Tauris.

Seekings, Jeremy. 2000. *The UDF*. Cape Town: David Philip.

Segal, Ronald. 1964. *Sanctions against South Africa*. London: Penguin.

Sen, Amartya. 2001. *Development as freedom*. London: OUP.

REFERENCE LIST 215

Serfontein, Hennie. 1970. *Die Verkrampte Aanslag.* Cape Town: Human and Rousseau.

Shubane, Khela. 1995. *The wrong cure.* Johannesburg: CPS.

Shubane, Khela, and Shaun Mackay. 1999. *Down to business.* Johannesburg: CPS.

Simkins, Charles. 1986. *Reconstructing South African liberalism.* Johannesburg: SAIRR.

———. 1987. Democratic liberalism and the dilemmas of equality. In *Democratic liberalism in South Africa,* ed. Jeffrey Butler, R. Elphick, and D. Welsh. Cape Town: David Philip.

———. 2005. Income distribution and poverty. Available at http://sarpn.org.za.

Simons, H. J., and R. E.. 1969. *Class and colour in South Africa.* London: Penguin.

Slabbert, F. van Zyl. 1975. Afrikaner nationalism, white politics and political change. In *Change in contemporary South Africa,* ed. L. M. Thompson and J. Butler. Berkeley: University of California Press.

———. 2006. *The other side of history.* Johannesburg: Jonathan Ball.

Slabbert, F. van Zyl, and D. Welsh. 1979. *South Africa's options.* Cape Town: David Philip.

Smith, Ken. 1988. *The changing past.* Athens, OH: Ohio University Press.

Spandau, Arnt. 1979. *Economic boycott against South Africa.* Cape Town: Juta.

Sparks, Allister. 1994. *Tomorrow is another country.* Johannesburg: Struik.

———. 2003. *Beyond the miracle.* Chicago: University of Chicago Press.

Spence, Jack. 2006. "Point man on Zimbabwe": South Africa's role in the crisis. *Round Table* 95 (384): 191–99.

Stadler, Alf. 1969. The Afrikaner in opposition, 1910–48. *Journal of Commonwealth Political Studies* 7:204–15.

———. 1987. *The political economy of modern South Africa.* London: Croom Helm.

Stolten, Hans Erik. 2007. The relationship between capitalism and apartheid. In *History making and present day politics in South Africa,* ed. Hans Erik Stolten. Available at http://jakobsgaardstolten.dk. Forthcoming in 2007 by Nordiska Afrikainstitutet, Uppsala.

Tawney, R. H. 1964. The conditions of economic liberty. In *The radical tradition,* ed. R. Hinden. London: Allen and Unwin.

Taylor, Ian, and Paul Williams. 2002. The limits of engagement: British foreign policy and the crisis in Zimbabwe. *In International Affairs* 78 (3): 547–65.

Terreblanche, S. J. 1997. Testimony before the Truth & Reconciliation Commission. Johannesburg: TRC (SJT 7/2).

Thoalane, Thoalane, ed. 1974. *Black renaissance.* Johannesburg: Ravan.

Thompson L. M. 1960. *The unification of South Africa.* Cape Town: OUP.

Thompson L. M., and M. Wilson, eds. 1971. *Oxford history of South Africa.* Vols. 1 and 11. Oxford: Clarendon Press.

———. 1975. *The political mythology of apartheid.* New Haven, CT: Yale University.

Thompson, L. M, and J. Butler, eds. 1975. *Change in contemporary South Africa.* Berkeley: University of California.

Tickten, Hillel. 1991. *The politics of race discrimination in South Africa.* London: Pluto.

Trapido, Stanley. 1971. South Africa in a comparative study of industrialisation. *JDS* 7:309–20.

———. 1980. The friends of the natives. In *Economy and society in pre-industrial South Africa,* ed. Shula Marks and A. Atmore. London: Longman.

Truth and Reconciliation Commission of South Africa. 1998. Report. Cape Town: Juta.

Vail, Leroy, ed. 1989. *The creation of tribalism in Southern Africa.* London: James Currey.

Van den Berg, Servaas. 2001. *Fighting poverty: Labour markets and inequality in South Africa.* Cape Town: University of Cape Town Press.

Van der Horst, Sheila. 1942. *Native labour in South Africa.* Cape Town: OUP.

———. 1971. *Progress and retrogression in South Africa.* Johannesburg: SAIRR.

Van der Merwe, P. J. 1938. *Die trekboer in die geskiedenis van die Kaap Kolonie.* Cape Town: Human and Rousseau.

Van Zyl, Johann, J. Kirsten, and H. Binswanger, eds. 1996. *Agricultural land reform in South Africa.* Cape Town: OUP.

Vigne, Randolph. 1997. *Liberals against apartheid.* London: MacMillan.

Waldmeir, Patti. 1997. *The anatomy of a miracle.* London: Viking.

Walker, Eric. 1957. *History of South Africa.* London: Longman.

Walshe, Peter. 1970. *The rise of African nationalism in South Africa.* London: Hurst.

Wassenaar, Andries. 1977. *The assault on private enterprise.* Cape Town: Tafelberg.

Welsh, David. 1969. Urbanisation and the solidarity of Afrikaner nationalism. *Journal of Modern African Studies* 7 (2): 265–76.

———. 1971a. The growth of towns. In *Oxford history of South Africa.* Ed. Monica Wilson and L. M. Thompson. 2 vols. London: OUP.

———. 1971b. *The roots of segregation.* Cape Town: OUP.

———. 1974. The political economy of Afrikaner nationalism. In *South Africa: Economic growth and political change,* ed. Adrian Leftwich. London: Allison and Busby.

Wilkins, Ivor, and H. Strydom. 1978. *The Broederbond.* London: Paddington.

Williams, Gavin. 1993. *Land distribution options*. Johannesburg. Land and Agriculture Policy Centre.

Wilson, Francis. 1971. Farming. In *Oxford history of South Africa*. Vol. 2. Ed. Monica Wilson and L. M. Thompson. London: OUP.

———. 1972. *Labour in the South African gold mines*. London: Cambridge University Press.

———. 1975. Political implications for blacks of economic changes in South Africa. In *Change in contemporary South Africa*, ed. L. M. Thompson and J. Butler. Berkeley: University of California Press.

Wilson, Monica, and L. M. Thompson, eds. 1969/1971. *Oxford history of South Africa*. 2 vols. London: OUP.

Wilson, Richard. 2001. *The politics of truth and reconciliation*. Cambridge: Cambridge University Press.

Wolpe, Harold. 1970. Industrialization and race in South Africa. In *Race and racialism*, ed. S. Zubaida. London: Tavistock.

———. 1972. Capitalism and cheap labour-power in South Africa. In *Essays from economy and Society*, ed. H. Wolpe. London: Routledge.

Worden, Nigel. 1994. *The making of modern South Africa*. Oxford: Blackwell.

World Bank. 1994. South African agriculture: Structure, performance and options. Southern Africa Dept discussion paper 6. Washington, DC: World Bank.

Wright, Harrison. 1977. *The burden of the present*. Cape Town: David Philip.

Yudelman, David. 1984. *The emergence of modern South Africa*. Cape Town: David Philip.

Index

Adam, H., 65, 195, 99–101, 201
Adler, G., 88
affirmative action, 112, 128, 137, 140, 149, 151, 152–54, 156, 159. *See also* Black Economic Empowerment
African National Congress (ANC), 1, 19–20, 22, 24–25, 46, 48, 50–51, 57, 61, 81–82, 84, 87, 89, 98, 107–8, 122, 138, 140–42, 144–45, 148–56, 159–62, 164, 198, 202
African Resistance Movement (ARM), 141, 220
Africanists, 97, 114, 148–49, 160–61
Afrikaanse Handelsinstituut (AHI), 46, 56, 59, 66, 177
Afrikaners, 3, 7, 13–16, 18, 25, 28–32, 28–29, 31–32, 64–79, 83, 99, 140, 144–47, 146, 188. *See also* Afrikaner National Party
Afrikaner National Party (NP), 11–12, 20–22, 33–35, 42, 44–51, 54, 63, 65–67, 68, 73, 82–83, 85–86, 94, 99–100, 105, 143–46, 176, 179, 181, 187, 198. *See also* Malan; Verwoerd; Botha, de Klerk; verkramptes/verligtes
agriculture/agrarian reform, 43, 54, 58, 66, 161–62
AIDS, 151, 158
Alden, C., 180

Alexander, N., 35, 107, 116, 117, 199
anarchism, 109
Anglo-American Corporation, 34, 36, 52, 151, 177
AngloGold Ashanti, 151–52, 154
Anglo-Vaal, 179
Angola, 50, 81–82
Anti-Apartheid Movement, 142
Antonie, F., 199
Apprenticeship Act and Boards, 76, 88
Ardington, E., 115
armaments industry, 91, 179
armed struggle, 6, 81–82, 102, 141, 200
army. *See* military
Armscor, 179
Arrighi, G., 194
Asmal, K., 60, 61, 138, 141, 181, 195
Assocom, 46, 56, 57, 59, 60, 62, 66, 176, 178, 187, 202
Atmore, A., 26, 27, 28, 29
Azapo, 83, 84, 97

Ball, C., 61, 84
Ballinger, M., 141–42
Bantu Education, schools boycott of, 142
Bantustans, 21–23, 33, 37, 42–43, 48, 50, 84, 94, 97–98, 176–77
Barlow Rand, 179
Barnard, N., 100
Basson, J., 46

Becker, C., 91–92, 201
Becker, G., 55, 155
Beeld, 67
Beevor, A., 132
behavioural theory, 6, 62–63, 118–22, 129
Beinart, W., 43, 117, 194
Bekker, S., 115
Bell, T., 51, 176, 182, 186, 187, 199
Berlin, I., 110, 112, 113–14
Biko, S., 97, 124, 139, 140
Black Consciousness Movement, 97
Black Economic Empowerment (BEE), 22, 148, 149, 153–56, 159, 160, 161
black elite, 30–31, 74, 154–58, 163
Black Management Forum, 152
Black Urban Councils, 84, 85
Bloom, T., 61, 84, 178
Blumenfeld, J., 197
Blumer, H., 34, 51, 55
Boer War, 27, 28, 29
Boers. *See* Afrikaners
Boipatong massacre, 146, 198
Bophuthatswana, 86, 145
Boraine, A., 62
Botha, P., 67
Botha, P. W., 50, 52–53, 60–61, 68, 86, 87, 93, 100, 166, 178, 181, 187
Boyce, W., 27
Bozzoli, B., 28, 132–33, 185, 192, 197, 199, 200
Brand, S., 100, 123
Brewer, J., 197, 198
Breytenbach, B., 68
Brink, A., 68
Broederbond, 68, 73
Bromberger, N., 51, 187, 194, 195
Brookes, E., 19, 21, 22
Brown, K., 125
Brown, P., 115, 142

Bundy, C., 108, 117, 132
Bunting, B., 65, 72, 142
Burma, 69, 94, 169
Burman, S., 115
business. *See* capitalists
Buthelezi, G., 97, 98
bywoners, 14, 65

Cape Colony, 15, 19, 23–26, 29
capitalists/capitalism, 1–2, 5–6, 9, 14, 17, 33–34, 48–55, 57–63, 66, 69, 76–78, 102–6, 108–9, 113, 117, 122–24, 128, 130, 148–52, 175–83, 187, 202
Carr, E. H., 133, 172
Cavalli-Sforza, L., 119–20
Celliers, S. P., 56
Cetshwayo, King, 27
Chamber of Mines, 11, 36, 39, 41–42, 46, 56, 58, 59
Chamberlain, J., 18, 27, 28
Chan, S., 201
Charney, C., 83
Chekhov, A., 107, 173, 200
Citation Index, 134, 173
class issues. *See* race-class debate
Codes of Conduct, 95
Coetzee, J. M., 12, 100, 158
Coetzee, K., 198
Cohen, R., 160–61
Coker, C., 198
collective action, difficulties of, 181–83
coloureds, 33, 50, 83, 140, 142, 145, 177, 178
complicity, 96–99, 104, 122–28
Conservative Party (CP), 59, 63, 71, 93, 182
Conservatives/neoconservatives, 13, 14, 17, 18, 21, 23, 27, 73, 109, 113, 140
constitution, 145–46; 1910 Constitution, 18, 28, 32
Constitutional Court, 146

Index

constitutional negotiations, 103, 144–45
Consultative Business Movement, 62
Cortwright, D., 169
Cory, G. M., 13, 14, 18
Cosatu, 53, 58, 88, 129, 149, 151, 154, 164
Cox, M., 2
Cox, P., 151
Crocker, C., 82
Cuito Cuanavale, 82
Currey, J., 141

Daily Despatch, 124
Daniels, E., 141
Danziger, K., 65
Davenport, R., 12, 17, 192–93
Davies, R. H., 37, 38, 40, 47, 52, 60, 61, 193–94
de Beer, Z., 62, 142
De Beers, 46
de Kiewiet, C. W., 9, 10, 12, 15, 17–18, 21, 26, 27–8, 31, 37, 192
de Klerk, F. W., 50, 70–71, 83, 87, 100, 105, 144–47, 199, 87, 180, 198–99; president, 1–2
de Klerk, W., 65
de Lange Commission, 49
de Tocqueville, A., 173
de Villiers, W., 62
decentralization policy. *See* Physical Planning Act
Degenaar, J., 70, 115
Delius, A., 117, 124, 192, 199
democracy, 129, 149, 165
Democratic Alliance (DA), 115, 139, 140, 143–44, 161, 164
Democratic Teachers Union, 129
"demographic representivity" proposal, 156
demographic trends, 55–56, 157
Dennett, D., 119

Dickinson, D., 201
Diederichs, N., 65
Dingane, King, 29, 31
Dlamini, S., 52
Dodge, T., 201
Doxey, G. V., 12, 37
du Plessis, J. C., 65
du Toit, A., 31, 65, 70, 115
Dube, J., 22
Dubow, S., 19, 117, 133, 188, 192
Dugard, J., 115
Duncan, P., 141, 220

education, 45, 48, 49, 51, 66, 142
Eglin, C., 100
Eliot, G., 121
Ellis, S., 82
Elphick, R., 15–16
Elster, J., 117
Eminent Persons Group, 61
English-speaking whites, 3, 7–8, 17–18, 26, 31–32, 44–45, 57, 61, 65, 72–73, 125, 136, 146–47, 180
Erwin, A., 58, 160, 201
Eskom, 56
Esterhuyse, W., 123
Etheredge, D., 62
Etherington, N., 135, 200
Evans, G., 115
Evans, M., 19, 21
Evans, R., 4, 132, 172
Evening Post, 124

Fagan Report, 47
falsifiability principle, 172
Federated Chambers of Industry (FCI), 46, 56, 57, 59, 60, 62, 176, 178, 187
Financial Mail, 124
Fine, B., 117
Focus (journal), 200, 201

Fosatu (later Cosatu), 58. *See also* trade unions
French trade unions, 129
Frank, G., 51
Frankel, S. H., 9, 10, 11, 37, 39
Frederickson, G. M., 15
Freund, W., 181, 182, 183, 185
Friedman, S., 58, 164
frontier conflicts, 13–15, 20, 27

Gagiano, J., 72, 115
Gandar, L., 124
Gelb, S., 117, 201
General Mining, 62, 65, 66
Gerhart, G., 197
Gerson, J., 199
Giliomee, H., 15–16, 24, 27, 31, 65, 74–75, 114, 132, 145–46, 151, 199
Ginwala, F., 138
Glaser, D., 29, 108, 117, 192, 199, 202
Godsell, B., 62, 151
gold mines. *See* mining industry
Goldstone Commission, 198
Goniwe, M., 124
Goodfellow, D. M., 191
Gorbachev, Mikhail, 57, 99, 101
Gould, S. J., 120
Gramsci, A., 117
Great Trek, 16, 192
Greenberg, S., 37, 52, 183–84, 186, 193
Guelke, A., 15, 90, 146, 197, 198, 201
Gumbi, M., 97
Gumede, W., 61, 125, 154, 164, 201
Gunnarson, G., 197
Gwala, H., 98

Hain, P., 142
Hanf, T., 72
Hani, C., 101

Hanlon, J., 197
Harris, J., 141
Hayek, F., 110, 111
Heard, T., 124
Hellman, E., 115, 194
Hepple, A., 65
Herstigte Nasionale Party (HNP), 34, 48, 63, 64, 70, 71, 93
Hertzog, General, 22
Herzen, A., 109, 137
Heunis, C., 100, 180, 202
Hindson, D., 194
historians, role of, 2–4, 6, 30–32, 131–47, 171–73
Hobsbawm, Eric, 99
Hoernlé, A., 20, 21
Hoernle, W., 26
Hofmeyr, J., 45, 93, 115
Holomisa, B., 98
"homelands." *See* Bantustans
Horace, 118
Horrell, M., 194
Horwitz, R., 9, 12, 18, 37, 41–42, 42, 65
Hughes, K., 135, 155, 181, 183, 194, 199
Hufbauer, G., 201
human agency, role of, 99–102
Human Rights Commission, 114
Hutt, W. H., 9, 11

IDASA, 198
imperialism, British, 3, 7, 14, 26–32
Improper Political Interference Act (1968), 48
Indians, 33, 50, 83, 140, 145, 177, 178
Industrial, Apprenticeship and Wage Councils, 63, 88
Industrial Conciliation (IC) Act, 46, 49, 58, 59, 88, 182
inequality in post-Apartheid Africa, 160–61

INDEX 223

influx control. *See* pass laws
Inkatha, 84, 98, 143
Innes, D., 195
Innes, R., 27
Institute of Commonwealth Studies, 132
institutions, 28, 99–102, 117
international pressures, 94–95, 103, 104. *See also* sanctions
Iraq, 69, 94, 201
Iscor, 41

Jaspers, K., 124
JCI, 61
Jeeves, A., 188
Jeffrey, A., 115
job color bar, 11, 35–44, 48, 51, 54, 60, 63, 66, 78, 195
Johnson, R. W., 197
Johnson, Dr. S., 118
Johnstone, F., 37, 116–17, 193
Jordan, P., 139, 140
Joubert, E., 68

Kahn, Sam, 142
Kane-Berman, J., 96, 197
Kant, I., 67, 113
Kaplan, D., 38
Keegan, T., 26
Kershaw, I., 132
Keynes, M., 108
Kissinger, H., 113
Krikler, J., 40
Krogh, A., 181
Kumar, D., 115
Kuper, A., 26, 119
Kuper, H., 114
Kuper, L., 26, 143, 191, 193

labor, black, 9–11, 36, 39, 41–45, 48–49, 54, 96, 123, 160–61.
See also trade unions

labor, white, 37–42, 63–64, 66, 75.
See also trade unions
Labour Relations Amendment bill, 71
Labour-Pact government, 39, 42, 44
Land and Land Acts, 10–11, 18, 30, 40, 42, 43, 70
Landsberg, C., 146
Lapchick, R., 90
Lawrence, P., 124, 201
"Left," "The," 117, 137, 140, 148–50, 159, 161, 164, 201
Legassick, M., 13, 14, 15, 19, 51, 82, 195
Legum, C. and M., 142
Lekota, T., 100
Lemon, A., 115
Lenin, V., 141, 220
Leon, T., 139, 151, 200
Lewin, H., 141
Lewsen, P., 22, 192
liberals, 3, 5–7, 18, 19–28, 31–32, 35, 37–43, 47–48, 54–64, 69–70, 75–77, 109–115, 138–44, 149, 151, 161, 183–89
Liebenberg, B. J., 32
Life of Brian (film), 193
Lipton, M., 13, 51, 177, 181–87, 194–95
Lodge, T., 30, 82, 158
Lonsdale, J., 9
Lopez, G. A., 169
Loram, C. T., 19, 21
Lugar, R., 198
Lundahl, M., 55, 201
Luthuli, A., 30, 140, 142

Mabuza, E., 98
McCracken, L., 22
MacCrone, I. D., 15
Mackay, S., 151
McKinley, D., 82, 117, 197

MacMillan, W. M., 9–10, 14, 17–18, 21, 26–27, 65, 114, 192
Macozoma, S., 97, 152
Magubane, B., 30–31, 65, 74, 191*n*
Mail & Guardian, 30, 125, 156, 158, 201
Makgoba, M., 138, 157–58
Makhanyi, M., 125
Malan, Prime Minister, 73
Maller, J., 88
Mamdani, M., 127
Mandela, N., 1, 2, 50, 53, 61, 81, 83, 87, 97–98, 100, 125, 142
Mangcu, X., 125
Manuel, T., 160
Maphai, V., 153, 156, 197
Marais, J., 14, 56
Marks, S., 8, 11, 14, 19, 26, 28, 29, 36, 43, 64–65, 188, 191–92, 195
Marquard, L., 188, 189, 192
marriage, interracial, 48, 49, 60, 67–68, 108
Marx, A., 83
Marx, K., 115–16, 130–31, 133
Mass unrest and actions, 6, 57, 83–88, 97 102–4, 58–59, 67, 86–88, 103, 178–79
Masters and Servants Laws, 11
Matanzima, K., 98
Matshiqi, A., 125
Matthews, T., 115
Matthews, Z. K., 30
Mayer, P., 196
Mayal, J., 197
Maylam, P., 8, 13–14, 19, 21, 23, 44
Mazwai, T., 124, 125, 138
Mbeki, M., 155
Mbeki, T., 61, 98, 100, 144, 145, 148, 150–52, 155, 158–59
Mboweni, T., 156, 160
Mckinley, D., 117

media, 67, 124–25, 149, 158
Meiring, General, 199
Meli, F., 96
Merriman, J. X., 21
Meyer, R., 100
military, role of, 56, 58–60, 77, 82, 86, 178–81, 197, 199
Mill, J. S., 25, 113
Mills, G., 115
Milner, A., 27
Mine Workers Union (MWU), 88, 194–95
mining industry, 37–43, 45–46, 54, 58, 62–63, 116
Moleketi, J., 138
Molema, M., 30
Moll, P., 201
Moll, T., 195
Moodie, D., 12
Morris, M., 38, 186
Mosala, I., 97
Moshesh, King, 25
Moss, G., 202
Motlatsi, J., 151
Motsepe, P., 152
Mpande, Prince, 29
Mulder, C., 179
Muller, T., 13, 21
Murray, M., 197, 200
Myburgh, J., 158, 200–1

Naidoo, J., 58
Namibia, 94, 128
Napoleon III, 130
Nathan, L., 197
National African Federated Chambers of Commerce (Nafcoc), 60, 96
National Forum, 83, 84, 97
National Manpower Commission, 88
National Party. *See* Afrikaner National Party

INDEX

National Security Management System (NSMS), 60, 178, 180
Nationalists/nationalism: African, 6, 16, 22, 30–31, 73–76, 81–87, 97, 110, 116, 121–22, 137–42, 148, 157–58 (*see also* African National Congress; Pan Africanist Congress; Africanists); Afrikaner, 6, 13–14, 17, 20–21, 23, 28–32, 64–76, 110, 116, 121–22, 144–47. *See also* Afrikaner National Party; Herstigte Nasionale Party; Conservative Party
Native Affairs Department (NAD), 175, 176
Nattrass, N., 195, 201
Naude, B., 46
Nazism, 119, 132, 157
Ndebele, N., 30, 138
Ndlovu, S., 31
Neo-Marxist revisionists, 3–9, 12–14, 17–23, 26–27, 31–32, 35–38, 41–48, 51–53, 57–56, 64–65, 69, 72–74, 77–78, 90, 102–4, 109, 115–31, 134–36, 175–81, 183–89, 194–95; mass actions and uprisings, 6, 58–59, 67, 83–88, 97, 102–4
Netshitenzhe, J., 97
Neumark, S. D., 9, 10, 12, 14
NGOs, 49, 50, 89, 99, 168
Niehaus, I., 120
Nolutshungu, S., 65, 74, 75, 85
Nzo, General, 81–82

O'Dowd, M., 34, 51, 54, 75–76, 78
Olivier, N., 46
Olson, M., 112, 183
O'Meara, D., 17, 19, 32, 38, 47, 52–53, 57, 64, 66, 83–84, 108, 116, 185–88, 194–96, 202
Operation Vula, 87

Oppenheimer, H., 46, 52, 56, 59, 62, 66, 176, 177, 178, 181, 187
Oppenheimer, N., 62
Orkin, M., 92
Ovenden, K., 91, 198
Owen, K., 124

Pahad, E., 139, 140
Pan Africanist Congress (PAC), 46, 48, 97, 141, 148
pass laws, 11, 16, 18, 23, 40, 44–45, 48–49, 54–55, 175–76, 194
passive resistance campaign, 141
Paton, A., 141, 142
Peires, J., 15, 136
Philip, J., 9, 20, 23, 25, 27
Physical Planning Act, 48, 49, 54, 76, 176–77, 186
Pigou, P., 199
Pim, H., 19, 21, 22
Pinker, S., 120
Pityana, B., 97, 114, 139, 144
Plaatje, S., 30
Plitz, R., 170–71
Pollard, P., 91–92
Popcru, 129
Popper, K., 172
Population Registration Act, 48, 70
Posel, D., 175, 176, 194, 202
post-apartheid South Africa, 137–73
postmodernism, 4, 117, 172
Poulantzas, N., 38, 194
poverty and anti-poverty policies, 10, 45, 54, 115, 159–62
power-sharing strategy, 50, 85
Pratt, D., 141
Preller, G., 13, 21
privatization, 159
Progressive Party, 54, 56, 62, 71, 93, 114, 178, 195
Prohibition of Political Interference Act, 49–50

property rights, 2, 48–49, 60, 111–12, 130, 161
proportional representation, 146
Putnam, R., 121

racism, 3, 7, 8–15, 11–26, 32, 40, 45, 55, 67–68, 119–22, 146–47, 153–58
race-class debate, 3, 5, 7, 8, 37, 40, 46, 63, 73–76, 85, 88, 96, 116, 118, 129–30, 143, 150–59, 163–65, 194–95
Ramaphosa, C., 89, 100, 145, 152
Ramogale, M., 157–58
Ramphele, M., 155, 156, 158
Rand Daily Mail, 124
Rand Rebellion, 36, 40, 44, 77
Rapport, 67
Rathbone, R., 43
Rawls, J., 112
reform(s), 5, 44–46, 49–64, 70, 78, 105, 108, 187–88
Renwick, R., 145, 197
reserves, African. *See* Bantustans
revisionists. *See* neo-Marxists
Reyburn, H. A., 14
Reynders Commission, 63–64
Rhodes, C., 18, 27
Rhodesia, 69, 94, 105, 170
Rich, P., 21, 192
Riekert Commission, 177
Roamer, J., 117
Roberts, M., 65
Roberts, R. S., 138
Robertson, H. M., 9, 10–11, 191
Rogerson, C., 115
Ross, A., 15
Roux, E., 188, 189, 192
Rubin, N., 141
Runciman, G., 119
Rupert, A., 46
Russell, B., 108

Sachs, S., 40

SACOL, 59
Sadie, J., 46, 56
SALDRU conference, 194
Salomon, L., 9, 12, 65
Sampson, A., 159, 197
Samuelson, P., 112
sanctions, 6, 70, 90–96, 103, 142, 165–71, 197
Sanders, M., 20, 21
Sanlam, 62, 65
Sasol, 56, 151
Sauer, J. W., 21, 27
Sauer, P., 46, 47
Saul, J., 117
Saunders, C., 2, 9, 20, 22, 35, 38, 64–65, 192–93, 195
Schlemmer, L., 68, 72, 92, 115, 147, 154, 182
Schreiner, W. P., 24
scientific racism, 119
Seabright, P., 120–21
Sechaba, T., 82
security/defence forces, 86–87, 178, 197
Seekings, J., 83–84, 201
Seepe, S., 125
SEIFSA, 59
self-interest. *See* behavioural theory
Sen, A., 110
separate development policy, 33, 47, 50, 54, 77, 78, 85, 94, 176
Serfontein, H., 65
Sexwale, T., 152
Shaka, King, 31
Sharpeville, 46, 57, 71, 73, 86, 93
Shaw, G., 124
Shepstone, T., 18, 22
Shubane, K., 151, 155
Simkins, C., 115, 151, 201
Simons, J and R., 142
Slabbert, F. van Zyl, 54, 65, 71, 100, 139, 142
slavery, 16, 23, 27
Slovo, J., 82, 100, 200

Smith, A., 27, 112, 133
Smith, I., 69, 105
Smith, K., 64–65, 94, 117, 134, 135, 192, 196
Smuts, J., 42, 45
Sobukwe, R., 148
Solidarity, 92
Solomon, P., 23, 27
Soros, G., 198
South Africa Foundation, 95
South African Agricultural Union, 59
South African Broadcasting Corporation, 125
South African Communist Party (SACP), 10, 20, 48, 51, 57, 72, 87, 138, 141–42, 149–50, 164
South African Native Affairs Commission (SANAC), 19, 21, 22
Soviet Union, 2, 82, 94–95, 99, 101, 103, 141, 144
Soweto uprising. *See* under mass action
Sparks, A., 124, 197
Spence, J., 115, 201
Spicer, M., 62, 197
Stadler, A., 65
Stals, C., 100
state of emergency, 82, 83, 86, 105
State Security Council, 178
State Security System, 179
state-market debate, 38, 40–41, 109, 111–12, 115–16, 152, 159–62, 176, 179–81
Seifsa, 46, 56
Steyn, J., 57
Stiglitz, J., 112
Stolten, H. E., 76, 183, 185
strikes. *See* trade unions
Sunday Independent, 125
Sunday Times, 124
"sunset clauses," 64
Sunter, C., 62
Sutherland, J., 124

Suzman, H., 56, 100, 139, 142–43, 151, 198–99
Swart, B., 73

Tambo, O. R., 61, 140
Tawney, R. H., 112
Terreblanche, S. J., 53, 176, 181
Theal, G. M., 13, 14, 17, 21, 27
Third Force, 145, 146, 198
Thompson, L. M., 11–12, 17, 18, 22, 27, 28
Tickten, H., 117
Tomlinson, F. R., 20–21
Total Strategy, 52, 53, 60, 61, 178, 181, 187
trade unions, black, 6, 46, 49, 57–59, 67, 87–90, 128–30
trade unions, white, 5, 35–49, 59, 63, 88, 116, 128–30, 187
Traher, Tony, 151
Transvaal, pass laws in, 11
Transvaler, Die, 72–73
Trapido, S., 19, 23–24, 27, 132
Treurnicht, A., 59
Tricameral Constitution & Parliament, 50, 84, 145, 177–78
Tripartite Alliance, 148–65, 163
Trollip, A., 65
Truth & Reconciliation Commission (TRC), 5, 53, 123, 124, 125–26, 128, 181, 198
TUCSA, 195
Turgenev, I., 201
Tutu, D., 125, 154, 157, 168

ubuntu, 140
"ultra-leftists," 149, 201
Umkhonto we Sizwe. *See* armed struggle
unemployment, 56, 86, 88, 160, 161
United Democratic Front (UDF), 83, 84, 85, 86, 87, 177–78

United Party (UP), 45, 46, 47, 62, 71
Unity Movement, 142
universal suffrage, 23
uprisings. *See* mass action
Urban Foundation, 57, 62, 179
Uys, S., 124, 139, 201

Vail, L., 120
Van den Berg, S., 201
Van den Berghe, H., 179
Van der Horst, S., 9, 10,11, 12, 17, 18, 37, 42, 114
Van der Merve, P. J., 9, 14–15, 65, 129, 132
Van der Stel, S., 28
Van der Walt, H., 14
Van Jaarsveld, F. A., 13, 31
Van Onselen, C., 117
Van Wyk Louw, N. P., 20
verligte/verkrampte dispute, 34, 51, 55, 59, 63–66, 68–69, 70–71, 78, 93, 104, 114, 129, 145
Verwoerd, H., 22, 33, 34, 46–47, 54, 68, 94, 141
Vigne, R., 141, 200
Viljoen, G., 100
Viljoen Commission, 177
Volkskas, 65
Voortrekkers, 16, 24
Vorster, J., 34, 47–48, 50, 51, 67, 73, 100, 187
voting trends, 70–71, 93, 145, 166

Waddell, G., 61, 62
wages, 11, 39, 48–49, 51, 63–64, 88–89
Wages & Productivity Improvement Association, 46
Waldmeir, P., 145, 195, 197, 198
Walesa, L., 92
Walker, E., 14, 18, 132, 192
Walshe, P., 12
Wassenaar, A., 62, 177
Weber, M., 165
Webster, E., 88
Welsh, D., 12, 18, 65
Wentzel, E., 142
Wessels, Albert, 62
Westlake, N., 26, 27
white labor. *See* labor
Wiehahn Commission, 49, 58
Williams, G., 201
Wilson, F., 2, 9, 12, 18, 37, 115, 194
Wilson, M., 11–12, 42
Wilson, President, 113
Witwatersrand History Workshop, 130, 132–33, 199
Wolpe, H., 42–43, 51, 116
Woods, D., 124, 142
Worden, N., 8, 19, 36, 188
Worrall, D., 196
World Bank, 149, 159, 162
Wright, H., 13

Xhoza, R., 152

Yengeni, T., 139
Yudelman, D., 193

zeitgeist, 94, 103
Zimbabwe, 50, 69, 87, 92–93, 128, 158, 161